MW00444906

The Soviet Union

The Soviet Union

A Short History

Mark Edele

WILEY Blackwell

This edition first published 2019
© 2019 John Wiley & Sons, Inc.

All rights reserved. No part of this publication may be reproduced, stored in a retrieval system, or transmitted, in any form or by any means, electronic, mechanical, photocopying, recording or otherwise, except as permitted by law. Advice on how to obtain permission to reuse material from this title is available at http://www.wiley.com/go/permissions.

The right of Mark Edele to be identified as the author of this work has been asserted in accordance with law.

Registered Office
John Wiley & Sons, Inc., 111 River Street, Hoboken, NJ 07030, USA

Editorial Office
111 River Street, Hoboken, NJ 07030

For details of our global editorial offices, customer services, and more information about Wiley products visit us at www.wiley.com.

Wiley also publishes its books in a variety of electronic formats and by print-on-demand. Some content that appears in standard print versions of this book may not be available in other formats.

Limit of Liability/Disclaimer of Warranty
While the publisher and authors have used their best efforts in preparing this work, they make no representations or warranties with respect to the accuracy or completeness of the contents of this work and specifically disclaim all warranties, including without limitation any implied warranties of merchantability or fitness for a particular purpose. No warranty may be created or extended by sales representatives, written sales materials or promotional statements for this work. The fact that an organization, website, or product is referred to in this work as a citation and/or potential source of further information does not mean that the publisher and authors endorse the information or services the organization, website, or product may provide or recommendations it may make. This work is sold with the understanding that the publisher is not engaged in rendering professional services. The advice and strategies contained herein may not be suitable for your situation. You should consult with a specialist where appropriate. Further, readers should be aware that websites listed in this work may have changed or disappeared between when this work was written and when it is read. Neither the publisher nor authors shall be liable for any loss of profit or any other commercial damages, including but not limited to special, incidental, consequential, or other damages.

Library of Congress Cataloging-in-Publication data applied for

Hardback [9781119131168]
Paperback [9781119131175]

Cover image: (map) © woewchikyury/Getty Images; (sickle & hammer in star) © Cvetkovic Nenad/Shuttertock; (back cover) © OnstOn/iStockphoto
Cover design by Wiley

Set in 10/12.5pt Bembo by SPi Global, Pondicherry, India
Printed in Singapore by C.O.S. Printers Pte Ltd

10 9 8 7 6 5 4 3 2 1

For Jane Hansen

Contents

Preface

This book tells the story of the Soviet Union's making, evolution, and breakdown. The Union of Soviet Socialist Republics (USSR) was the successor to the Romanov Empire, which had broken apart in war and revolution. It became the predecessor of 15 nation states in a region, which once encapsulated my generation's hopes for democratic change in Eastern Europe. Today, it is a hotbed of authoritarianism, crony-capitalism, and war, although democrats still hold their ground. The history of the Soviet Union has been told numerous times, in some very good and some not-so brilliant tomes. Historians have conceived this history as the story of Russia and the Russians, as a tale of the rise and fall of a specific form of modernity, as the instantiation and failure of an ideological project, or as a repressive empire, a "prison house of nations" in the catchy formulation of a 1958 publication that adapted Lenin's description of the Tsarist state for its successor.[1]

This book focuses on three themes: welfare, warfare, and empire. The Soviet Union was a socialist state with the aspiration to build a better, fairer, and more prosperous society than capitalism could. It inspired generations of leftists all over the world and disappointed as many of them over the decades. It promised a superior level of welfare but seldom delivered it. Instead, its second major trait often won out: The USSR was also a police state, which devoted much of its resources to preparation and execution of warfare. A nightmare to liberals and conservatives in the West, it served as a warning to anybody contemplating an alternative to capitalism. Finally, while this country was dominated by Russia and the Russians, it was not identical to them. The Soviet Union was a multinational state, an "empire of nations,"[2] or, indeed, a Red Empire. Following much recent writing, then, this book tries to escape the narrative of Russia = USSR = Russia. Such a Russocentric tale marginalizes all the non-Russian societies and current nation states. It thus obscures, rather than aids, our understanding of the contemporary world in its historical context.

This book is organized chronologically. Part I, *The First Age of Violence*, chronicles the years 1904 to 1924, when the Romanov Empire was unmade in two wars and two revolutions, and then reconstituted as a Bolshevik empire in an immensely destructive civil war. Chapter 1 covers the twilight of the old empire from the beginning of the Russo-Japanese War in 1904 to the outbreak of World War I a decade later. These were years of political upheaval, with a first revolution in 1905/1906 forcing the Tsar to grant major political concessions without giving up on his claim to autocratic power. They were also years of rapid cultural, social, and economic transformation, providing the contradictions that would explode in the subsequent period, but also containing the possibility for alternative, less dictatorial historical paths.

Chapter 2 chronicles the empire's World War I, all the way through to the German defeat in the west in November 1918. After initial successes against their German, Austrian, and Ottoman foes in 1914, the Tsar's armies increasingly struggled with the demands of modern war. 1915 became a year of military catastrophe when, during the Great Retreat, Russian forces abandoned large swathes of the Romanov's western lands, destroying the country and deporting populations as they went. After a partial stabilization in 1916, political catastrophe followed in 1917. The Tsar was deposed in a first revolution in February, which began the breakdown of the empire. Russia itself was ruled by an uneasy alliance of a caretaker government staffed by liberals with the socialist Petrograd Soviet overseeing its actions. Meanwhile, other regions – Finland, Ukraine, Central Asia, and the Trans-Caucasus – became increasingly autonomous from the imperial center in Petrograd. While the periphery thus started to break away, in the capital, the refusal of the Provisional Government to end the war, the ongoing economic crisis, and the relentless agitation for a more radical revolution by Vladimir Lenin's radical communists (the Bolsheviks) pushed the Petrograd Soviet further and further to the left. In October, the Provisional Government was thoroughly discredited and moderate socialists had lost support among the revolutionary masses of Petrograd. Lenin's men now took power in the name of the Soviet. This second revolution accelerated the imperial breakdown amidst the world war. The further fragmentation of the Tsar's domains would become the major story of 1918. Bolshevik Russia was increasingly restricted to the old heartland around Moscow. The rest of the old empire was ruled either by German occupation troops or their local puppets, by non-Russian politicians, or by competing Russian governments. Once the defeated Germans retreated from Ukraine and the Baltics after their defeat in November 1918, the Russian Empire thus was no more. The Bolshevik Revolution of October 1917, then, was only one moment in a larger process of military and revolutionary dissolution of the old empire.

However, the Bolshevik revolution was also a beginning, as chapter 3 shows. It tells the story of how and why the Bolsheviks managed to re-gather most of the old empire under the Red flag. This process was violent: a civil war. We can distinguish several steps, easily summarized by year. 1919 was the year of a struggle between "Reds" and "Whites" – labels deriving from the French Revolution, which can easily mislead, as we shall see. Not only were some of the "Whites" socialists flying the red flag; but in Ukraine and elsewhere, the civil war also had ethnic and national components. From early 1920, the reconquest of the empire continued with the military acquisitions of the Transcaucasian republics, the brutal pacification of Central Asia, a hard-fought war against the new Polish state, and bloody counter-insurgencies against peasant and military rebels in the Bolshevik heartland. By 1923, the new empire was more or less complete, although in some areas fighting continued. The new Union of Soviet Socialist Republics was enshrined in the constitution of 1924. It covered much of the old Romanov Empire, except Finland, the Baltic Republics, and Poland.

Part II, *The Interwar Years*, contains only one chapter, which focuses on how the new empire was consolidated during the 1920s. As fighting ended at different moments in different parts of the empire, there is some chronological overlap with the previous chapter. The short "decade" from 1921 to 1928 was a period of economic recovery from the prolonged fighting. State building, strengthening of the dictatorship, and the formalization of the legal and constitutional structure of the new empire were the orders of the day. Yet, the new Bolshevik rulers engaged in fierce political fights about both the further direction of the country and the composition of its leadership team. By 1928, Stalin's faction had won and proceeded to push the country into its second period of upheaval.

Part III, *The Second Age of Violence*, comprises two chapters, covering the years from 1928 to 1949, a period of renewed internal and external warfare. Chapter 5 shows how Stalin and his men transformed the exhausted empire into a warfare state ready for the next engagement. This transformation came in the form of two extremely violent "revolutions from above" (1928 to 1932 and 1937 to 1938), separated by three years of relative calm in most areas. Chapter 6 then turns to World War II, which began in Asia in 1937, in Europe in 1939, and in the Pacific in 1941. The chapter contains an analysis of the extent and nature of Soviet participation in these interconnected wars: from a defensive posture at its Asian frontier in 1937 to 1939, to aggression in Europe in 1939 to 1941 (when the regathering of the old empire was completed), to catastrophe when the Germans attacked on June 22, 1941, the starting point of the "Great Patriotic War" of the Soviet Union. Once the initiative had been regained in the Battles of Moscow (Winter 1941) and Stalingrad (1942–1943), the Red Army returned to the offensive and won the war in Europe before turning east to help defeat Japan in the summer of 1945. Fighting against local guerilla forces continued along the new and expanded western frontier of the empire well into the 1940s, with a final round of deportations in 1949 marking something of an end point.

In neighboring China, too, the war only ended with the victory of the communists in the civil war in 1949.

Part IV, *From Warfare to Welfare*, is made up of two chapters analyzing how the Soviet Union recovered from the prolonged periods of violence that had shaped its form, character, and content. Chapter 7 describes the years of post-war normalization. Its chronological boundaries overlap with both the previous and the following chapters. The narrative starts with the completed liberation of Soviet territory in 1944, covers the years between the war's end in 1945 and Stalin's death in 1953, as well as the early post-Stalin years when collective leadership of the dictator's closest underlings ran the empire. It ends with Nikita Khrushchev's 1957 victory in what in effect was a prolonged succession struggle. Stalin tried to reconstruct the prewar dictatorial structure at home after the war was won, and he consolidated his empire abroad by surrounding it with nominally independent states in Europe. In Asia, he attempted to continue the pre-1941 tactic of encouraging proxy wars as a means of securing the Soviet Union's "eastern front." This attempt backfired in the Korean War (1950–1953), which threatened to lead to a direct confrontation with the United States. After Stalin's death this war was quickly brought to an end and the dictator's deputies put in place a variety of reforms they had long considered but had not been able to implement as long as the dictator was alive. Now, first attempts were made to dismantle his warfare state and normalize life within the new empire. The political liberalization of the 1950s, however, constantly threatened to undermine the very empire Stalin had built – the foundation of the security of the Soviet project.

Eventually, then, efforts were made to build a socialist welfare state to reward the population for the years of exhausting warfare. The contradictions, dead ends, but also successes of this process are covered in Chapter 8. It begins the years of mature socialism with the pension reform in 1956 and ends it with the start of economic and political reform (*perestroika*) in 1985. It thus covers most of the years Khrushchev was First Secretary of the Communist Party of the Soviet Union (1953–1964, until 1957 as part of a leadership team, from then on his own) as well as those of the successors Leonid Brezhnev (1964–1982, from 1966 with Stalin's title of "General Secretary"), Iurii Andropov (1982–1984), and Konstantin Chernenko (1984–1985).

The final two chapters, forming Part V, deal with *Imperial Discontent*. From 1985, the new General Secretary, Mikhail Gorbachev, made a concerted attempt to end the Cold War, dismantle the empire of satellites in Europe, and decisively to demobilize the remnants of the Stalinist warfare state. The goal was to finally shift to building a democratic, socialist welfare state within the borders of the Soviet Union. This attempt failed spectacularly. Reform led to crisis, crisis to breakdown, and in 1991 the Union broke apart along national lines. We are still living with the fallout of this momentous event, which created a whole new world of nation states with roots deep in the first and second epochs of violence, but no longer held together by an empire. A short final Chapter 10 serves as an afterword. It sketches the trials and tribulations of the successor states, their struggles with and against democracy, capitalism, authoritarianism, and war.

This book is the result of explaining Soviet history for over a decade to undergraduate students, first at the University of Western Australia, then at the University of Melbourne. My teaching during these years was supported by immensely influential histories written by Geoffrey Hosking, Ronald G. Suny, Alec Nove, and Stephen Lovell, which are listed at the end of this preface together with other useful overviews. Kevin McDermott's "war-revolution model," served as a conceptual starting point and Joshua A. Sanborn's path-breaking *Imperial Apocalypse* inspired the early chapters, with profound implications for the rest of the narrative. The influence of Richard Pipes will be obvious to anybody who has read his classic book on how the Russian Empire was unmade but reborn as the Soviet Union. My views of the pivotal Stalin and his world are informed by Oleg Khlevniuk's and Sheila Fitzpatrick's masterful books. For demographic information I relied heavily on *Naselenie Rossii v xx veke. Istoricheskie ocherki*, 3 vols (Moscow: Rosspen, 2000–2011), as well as the census data now available online at http://demoscope.ru/weekly/pril.php. For the 1937 census I consulted V. B. Zhiromskaia, I. N. Kiselev, and Iu. A. Poliakov, *Polveka pod grifom "sekretno": vsesoiuznaia perepis' naseleniia 1937 goda* (Moscow: Nauka, 1996), and V. B. Zhiromskaia and Iu. A. Poliakov, *Vsesoiuznaia perepis' naseleniia 1937 goda: obshchie itogi. Sbornik dokumentov i materialov* (Moscow: Rosspen, 2007). David Stahel, Josh Sanborn, and Ben Mercer read and commented on parts of the manuscript, Elizabeth Gralton and Yuri Shapoval on a full draft. Debra McDougall worked persistently on making the penultimate product more readable. Caroline Maxwell (elmindexing.co.uk) took on the task of indexing at short notice and with admirable efficiency. Parts of Chapter 2 were first presented as the Inaugural Hansen Lecture at the University of Melbourne in October 2017. A companion essay to the lecture was published in the *Australian Book Review* (October 2017): 10–15.

That I could step back, reassess, and consolidate what I have learned over a decade was due to an Australian Research Council Future Fellowship (FT140101100). Several chapters were drafted while I was an Academic Visitor at The Australian National University in Semester 2, 2016. I would like to thank the School of History and in particular its Head, Nicholas Brown, for being so welcoming and for providing office space and library privileges, and ANU Apartments for accommodating our changing plans in the delightful Judith Wright Court. Turner School made our daughter Anna welcome and soothed her longing for her North Fremantle friends. A first draft of the manuscript was finished while on a research trip to Kyiv, Ukraine, at the end of 2016. The final revisions were made during my first half year as Hansen Chair at the University of Melbourne in 2017. Una McIlvenna's invitation to lecture on Russia and the Soviet Union in a team-taught course on the history of empires helped to finalize the early chapters.

A book like this volume is a serious effort in compression. Decisions need to be made about what to include, and more importantly, what to exclude. I attempted to highlight scholarly controversies without transforming what is essentially a narrative interpretation into a historiographical discussion. I also tried to strike a balance between historicism and writing a history of the present, which explains a part of the world we live in. For reasons of space I was not able to document my intellectual debts in my usual "Germanic" fashion. The footnotes in this volume only document direct quotations and the bibliographies at the end of each chapter are reading lists for an English-language audience, not a list of all works consulted. They do not include Russian, Ukrainian, German, or French literature and are by necessity incomplete. Updates on these reading lists will be posted periodically on www.markedele. com, which also includes links to maps and a page with annotated links to primary sources in English, Russian, and other languages, for readers who want to study aspects of this history in more depth. Wherever possible, I quoted from English translations and if available from free online sources. Dates are according to the Julian calendar until February 1918, when Russia adopted the Gregorian calendar then already used in the West. In cases where events are of international interest, both the Julian and the Gregorian date are given, with the earlier date denoting the old style, the later the new style.

Notes

1 *The Soviet Empire: Prison House of Nations and Races: A Study in Genocide, Discrimination, and Abuse of Power* (Washington, DC: US Government Printing Office, 1958).
2 Francine Hirsch, *Empire of Nations. Ethnographic Knowledge and the Making of the Soviet Union* (Ithaca, NY and London: Cornell University Press, 2005).

Bibliography

Colton, Timothy. *Moscow. Governing the Socialist Metropolis* (Cambridge, MA: Belknap Press, 1995).

Fedor, Julie. *Russia and the Cult of State Security: The Chekist Tradition from Lenin to Putin* (New York: Routledge, 2011).

Fitzpatrick, Sheila. *On Stalin's Team. The Years of Living Dangerously in Soviet Politics* (Melbourne: Melbourne University Press, 2015).

Hansen, Philip. *The Rise and Fall of the Soviet Economy. An Economic History of the USSR from 1945* (London: Longman, 2003).

Hosking, Geoffrey. *A History of the Soviet Union 1917–1991*, final edition (London: Fontana Press, 1992).

Hosking, Geoffrey. *Rulers and Victims: The Russians in the Soviet Union* (Cambridge, MA: Belknap Press, 2006).

Khlevniuk, Oleg. *Stalin. New Biography of a Dictator* (New Haven, CT and London: Yale University Press, 2015).

Kirby, David. *The Baltic World 1772–1993. Europe's Northern Periphery in an Age of Change* (London and New York: Longman, 1995).

Kirby, David. *A Concise History of Finland* (Cambridge: Cambridge University Press, 2006).

Kuromiya, Hiroaki, and Georges Mamoulia. *The Eurasian Triangle. Russia, the Caucasus and Japan, 1904–1945* (Warsaw and Berlin: De Gruyter Open, 2016).

Lovell, Stephen. *The Soviet Union. A Very Short Introduction* (Oxford: Oxford University Press, 2009).

Lovell, Stephen. *The Shadow of War. Russia and the USSR 1941 to the Present* (Oxford: Wiley-Blackwell, 2010).

Marples, David. *Belarus. A Denationalized Nation* (London: Taylor and Francis, 2013).

McDermott, Kevin. *Stalin* (Basingstoke and New York: Palgrave Macmillan, 2006).

Newton, Scott. *Law and the Making of the Soviet World: The Red Demiurge* (New York: Routledge, 2015).

Nove, Alec. *An Economic History of the USSR 1917–1991*, new and final edition (London: Penguin, 1992).

Pipes, Richard. *The Formation of the Soviet Union. Communism and Nationalism 1917–1923*, 3rd revised edition (Cambridge, MA: Harvard University Press, 1997).

Plokhy, Serhii. *The Gates of Europe. A History of Ukraine* (New York: Basic Books, 2015).

Sanborn, Joshua A. *Imperial Apocalypse. The Great War and the Destruction of the Russian Empire* (Oxford: Oxford University Press, 2014).

Sanchez-Sibony, Oscar. *Red Globalization: The Political Economy of the Soviet Cold War from Stalin to Khrushchev* (Cambridge: Cambridge University Press, 2014).

Shaw, Claire L. *Deaf in the USSR. Marginality, Community, and Soviet Identity, 1917–1991* (Ithaca, NY and London: Cornell University Press, 2017).

Siegelbaum, Lewis, and Leslie Page Moch. *Broad Is My Native Land. Repertoires and Regimes of Migration in Russia's Twentieth Century* (Ithaca, NY and London: Cornell University Press, 2014).

Slezkine, Yuri. *The Jewish Century* (Princeton, NJ: Princeton University Press, 2004).

Suny, Ronald G. *The Soviet Experiment. Russia, the USSR, and the Successor States*, 2nd edition (Oxford: Oxford University Press, 2011).

Yekelchyk, Serhy. *Ukraine: Birth of a Modern Nation* (Oxford and New York: Oxford University Press, 2007).

Part I

The First Age of Violence

1

Twilight of Empire (1904–1914)

For the lands that would form the Soviet Union, the twentieth century began in Asia. It began during the night of January, 26/27 (February, 8/9) 1904 when a group of Japanese torpedo boats attacked the Russian Pacific Fleet at Port Arthur (Lüshun). Russia had effectively annexed this Chinese warm-water port in the late nineteenth century, to the chagrin of an increasingly self-confident Japan that was also intent on expansion in China. Negotiations between the two imperialists had led nowhere. Now weapons did the talking.

In Petersburg, which had been the capital of the Russian Empire since Peter the Great (1672–1725) had built this city in the northern swamps, the reaction was mixed. Tsar Nicholas II (1868–1918) was taken aback, as no prior declaration of war had been received. Nevertheless, he was confident of victory against these Japanese "baboons." Others looked forward to what surely would be a "victorious, little war" distracting the Tsar's subjects from their many grievances.[1]

The Late Tsarist Regime

Indeed, the Tsarist regime needed all the help it could get. In the nineteenth century, a once highly successful formula for expansion had turned from a motor of imperial growth to a brake on the further development of Russia's power. The historical core of Russia, the Principality of Moscow, had not been a particularly well-resourced or strategically well-located place during its establishment in the late thirteenth century. It was surrounded by stronger competitors who

The Soviet Union: A Short History, First Edition. Mark Edele.
© 2019 John Wiley & Sons, Inc. Published 2019 by John Wiley & Sons, Inc.

threatened its independence. Its climate was harsh and its human resources scarce. And yet, this rural backwater rose from an insignificant trading outpost deep in the Eurasian woods to become the largest state in the world and one of the great powers of Europe. At the height of its might in the early nineteenth century, it would play a pivotal role in defeating Napoleon's armies and redefine Europe in the Congress of Vienna of 1814–1815.

It could do so, because its rulers – first the Rurikids, then the Romanovs – had mobilized the population into service classes harnessed to an increasingly strong state headed by an autocratic ruler. The service classes came in the form of legally defined estates (*soslovie,* pl.: *sosloviia*) on the one hand, and positions in a "table of ranks" on the other. The *soslovie* group defined a person's relationship to the state: Peasants tilled the land, served the landlord, and paid taxes. Some of them would be forced to serve in the autocrat's armies and die in never-ending wars. Townspeople were engaged in trade or artisanal work in the towns, servicing the state's servants in the urban military and administrative centers. They also paid taxes. The term *dvoriane* is sometimes translated as "nobles" or "gentry," but this group had fewer rights and less freedom than their peers in Europe. They did not pay taxes, relied on the exploitation of the peasantry for their livelihoods, and staffed the empire's bureaucracy and officer corps. Their internal hierarchy was legislated in the table of ranks, which defined a parallel structure for army and civil service. The highest ranks led to hereditary nobility, which served as a conduit for ambitious and talented commoners to enter state service at the highest levels. The role of the clergy, finally, was to pray, and also to serve as the Tsars' ideologists manning the state church. The economic base of this warfare state was serfdom: peasants were bound to the land to support the service elite that ran the administration and the army. This peculiar form of resource mobilization for war and imperial expansion was invented by Ivan III (1440–1505) and perfected by Peter the Great (who introduced the table of ranks in 1722). It served the Romanovs well who ran this state since 1613 and grew it into the largest continuous land empire in the world.

By the middle of the nineteenth century, however, this once-successful formula ran into trouble. Russia now faced competitors who had combined the exploitation of overseas empires with the new might of the dual revolutions that rocked Europe: The French Revolution provided a new model of military mobilization of entire nations, while the industrial revolution, emanating from England, added higher quantities of more lethal weaponry that could be transported more quickly over longer distances by the railways. An agricultural empire based on the exploitation of peasant serfs could not compete with these new, industrialized empires. This fact was driven home in the Crimean War (1853–1856). Only decades after its brilliant victory over Napoleon in 1812, Russia was defeated comprehensively by a coalition of France, Britain, and the Ottoman Empire.

The defeat jolted Alexander II (1818–1881) into action. The Great Reforms of the second half of the nineteenth century were meant to modernize Russia to keep it competitive in this new world of industry and mass politics. These reforms saw the end of serfdom in 1861, an introduction of local self-government (*zemstvo*, 1864; town dumas 1870), judicial reform (1864), and universal military service (1874). Under the next two tsars, Alexander III (1845–1894) and Nicholas II (1868–1918), fast-paced industrialization fundamentally altered the urban landscape from the 1890s onwards. Cities were growing creating over-crowded working-class districts adjacent to new factories billowing smoke. Literacy was on the rise and a growing number of cheap publications catered to this new, lower-class reading public.

Meanwhile, the Russian monarchy was reluctant fully to enter this new age of industrial capitalism and mass society. The tsars continued to insist on the principle of uninhibited personal power that was above the law and beyond the functioning of a routinized bureaucracy. A maze of laws remained on the books, many no longer reflecting the needs of the economy and the growing urban society. They had to be circumvented constantly by imperial decree. This situation enhanced the authority of the tsar, who could make these exceptions, but it also put an incredible amount of negative power into the hands of civil servants at all levels who could refuse to forward an issue to the next level. Only requests that reached the ministers, who reported directly to the tsar, had a chance of being heard unless, that is, direct connections in the court itself could be mobilized. Administrative arbitrariness thus combined with unpredictability; bureaucratic inefficiency combined with corruption. The fact that every minister reported separately, and without consultation with his colleagues, to the sovereign encouraged competition between them, enabled the perpetuation of contradictory policies, and promoted back-stabbing and intrigue. The political system was also top-heavy and much of the country was under-governed by the comparative standards of the time. Strikingly for a country known as a police state, there were fewer police per population than in the Great Britain or France. Russia was big, as the saying went, and the tsar far away.

Indeed, the empire was huge. The Tsars' domains stretched from the Baltic and the Arctic Sea in the north to the Black Sea, the Caucasus and the Caspian in the South, from the Bering and Okhotsk seas in the east to central Europe in the west. Its 8.7 million square miles covered parts of Europe and Asia, altogether nearly one-sixth of the globe and more than 128 million inhabitants (125.6 million in its first census of 1897 plus 2.6 million in Finland), making it the third most populous country in the world (after China and India). And it included much more than just "Russian," or even eastern Slav areas. From the late eighteenth century and throughout the nineteenth century the Tsarist empire had gobbled up Poland, acquired Finland from Sweden and Bessarabia from the Ottoman Empire, subdued the Caucasus and Trans-Caucasus, won

Central Asia in the "Great Game" with Great Britain, and expanded into what used to be Chinese possessions in the far east. By 1904, it bordered Norway and Sweden in the north, in the west Germany and Austria-Hungary, in the south the Ottoman Empire, Persia, Afghanistan and China, and in the south-east it even had a small border with Korea. Japan was only a short stretch of water away from Russian Sakhalin. This was an enormous empire in which large distances and ever poor communications added to the problems of the political system.

To make things worse, the man, who since November 1894 ruled over this complex inefficiency, was not up to the task. With Nicholas II, the empire was stuck with a pathetic autocrat ruling within an archaic political system that he was unable and unwilling to adjust to the realities of industrial war and the emerging mass society. The last Tsar was a textbook example of the dangers of dynastic and autocratic rule. Mild mannered, soft spoken, and slim, he could never live up to the example of his loud, large, and self-confident late father, Alexander III, against whom he constantly measured himself. In a meritocratic political system he would have never been put in charge. He would not have volunteered for a role he did not desire and nobody would have chosen a man for the top job who seemed to change his opinions the moment one advisor left and another one walked through the door. A strong sense of duty, however, kept him from the only reasonable course of action: to resign and go hunting, letting someone else handle the affairs of state. Even a better man, however, would have had his work cut out. What transpired after January 26, 1904, was not a "successful little war" of a European great power against some inferior Asiatics, as had been the hope of the Tsar's more arrogant (and more racist) servants. Instead what Russia faced was a dress rehearsal for modern war leading to revolution.

The Russo-Japanese War (1904–1905)

The fighting was terrible and in the course of the conflict some 400,000 of the Tsar's subjects lost their lives. The Russian armed forces suffered defeat after defeat: Port Arthur fell in December 1904; the battle of Mukden was lost in February and March 1905; the Baltic Fleet, which had hurried around the world to relieve its Pacific sister, was annihilated in May. The empire was beaten at sea, but also on land. Both sides sent their soldiers into suicidal frontal attacks on entrenched positions defended by barbed wire enclosures and machine guns.

Contemporary descriptions of such battles are reminiscent of the killing fields at World War I's Western Front, where German, French, British, and US troops would confront the terror of the modern battlefield. This similarity is significant. While older histories have seen the 1914 to 1918 war as the birth pangs of the twentieth century, more recently the 1904 to 1905 war has received more attention. As the history of the twentieth century becomes less and less

Eurocentric, historians have started to understand the Russo-Japanese war as the first major conflict of this terrible epoch: "World War Zero," as one pithy formulation has it. In this foundational carnage, the Russian army faced defeat despite numerical superiority (as it would later, in World War). Incompetently led, poorly equipped, and suffering from the logistical problems of long lines of communication, the Tsar's army bled and bled.[2]

The unbelievable carnage of this war; the humiliation of being beaten by an Asian foe, who, somewhat annoyingly, accepted all extant rules of war making (proving that there was nothing European about "civilized warfare"); and the clearly inept political and military leadership of this catastrophe all stirred opposition in Russian society. Critics of autocracy had multiplied since the middle of the nineteenth century; they were joined by others unhappy about their living conditions, their working lives, their access to land, or the status of their national group within the Tsarist multinational empire. In the context of the debacle of the war against Japan, the opposition of a variety of groups first grew, then merged, and then exploded.

Forces of Discontent

First was "liberal society," whose campaign for political reforms heated up considerably in the context of the war. Its backbone was the class of professionals – lawyers, doctors, pharmacists, engineers, teachers, journalists, academics – which had been growing since the nineteenth century as an unintended outcome of Alexander II's reforms. Their outlook was European, like their training, which they had often received abroad. For them, Russia was hopelessly backward and needed to "modernize", that is, be dragged out of its stinking sheepskin coat and become more like Western Europe. The peasants needed to be washed, taught to read and write, and educated in the ways of the world. Superstition had to be replaced by enlightenment, the wooden spoon and the communal bowl by more hygienic eating implements, drunkenness by sobriety, and sloth by discipline. Healthcare, education, and transport had to become state of the art, and the political system needed to listen to its people, or at least to the voices of experts and professionals. Liberal society also included some industrialists and other businessmen who elsewhere would have been considered a bourgeoisie. While some of them were critical of autocracy, others wanted a more efficient government and a predictable legal system, but were otherwise content with the state of affairs.

Partially overlapping with "liberal society" was the most Russian of social groups – "the intelligentsia." Historians have struggled to define its essence. Was it a social stratum, emerging from the most peculiar of the estate categories, the "people of various ranks" (*raznochintsy* which included a variety of people who had fallen between the original service classes)? Was it the result of rising education levels and the expansion of university education? Or was it an "imagined community," defined by those who understood themselves as intellectuals and critics of the established order? It was all of the above and its boundaries were therefore constantly challenged, redrawn, and negotiated. Membership of this group did require a certain level of education; most university students understood themselves as *intelligenty*, as did many doctors or lawyers. At the same time, not all were recognized as such, either by themselves or others. Many did come from the people of various ranks, but neither were all *raznochintsy* also *intelligenty* nor vice versa. A critical attitude to the regime and to the social and economic realities of contemporary life was another essential attribute, but it alone did not make an *intelligent* either. Worker-revolutionaries, too, were critical of the existing regime that was estranged from "the people." They adopted many of the practices, rituals, and even language of the intelligentsia but saw themselves as "conscious workers," not intellectuals.

One of the late Tsarist intelligentsia's foundational moments was one of fundamental alienation from the "common people." During the "crazy summer of 1874" thousands of university students "went to the people." Enthused about the supposed revolutionary potential of the peasantry they had read about in books, they hoped to stir the lower orders into rebellion. What they found in the Russian villages, however, were not the naive socialists of their imagination, but hard headed and often hard hearted patriarchs. Freed from serfdom only in 1861, most Russian, Ukrainian, and Belarusian peasants seemed to live in a different century. Their agricultural practices were unproductive and often archaic with no or only very little mechanization. Village life could be violent, and power was in the hand of older men, who could make decisions over the life of "their" youth and womenfolk alike.

When confronted with the radicals who had come "to the people," peasants were more likely to ridicule, beat, or denounce the idealistic city youth with the strange ideas than to make common cause with them. In a country still made up largely of villagers, this experience was sobering. Several reactions are recorded. One path was to take the notion of "going to the people" seriously and join them, going native. This group must have been successful enough, as we no longer hear about them in later accounts. A larger number compensated for their fundamental impotence by taking up that ultimate "weapon of the weak" – terrorism. After 1874 a frightening wave of revolutionary violence engulfed the country. Governors, ministers, police chiefs – and in 1881, the biggest prize of all, Tsar Alexander II himself – fell victim to bombs thrown, shots fired, or daggers drawn. Terrorism would continue to score its dubious successes all the way to 1918 (when Lenin managed to escape an attempt). The state reacted with increasingly heavy-handed policing, which only helped in the recruitment of new "revolutionary martyrs."

A third path after 1874 was to turn away from the peasants and find a better revolutionary subject. Here Marxism came to the rescue; the *Communist Manifesto* was published in Russian in 1869 and *Kapital* in 1872. They would deeply influence Vladimir Il'ich Ulianov (1870–1924), whose brother Alexander was hanged as a terrorist in 1887 after a botched attempt on the life of Tsar Alexander III. As "Lenin," Ulianov would lead the maximalist faction of Russian Social Democracy, the Bolsheviks, to victory in October 1917. But Marxism influenced a much wider field of political radicals, most prominently the more moderate Mensheviks under Iulii Osipovich Martov (1873–1923). The new doctrine promised that industrial development, driven by competition between countries, was the future of humanity. Agrarian societies had to industrialize or perish. Peasants would become workers. Within industrial capitalism a polarization would occur between a few owners of the "means of production" and the majority who had "nothing to lose but their chains." Marxists saw themselves as "materialists" and scoffed at other "idealist" brands of revolution making. In Russia, however, there were Marxists before there was a working class, an idealist situation if there ever was one. The paradox of Marxist revolutionaries attempting to take power in an agrarian land would continue to haunt them once they succeeded in 1917.

Before they could do so, however, the revolutionary subject they relied upon had, first, to come into existence: the proletariat. Luckily, it did, and for reasons quite compatible with Marxist theory: the Romanov Empire was a great power; a great power needed to be able to win wars; winning wars depended on the latest military technology; this technology in turn depended on industrial production of trains, tracks, guns, rifles, shells, and ammunition; hence, Russia needed to industrialize or perish, despite serious misgivings among its leadership and the broader imperial elite, spooked as it was by what Karl Marx and Friedrich Engels had called the "specter of communism" (an oppositional working class, the European experience suggested, was an inevitable byproduct of industrialism). With state funding coming to the aid, the empire industrialized with a vengeance from the 1890s onwards. In the final decade of the nineteenth and the first decade-and-a-half of the twentieth century, Russian industry grew at a faster rate than not only Germany and Great Britain, but also than the rising capitalist power across the Atlantic: the United States.[3]

The result of this spurt was a growing, highly centralized working class particularly in St. Petersburg, but also in the oil-rich Baku, Ukraine's Donbass, or in the old capital Moscow, which became a center of the textile industry. Pay was low, workdays were long, regulation sketchy, and life hard. From the very start, therefore, a group of worker revolutionaries interacted with the radical intelligentsia but also remained distinct from it. They were a minority among the new proletarians, but their influence grew. Many more were disgruntled with their living and working conditions, but grumbled that were their "little father Tsar" to know about their plight, he would help them against the often foreign employers.

9

The restlessness of the working class communicated itself to the countryside, where the overwhelming majority of the population still lived (even as late as 1914, only 18% of the population resided in cities). Most of the new proletarians remained connected to their village of origin. As "peasant-workers" they moved between the city and the countryside, where they would return to help with the harvest, to participate in holiday festivities, or to marry. Strikers were routinely exiled to their rural homes, further strengthening the stream of radical thought from the city. Thus, the unhappy mood in proletarian quarters also circulated through the peasant huts, where it mingled with centuries-old resentments of the toilers of the soil against those who owned land without tilling it. Throughout 1905 the land-hungry peasantry revolted in many regions. Their brothers in uniform also mutinied during this revolutionary year, but were later mobilized to put down peasant rebellions. This basic loyalty to the regime of conscripted peasants has been explained by their perception that the regime's crisis was over, and rebellion thus dangerous. This assessment, by those serving in the armed forces, of the continued strength of the regime set the first Russian revolution apart from its replay in 1917.

Finally, minorities at the periphery of this multinational empire joined the melee. Non-Russians made up well over half of the empire's population – overwhelmingly Slavs, such as Ukrainians, Poles, or Belarusians, but also Finns, Germans, Latvians, Lithuanians, and Estonians, various peoples of the Caucasus and Trans-Caucasus, Tatars, Uzbeks, Kazakhs and other Central Asians, even Iranians and Eskimos. This multiculturalism was not new. Ever since it had begun to expand beyond the lands around Moscow under Ivan III, but in earnest since Ivan IV's (1530–1584) conquest of Kazan in 1552 and the subsequent incorporation of Siberia from 1580, the Russian Empire had to contend with non-Russian peoples. Not only did the empire constantly incorporate non-Russian ethnicities but the tsars also coopted foreign elites into running their state. The result was not a nation state but a multinational empire, held together with force, but also with special concessions, legally prescribed exclusions and privileges for a plethora of peoples.

The fact that the Russian Empire was not ethnically Russian was so central to the life of the Romanov realms that the language that ran this empire even developed a special word to describe it. In Russian, there are two words for "Russian" – *Russkii* and *Rossiiskii*. The former describes the ethnos, the latter the empire. Hence, you can meet an ethnically Russian peasant (*russkii muzhik*) in this imperial Russian state (*Rossiiskoe gosudarstvo*). But you cannot have an imperial *Rossiiskii muzhik* or an ethnically *Russkoe gosudarstvo*, which both would be contradictions in terms.

In the nineteenth century, the sophisticated legal and ideological apparatus holding this empire together came under strain as nationalism became a serious ideological alternative to autocracy. This infiltration of nationalism went both ways: on the one hand, the Russian state became more *Russkii* – which annoyed some of the recently acquired nationalities. Finns and Poles had thought of themselves as constituting specially privileged peoples connected to the empire through the person of the Emperor. Now they found their languages and customs under assault by Russification. On the other hand in the Caucasus and Central Asia, Russia began to behave much more like a European colonial power than as the elite-coopting land empire of old. Non-Russian minorities now grew restless. In particular the relatively recently acquired Poles and Finns, the Baltic and Trans-Caucasian peoples, but also longer-term subjects of the empire like the Ukrainians bristled under Russian rule. In the context of the war with Japan, the unhappiness increased. The end of 1904 saw demonstrations against conscription in Ukraine and Poland (ruled by the Russian emperor as King of Poland since 1815 and a formal part of the empire since 1867).

Revolution

Then came January 9, 1905: "Bloody Sunday." A strike wave had been building since late the previous year and had grown to a de facto general strike in the capital. It paralyzed industrial production, plunged the city into darkness, stopped public transport, and brought life in theaters and restaurants to a halt. On that morning tens of thousands of workers began marching from several assembly points into the center of the capital. Some 100,000 strikers and onlookers, including many women and children, congregated in Palace Square, where they hoped to present a petition to their sovereign and hear their "little father tsar" address his people. Instead, they were greeted, without warning, by bullets; 299 were seriously wounded and at least 130 killed. The Tsar declared martial law.

If the Russo-Japanese war had made the crisis of autocracy acute, Bloody Sunday served as the trigger for revolution. The disparate social groups who had earlier protested, struck, rioted, petitioned, or written pamphlets to voice their discontent with autocracy now merged into one revolutionary movement and their actions into an anti-Tsarist explosion. Worker and professor, professional and peasant, student and soldier, industrialist and intellectual, woman and man, Russian and Chechen, Pole and Jew – all wanted change and they wanted it fast. Workers and professionals were striking, students and professors protesting, and entrepreneurs offered financial assistance to the opposition. Peasants were burning estates. Soldiers were rioting, unwilling to be machine gunned in the killing fields of the war against Japan. There were strikes, armed clashes, and full-blown uprisings in the borderlands: in Finland, the Baltic provinces, Poland, Ukraine, and the Trans-Caucasus. In Moscow, the Tsar's uncle, Grand Duke Sergei Aleksandrovich, a well-known reactionary, became the latest victim of a left-wing terrorist bomb.

11

Confronted with such broad and deep opposition, the Tsar had only two options: to move in troops to quell the unrest, or to drop his usual dismissal of any constraints on his power and make concessions. The first option turned out not to be an option after all: Because of the war in the east, there were too few soldiers available to repress a revolution of this size. Hence, the only course of action was to buckle to popular pressure. First, the Tsar ended the war and made peace with Japan, signing the Treaty of Portsmouth in late August (early September according to the Western calendar). Russia removed its troops from Manchuria, handed over its mines and the South Manchuria Railway, lost Port Arthur and the southern part of the Island of Sakhalin and recognized Korea as part of the Japanese sphere of interest. The empire contracted to 8.4 million square miles, its size at the outbreak of World War I.

More important were internal modifications. They came in the form of the "October Manifesto," an imperial edict issued on October 17 (October 30). It promised inviolability of the person, the freedoms of speech, conscience, assembly and association, universal (male) suffrage, and an elected body representative of all classes of the population (the Duma), which would have the right to discuss and develop legislation. By international standards of the time these were not very radical proposals but, in the Russian case, they amounted to an end to the repressive policies of the late Tsarist police state, at least some checks on autocratic power, and an unleashing of the political and creative energies of society.

For the national minorities, the Manifesto marked a return to a more traditional, pragmatic nationality policy, which coopted elites and left national cultures alone. The freedoms of communication, conscience, speech, and assembly, which the Manifesto promised, and the end of advance censorship, gave the national movements more room to maneuver, to express themselves in the language of their choice. What followed has been described as "springtime of the peoples."[4] Most active were the Poles, the peoples of the Trans-Caucasus, and of the Baltic, especially Estonians and Latvians. Their restlessness pointed to things that came later in the century. Another aspect of the national awakening of 1905 would prove to have an afterlife: inter-ethnic violence, most prominently a wave of terrible anti-Semitic pogroms in the so-called "pale of settlement" for Jews in the Empire's western regions. The pogrom in Kyiv went on for three long days.

Dual Polarization

The October Manifesto was a stroke of Machiavellian genius. Written by Count Sergei Iulevich Witte (1849–1915), one of the most gifted statesmen of the late Tsarist Empire, it served to split the revolutionary movement. The better off, more "respectable" and "liberal" opposition received what it had hoped for: the rule of law, the end of censorship, and an elected representative body. They were inclined, therefore, to close ranks with the civil service and the autocratic state that after all also protected their property from thieves and revolutionaries (but during the chaos of revolution were unable to do so). Mutinous soldiers, rioting peasants, unruly national minorities, and striking workers, meanwhile, were left alone to deal with the wrath of the counter-revolution. With peace in the East, troops became available to quell the unrest. Punitive expeditions put down peasant and national rebellions and strikes were broken by military force. Thousands were executed in these "pacifications."

Soon, counter-revolution also extended to the liberal gains of 1905. Civil liberties were again curtailed and the Duma's rights carefully circumscribed. As these steps did not prevent the new legislature from attempting further political and social reform, the Tsar dissolved it after less than three months in 1906. After new elections, the second Duma of 1907 again ran into the obstructionism of a government never committed to sharing power with a popularly elected legislature. After dissolving the Duma again, the emperor introduced a new electoral law that skewed the vote towards the wealthy and against national minorities. But even the resulting, much more conservative, third and fourth Dumas found it hard to work with a government that never saw the parliament as more than as a consultative body. This stubborn refusal to share power frustrated even staunch supporters of the monarchy. "Respectable society" thus again became alienated from the regime, without ever feeling comfortable again rubbing shoulders with the increasingly aggressive plebeian revolutionaries. Thus, a "dual polarization" – between the regime and "society," and between "society" and "the people" – characterized the last years of peace. It re-emerged in 1917.[5]

Some historians, therefore, have constructed a straight line from the dual polarization after 1905 to the Bolshevik revolution of 1917: given the failed liberal revolution, more radical upheaval was inevitable. And indeed, many of the revolutionaries in 1917 could draw on their experience of 1905, the "dress rehearsal," in Lenin's words.[6] They could also mobilize an original organizational form of revolutionary governance: the councils of workers' deputies, or "soviets" (Russ.: *sovety*), institutions of revolutionary democracy that emerged in 1905 to coordinate strikes and other revolutionary action. While they had precursors in one of the mythical moments of European radicalism – the Paris Commune of 1871 – they were a genuinely Russian invention of working-class self-organization. They served as elected and directly accountable representations for workers of several enterprises, or even an entire city. Dissolved at the end of 1905, they have inspired proponents of "revolutionary democracy" ever since, despite the fact that the Bolshevik dictatorship would, somewhat misleadingly, take over the term as a designation of a fundamentally undemocratic regime. The idea and the practice of "council democracy" forms a bridge between 1905 and 1917, a model readily available once the Tsarist regime broke down under the strains of war. The reformed Petrograd Soviet in particular played a leading role in the events that led to the Bolshevik insurrection.

Another school of history writing has gained in prominence in late twentieth and early twenty-first centuries. In explaining the revolutions of 1917, it puts more weight on the unsettling effects of World War I. While nobody denies that the late Tsarist empire was riven with conflicts, these historians tend to emphasize more positive developments, indicating that Russia might have been on the way to a more west-European model of political, social, and economic development, had the war not intervened. The revolutions of 1917, then, were not inevitable, but maybe the result of a bit of bad luck, as already the first émigré historians teaching at US universities had professed. Much of the recent historiography on Russia in World War I, likewise, stresses the destructive force of the war on the one hand, and its "creative" aspects on the other: the building of a modern warfare state (see Chapter 2).

Where one comes down in such debates about alternative pasts or their impossibility is more a matter of philosophy and politics than of historical record: Is everything that happens over-determined or are there chance and choice in history? Was the Bolshevik revolution a legitimate popular response or an illegitimate coup? There are no definitive, empirically verifiable answers to such questions.

Contradictions

What cannot be doubted, though, is that in the few years between the end of the 1905 Revolution and the outbreak of World War I, the Russian Empire was a cauldron of intense contradictions. The principle of autocracy asserted itself side-by side with a pseudo parliament, the State Duma. Despite all efforts by the tsar and his ministers to destroy it as a political force of consequence, it remained a center of debate, the focal point of a multiparty system, enabling a wide field of legislative activity and political discourse. It showed that the peoples of the Russian Empire were not genetically prone to one-man rule but longed for freedom of expression and self-determination as much as anybody. The Duma's very existence was crucial in the next revolutionary crisis, as we will see in Chapter 2. At the same time, the Duma remained emasculated, both by an electoral law which under-represented the vast majority of the Tsar's subjects, and by the tsar's continued claim to absolute power.

The political absurdity of "parliamentary autocracy" also contributed to the many fissures within late Tsarist society. The October Manifesto had not united reactionaries with the liberal wing of professionals and intelligentsia; at the same time, however, its minor concessions had estranged the latter from more plebeian revolutionaries with their angry slogans and crude disregard for the sacred laws of private property. The clear expectation that revolution would not only come, but would also be successful, which radical students had shared widely before and during 1905, had given way to confusion, and also to reorientation towards other, less heroic but not less taxing life goals. A collection of essays of 1909 tried to distill these new "signposts" (*vekhi*) for the intelligentsia. Students should stop masturbating (both literally and figuratively), it counseled, respect their elders, and devote themselves to their studies. A proper intellectual, in the estimation of this contentious publication, was not somebody who dreamed of revolution, but a hard-working professional with a disciplined mind and detailed knowledge of his or her chosen specialty.[7]

Meanwhile, working-class activism continued. A new strike wave started in 1912. Even at its height, in 1914, however, less than a third of the number of workers were involved than had been in 1905. The strike wave was largely concentrated in the capital's metal-working industry. Elsewhere, the working class was more likely to be engaged in organizing self-help societies than fighting management. Much of industrial action, moreover, was about pay and conditions, not revolution. Even political strikes were usually not anticapitalist, but focused on the abuses of power inherent in the Tsarist political system, concerns similar to those of liberal critics of the regime. Once war broke out, the strikes evaporated into thin air.

Public Sphere

As a growing number of historians have shown, then, the polarizations in late Tsarism were much less pronounced than the older literature would have us believe. Social divisions were deep and real, but they were transcended by broadly shared dreams and aspirations, circulating in the growing public sphere of print media, film, and popular entertainment. During the decades "when Russia learned to read," workers often aspired to the same kind of "respectability" as their social betters and urban culture was more a meeting ground for diverse life forms than a clash of segregated class cultures.[8] The countryside was increasingly drawn into the new nexus of markets for goods and dreams, and villagers, too, participated in these new forms of exchange and consumption, although to a lesser degree than city folk. Film made its debut in Russia well before the revolution, and the Russian film industry developed its own distinctive style of often melodramatic entertainment.

Social identities were complex. The old estate categories – nobles, clergymen, peasants, townspeople, Cossacks, etc. – had defined a person's rights and duties vis-à-vis the service state. They made less and less sense in the more complex world that had come into existence in the nineteenth century. They were overlaid by professional, class, lifestyle, and sexual identifiers. Social mobility was such that it was hard to describe a particular person with only one category, despite the attempts of Marxist analysts, both then and later, to allocate every person to a neat box. The most successful press-tsar of the late years of this empire, Ivan Sytin (1851–1934), was by legal estate a "peasant," by social origin the son of a country clerk, and to Marxists would certainly have been "bourgeois." His newspapers catered to a wide range of readers, from rural folk to city slickers. Nevertheless, the Bolsheviks, whose revolution ruined his business, awarded him a personal pension in recognition of his efforts to spread enlightenment among the masses.

Thanks to men like Sytin, but also thanks to the vast and complex intelligentsia serving an expanding reading public, and despite continuing censorship and police harassment, the Tsar's subjects could read a greater diversity of books, journals, broadsheets, and watch more varied movies than they would for decades after the Bolshevik takeover. Despite everything, this was a much more liberal, and a far more diverse society than anything that would come in the period from 1917 to at least 1985, if not 1991. Revolutionaries were locked up, to be sure, but in confinement they could not only catch up on reading Marx and Engels, but also consort with other radicals of various stripes. Many would remember their prison stints later as their "university." The faction that came to power at the end of 1917 would make sure that their own prisons did not create such favorable conditions for oppositional thought. The Bolsheviks also made every effort to disrupt links to the outside world, resulting in an intellectual, economic, and social isolation unheard of in Russian history. Before 1914, it was not only radicals who had links to foreign countries, where often their leaders sat to plot future revolution. Scholars, too, were integrated into international networks, as were professionals of all kinds. The Russian economy was thoroughly enmeshed in global markets and the Russian state in international treaty systems. In many ways, then, the late Tsarist empire was a much more "normal" country than the victorious revolutionaries made it out to have been.

The growing public sphere also took an increasing role in the provision of welfare to the population. Voluntary associations began to take responsibility for the poor. By 1905, a confusing mixture of local government, religious, and secular philanthropic societies, provided, usually underfunded and ineffective help, to the sick, the poor, the unemployed, and the elderly. Employers, both state and private, increasingly covered their workers for accident, sickness, and invalidity, often directly offering aid through clinics or hospitals attached to the workplaces. Workers joined mutual-aid societies to lessen their risks. Between a quarter to a third of peasant households were members of agricultural cooperatives. They provided loans, served as savings banks, and helped access markets in a more efficient manner than individual peasants could. The central state, too, expanded its welfare functions beyond the workhouses, almshouses, and orphanages it had run since the late eighteenth century. The year 1912 was a key year in this beginning transformation of poor relief into rights-based welfare provision. New legislation now granted universal pension rights to disabled soldiers and war widows, as well as food allowances for families of servicemen. In parallel, the Health and Accident Insurance Law covered workers in many industries in European Russia and the Trans-Caucasus. Siberia and Central Asia remained outside this legislation.

A Warning

It was this country of contradictions, deep divisions, but also a high cultural and social diversity that went to war again in 1914, nine years after the debacle of the Russo-Japanese war. It is impossible to know whether or not it could have avoided the kind of destructive political and social revolution it later witnessed, had it somehow avoided being drawn into World War I. What we do know, however, is that the likelihood of political breakdown and eventually civil war was heightened by the strains of war. It was a war that had triggered the revolution of 1905; and it would be the new war that would lead to the next set of revolutions a decade later. As we will see in the next two chapters, it was war and civil war that deeply shaped the new empire that would emerge, bleeding and exhausted, by the early 1920s.

The risks of war were laid out in impressive clarity in a 1914 memorandum Petr Nikolaevich Durnovo (1848–1915) sent to Nicholas II several months before the start of hostilities.[9] In this brief, the one-time Minister for the Interior argued the case for peace. What he called "the ever-memorable period of troubles in 1905–1906" was bound to repeat itself. "This war," he wrote, "cannot turn out to be a mere triumphal march to Berlin. Both military disasters – partial ones, let us hope – and all kinds of shortcomings in our supply are inevitable." Severe repression of the opposition would be necessary. Even in the event of victory, he predicted "agrarian troubles … as a result of agitation for compensating the soldiers with additional land allotments" as well as "labor troubles during the transition from the probably increased wages of war time to normal schedules." However, he thought that with the army victorious, "the putting down of the Socialist movement will not offer any insurmountable obstacles." It had not so, after all, in 1905–1906.

This, then, was Durnovo's best case scenario: a war full of military setbacks but overall victorious; severe internal strife, which would be put down with an iron fist. The worst case was what later transpired:

> The defeated army, having lost its most dependable men, and carried away by the
> tide of primitive peasant desire for land, will find itself too demoralized to serve as

a bulwark of law and order. The legislative institutions and the intellectual opposition parties, lacking real authority in the eyes of the people, will be powerless to stem the popular tide, aroused by themselves, and Russia will be flung into hopeless anarchy, the issue of which cannot be foreseen.

Durnovo turned out to be right and his warning has been quoted ever since. A war was indeed imminent, and it could not be contained.

After Archduke Franz Ferdinand, heir to the Austrian throne, was murdered with his wife by a Serbian nationalist in Sarajevo on June 15/28, 1914, Austria-Hungary, backed by a diplomatic "blank check" from Germany, declared war on Serbia on July 15/28. This declaration of war triggered a whole series of events that would quickly bring all major powers into what became World War I. Tsarist Russia, backing Serbia, entered the war on the side of France and Britain against Germany and Austria-Hungary.

Why did the Tsar not listen to Durnovo? Part of the answer is political. Nicholas II would have known that Durnovo was a long-term opponent of any alliance with Great Britain and an advocate of a rapprochement with Germany. Much of his memorandum was indeed a review of the foreign policy of Russia since 1904, a series of diplomatic missteps in the view of its author. The Tsar might thus be excused for disregarding this now-famous note: read in the context it was written, it becomes less the clear-sighted prophecy it turned out in hindsight. Instead, a critical reader at the time would have seen it as attempting to bolster one policy position by using the threat of revolutionary apocalypse. After all, had not the Tsar survived the last revolution, by successfully implementing a policy of divide and rule, appease and suppress?

Moreover, the Tsar seems to have convinced himself that this time things would be different. In a war against Germany he would have the people on his side. Anti-German sentiment would be strong enough to mobilize popular patriotism, in effect overcoming rather than exacerbating social and political divisions. Clearly, Russia's great power status was at stake, and outside of some radical circles the people would understand this basic fact. While war was risky, as the empire was not ready for it, the risk was military rather than revolutionary. And this military risk was balanced by the political risk of losing the status of being one of the major players in European politics – the main reason that the many painful reforms of the nineteenth century had been forced upon the autocracy in the first place. Much, then, was at stake.

In the end, the Tsar followed Durnovo insofar as he tried to avoid war rather than provoking it. Russian actions during the July crisis were not intended to bring about a military showdown. Rather, a partial mobilization on July 16/29 was supposed to delay the conflict by convincing Vienna that St. Petersburg meant business but also to appease Germany by not mobilizing close to its border. The Tsar hoped that direct communication with his cousin, German emperor Wilhelm II, could avoid war. The Kaiser, however, informed his royal relation that it was Russia, not Germany, that could decide about war and peace, effectively daring Nicholas to give up any pretense to great power status if he wanted to avoid hostilities. This slight finally forced the Tsar's hand. On 17/30 July17/30, Nicholas II ordered general mobilization. It took effect on 18/31 July18/31. On July 19/ August 1, Germany took it as a pretext to declare war, casting itself a victim of alleged Russian aggression. Two days later, Germany declared war on Russia's ally France. World War I had begun.

Notes

1   Both reactions reported in *The Memoirs of Count Witte. A portrait of the twilight years of tsarism by the man who built modern Russia*, ed. Sidney Harcave (Armonk, NY, and London: M. E. Sharpe, 1990), 369 ("victorious"), 385 ("baboons").

2   John W. Steinberg, "Was the Russo-Japanese War World War Zero?" *The Russian Review* 67 (2008): 1–7.

3   Like many other Marxist texts, the Communist Manifesto, with its threat of the "specter of communism" can be accessed at the *Marxist Internet Archive*: https://www.marxists.org/archive/marx/works/1848/communist-manifesto/ (last accessed December 27, 2017).

4   Andreas Kappeler, *The Russian Empire: A Multiethnic History* (Harlow: Longman, 2001).

5   Leopold Haimson, "The Problem of Social Stability in Urban Russia, 1905–1917 (Part One)." *Slavic Review* 23, no. 4 (1964): 619–42; part two: ibid., 24, no. 1 (1965): 1–22; id., "'The Problem of Political and Social Stability in Urban Russia on the Eve of War and Revolution' Revisited." *Slavic Review* 59, no. 4 (2000): 848–75.

6   V. I. Lenin, "'Left-Wing' Communism: an Infantile Disorder," (1920), https://www.marxists.org/archive/lenin/works/1920/lwc/ (last accessed December 27, 2017).

7   Anon. *Vekhi. Sbornik statei o russkoi intelligentsii* (Moscow: Avalon, 1909).

8   Jeffrey Brooks, *When Russia Learned to Read. Literacy and Popular Literature, 1861–1917* (Princeton, NJ: Princeton University Press, 1985).

9   The Durnovo memorandum is available in a variety of source collections on Russian history. Several copies are available online, including the edition from which the quotations in this chapter are taken: http://www.archive.org/stream/documentsofrussi027937mbp#page/n17/mode/2up (last accessed December 27, 2017).

Bibliography

Ascher, Abraham. *The Revolution of 1905 2 vols. Volume 1: Russia in Disarray* (Stanford: Stanford University Press, 1988); volume 2: *Authority Restored* (Stanford: Stanford University Press, 1992).

Ascher, Abraham. *The Revolution of 1905. A Short History* (Stanford: Stanford University Press, 2004).

Brooks, Jeffrey. *When Russia Learned to Read. Literacy and Popular Literature, 1861–1917* (Princeton, NJ: Princeton University Press, 1985).

Bushnell, John. *Mutiny Amid Repression. Russian Soldiers in the Revolution of 1905–1906* (Bloomington: Indiana University Press, 1985).

Bushnell, John. "The Specter of Mutinous Reserves: How the War Produced the October Manifesto," in: *Russo-Japanese War in Global Perspective*, ed. John Steinberg, Bruce Menning, and David Schimmelpennick van der Oye (Leiden: Brill, 2005–2006), 333–48.

Clowes, Edith W., Samuel D. Kassow, and James L. West, eds. *Between Tsar and People. Educated Society and the Quest for Public Identity in Late Imperial Russia* (Princeton, NJ: Princeton University Press, 1991).

Dowler, Wayne, *Russia in 1913* (DeKalb, Northern Illinois University Press, 2010).

Engelstein, Laura. *Moscow, 1905. Working-Class Organization and Political Conflict* (Stanford, CT: Stanford University Press, 1982).

Engelstein, Laura. *The Keys to Happiness. Sex and the Search for Modernity in Fin-De-Siecle Russia* (Ithaca, NY and London: Cornell University Press, 1992).

Engelstein, Laura. *Slavophile Empire: Imperial Russia's Illiberal Path* (Ithaca, NY: Cornell University Press, 2009).

Enticott, Peter. *The Russian Liberals and the Revolution of 1905* (London: Routledge, 2016).

Ferro, Mark. *Nicholas II. The Last of the Tsars* (London: Viking, 1991).

Frank, Stephen P., and Mark D. Steinberg, eds. *Cultures in Flux. Lower-Class Values, Practices, and Resistance in Late Imperial Russia* (Princeton, NJ: Princeton University Press, 1994).

Gaudin, Corinne. *Ruling Peasants. Village and State in Late Imperial Russia* (DeKalb: Northern Illinois University Press, 2007).

Hellie, Richard. "The Structure of Russian Imperial History," *History and Theory* 44 (2005): 88–112.

Holquist, Peter. "Violent Russia, Deadly Marxism? Russia in the Epoch of Violence, 1905–21," *Kritika: Explorations in Russian and Eurasian History* 4, no. 3 (2003): 627–52.

Kappeler, Andreas. *The Russian Empire: A Multiethnic History* (Harlow: Longman, 2001).

Kotsonis, Yanni. *Making Peasants Backward: Managing Populations in Russian Agricultural Cooperatives, 1861–1914* (Basingstoke: Macmillan, 1999).

Kotsonis, Yanni. *States of Obligation. Taxes and Citizenship in the Russian Empire and Early Soviet Republic* (Toronto: University of Toronto Press, 2014).

Lieven, Dominic. *Nicholas II. Twilight of the Empire* (New York: St. Martin's Press, 1993).

Lincoln, W. Bruce. *The Great Reforms. Autocracy, Bureaucracy, and the Politics of Change in Imperial Russia* (DeKalb: Northern Illinois University Press, 1990).

Lindenmeyr, Adele. *Poverty is not a Vice: Charity, Society, and the State in Imperial Russia* (Princeton, NJ: Princeton University Press, 1996).

McDonald, David M. "The Durnovo Memorandum in Context: Official Conservatism and the Crisis of Autocracy," *Jahrbücher für Geschichte Osteuropas* 44, no. 4 (1996): 481–502.

McKean, R. B. "Social Insurance in Tsarist Russia, St Petersburg, 1907–17," *Revolutionary Russia* 3, no. 1 (1990): 55–89.

McReynolds, Louise. *Russia at Play. Leisure Activities at the End of the Tsarist Era* (Ithaca, NY and London: Cornell University Press, 2003).

Montefiore, Simon Sebag. *The Romanovs. 1613–1918* (London: Weidenfeld & Nicolson, 2016).

Moon, David. *The Russian Peasantry 1600–1930. The World the Peasants Made* (London and New York: Longman, 1999).

Morrissey, Susan K. *Heralds of Revolution. Russian Students and the Mythologies of Radicalism* (New York and Oxford: Oxford University Press, 1998).

Neuberger, Joan. *Hooliganism. Crime, Culture, and Power in St. Petersburg, 1900–1914* (Berkeley, Los Angeles, London: University of California Press, 1993).

Rogger, Hans. *Russia in the Age of Modernisation and Revolution 1881–1917*, 9th edition (London and New York: Longman, 1992).

Steinberg, John W., Bruce W. Menning, and David Schimmelpennick van der Oye, eds. *Russo-Japanese War in Global Perspective. World War Zero*, 2 vols. (Leiden: Brill, 2005–2006).

Tian-Shanskaia, Olga Semyonova. *Village Life in Late Tsarist Russia* (Bloomington and Indianapolis: Indiana University Press, 1993).

Verner, Andrew M. *The Crisis of Russian Autocracy: Nicholas II and the 1905 Revolution* (Princeton, NJ: Princeton University Press, 1990).

Watstein, Joseph. "Ivan Sytin – an Old Russia Success Story," *The Russian Review* 30, no. 1 (1971): 43–53.

Weeks, Theodore R. *Nation and State in Late Imperial Russia. Nationalism and Russification on the Western Frontier 1863–1914* (DeKalb: Northern Illinois University Press, 1996).

Wirtschafter, Elise Kimerling. *Social Identity in Imperial Russia* (DeKalb: Northern Illinois University Press, 1997).

Wolff, David. *To the Harbin Station. The Liberal Alternative in Russian Manchuria, 1898–1914* (Stanford, CA: Stanford University Press, 1999).

Wynn, Charters. *Workers, Strikes, and Pogroms. The Donbass-Dnepr Bend in Late Imperial Russia, 1870–1905* (Princeton, NJ: Princeton University Press, 1992).

Youngblood, Denise J. *The Magic Mirror. Moviemaking in Russia, 1908–1918* (Madison: Wisconsin University Press, 1999).

Zelnik, Reginald, ed. *A Radical Worker in Tsarist Russia. The Autobiography of Semen Ivanovich Kanatchikov* (Stanford, CA: Stanford University Press, 1986).

2

Imperial Apocalypse (1914–1918)

World War I brought unbelievable suffering to the Tsar's lands. By 1918, nearly two million, or 5%, of the male working-age population had died at the frontline or as a result of wounds or disease suffered in the trenches or while in captivity. Well over seven million had been deported or displaced as refugees. Jews and Germans had become victims of pogroms and dispossession. Industry as well as agriculture lay in ruins. The strains of war had exacerbated the social, ethnic, and political divisions and magnified Nicholas II's defects as a leader. Revolution and imperial collapse ensued.

By the middle of 1918, the Tsar and his family were dead, shot by revolutionaries. No less than 30 governments now claimed authority over various parts of the former Russian Empire: 13 in the Volga, Siberia, and North Russia, six in regions under German occupation, six others in nonoccupied regions of Russia, the Kuban, Don, Northern Caucasus, and Turkestan, plus the five newly independent states of Finland, Poland, Georgia, Armenia, and Azerbaijan. And such a snapshot does not even account for the constant changes in some regions. Crimea, for example, saw 10 different governments between 1917 and 1921, Ukraine experienced nine.

The war was central to this collapse of the Romanov Empire. Changes to conscription triggered the first major uprising of this period that occurred in Central Asia in 1916. The wartime economic boom and bust provided the broader context of the urban revolutions that shook the Russian heartland in 1917. It was food shortages caused by the war that triggered the demonstrations setting off the revolution in February, and war-related economic imbalances fueled the accompanying industrial strikes.

The Soviet Union: A Short History, First Edition. Mark Edele.
© 2019 John Wiley & Sons, Inc. Published 2019 by John Wiley & Sons, Inc.

Soldiers were crucial at every turning point in 1917. In February, it was their increasing refusal to shoot civilians that transformed a rebellion into a revolution; and throughout the year it was the soldiers in Petrograd and their increasing frustration with the continuing war that drove the radicalization leading to Red October. Vladimir Lenin's revolution, then, was carried out in the name of the workers. But it was soldiers who indeed made this revolution. The politics of war were central in this process. The caretaker government's reluctance to give up the Tsarist war aims after the February revolution hurt its legitimacy more than anything else. And its determination to continue the war on the side of the democratic countries ran into the increasing war-weariness of an increasing number of the long-suffering rank and file.

The rural revolutions, too, were entangled with the war in various ways. On the one hand, the rumors about land distribution (and its actual practice on the ground) increased the likelihood for peasants in uniform to abandon their posts and go home. This 'melting away of the army' had weakened the caretaker government that had been in charge since the abdication of the Tsar. It also brought men back into the villages, often armed not only with rifles but also with new revolutionary words. The military revolt, the rural and the urban revolutions thus mutually reinforced each other in complex spirals of radicalization and state breakdown.

World War I, then, was central to the emergence and success of the revolution. But the war continued after October 1917 and it continued to structure the choices of the actors in this drama. In 1918, the German presence in the western borderlands contributed decisively to the major story of this year: further breakdown of the empire. The persistence of a Ukrainian state throughout 1918 was guaranteed by German bayonets. The emergence of independent states in the Baltics and the Trans-Caucasus, likewise, was a result of the war, as was Allied intervention in the east of the crumbling colossus and the way anti-Bolshevik forces emerged in Siberia.

This chapter thus narrates the Revolutions of 1917 and the events of the following year as part of the history of World War I (1914–1918). It starts with the war's beginning and ends with the surrender of Germany in November 1918. An older literature has often shortened the history of this war and treated it as a prequel to the real story of the Revolution of 1917. More recent research has done the opposite: the revolutions became a moment in a "continuum of violence."[1] Where the standard treatments end Russia's War either in 1917, with the end of Tsarism, or with the Treaty of Brest-Litovsk (March 3, 1918), which formally ended hostilities between Russia and Germany, we can now see that the imperial breakdown, which had started with the war, did not stop until after the Germans had lost the war in the west. World War I and the first year of the Civil War bled into one "imperial apocalypse."[2]

Initial Successes

When the war broke out in 1914, military matters went well at first. Germany was distracted in France. Russian troops marched into East Prussia, won a victory at Gumbinnen, and laid siege to Königsberg, while a second pincer moved towards Tannenberg. In the South, successes were even more impressive. By 1915, Russia had occupied large swathes of Austrian Galicia. The military risk, it appeared, was smaller than initially apprehended. Russia was still a great power.

The outbreak of war silenced the strike movement. The cities witnessed an eruption of patriotic sentiment enveloping substantial minorities of all social classes. Popular anger directed itself at the German embassy in St. Petersburg, which was looted. Massive police presence saved the Austrian embassy from a similar fate. The village was more subdued. But here, too, identification with the nation went further than historians sometimes assume. In keeping with this patriotic frenzy, the government changed the name of the capital. "Petersburg" sounded much too Teutonic. It would now be a more Russian "Petrograd."

The Great Retreat of 1915

The euphoria was short-lived. Soon after the victory at Gumbinnen in East Prussia (7/20 August), the poorly led Russian army suffered a crushing defeat at Tannenberg on August 13/26 through August 17/30, 1914. Things worsened when the battle of the Masurian Lakes (August 27/ September 9, through September 1/14) initiated the Tsar's soldiers' complete withdrawal from German territory. Inept leadership asserted itself, as did poor organization and failing infrastructure. The shortage of shells, ammunition, and rifles was exacerbated by serious transport problems, not only from the railheads, where horse-drawn transport predominated, but also within the inadequate rail network itself. By 1915, things started to look catastrophic at the frontline.

When faced with an encirclement operation in Poland and Galicia, the Russian high command had no choice but to pull back, eventually abandoning all of Poland as well as Courland (today's Lithuania and parts of Latvia). This "Great Retreat" of 1915 was accompanied by a mass expulsion of civilian populations eastward, pogroms against Jews, and a brutal policy of scorched earth attempting to leave nothing to the enemy. The results were massive territorial losses, an enormous refugee crisis, and spreading lawlessness within the Russian army. In the longer term, the destructiveness of the retreat pulverized whatever goodwill towards Russia might have been left in Poland, which would remain outside of Russia's orbit until the end of World War II. Likewise, the fact that the Russian army treated Jews worse than the German occupiers would have a tragic afterlife during World War II, when many refused to evacuate because they remembered the Germans as the lesser evil.

Discontent Renewed, 1915–1916

The Great Retreat was a shock. The early signs of misgivings among the population – along with the patriotic demonstrations there had been draft riots in 1914 – now grew to a growing tremor of war weariness. The strike movement resurged in 1915. Peasant riots grew in frequency in 1916. In Central Asia, a violent uprising against conscription was drowned in blood in the same year. Elsewhere, draft evasion assumed massive proportion. Whatever support there had been for the war in the villages disappeared with the men drafted into the frontline's meat grinder.

Social and geographic dislocations were breathtaking. Men were drafted into the army and disappeared from farms, mines, and factories. Women, youth, prisoners of war (POWs), and labor migrants from China and Korea took their place. Villagers moved to the cities in even more astonishing numbers than had been the case before the war. Miners went from the coalfields to the industrial cities, where they could find better working conditions in the expanding war factories. Refugees flooded back from the frontlines as the Germans began to march east. Germans and Jews were dispossessed and deported. The war economy grew by leaps and bounds, churning out more and more of the lacking equipment, which a rail system struggled to deliver, charged to the breaking point as it was with transporting soldiers and civilians, refugees, deportees, and labor migrants.

State finances were in disarray. During the early patriotic days, the state had imposed prohibition, depriving its coffers of the quarter of revenue the state monopoly on liquor sales had provided in the final years of Tsarism. The enormous costs of the war were met by going deeper and deeper into debt and by printing paper money. Inflation skyrocketed. The economy, first fueled by a wartime boom, began to stutter. As skilled labor disappeared into the frontline's killing fields untrained hands took over. Productivity dropped. Consumer goods disappeared from shelves. Food in the cities became scarce as the peasants withheld more and more grain from a market that had nothing to offer but valueless paper bills. What little they did release got stuck on the over-burdened transport system. The fear of hunger raised its ugly head.

In this situation, the gulf between the Tsar's bureaucrats and educated society became wider. Publicly minded citizens asserted themselves during the war, both in the sphere of warfare and in the provision of welfare. As men went off to the front, women joined the Red Cross or charity organizations. War–Industrial committees provided another avenue for patriotic work open to both men and women, as did the Union of Towns and Zemstvos (*Zemgor*). Citizen-technocrats now took over the care of refugees and the management of diseases they brought with them. They also looked after wounded and convalescing soldiers. Increasingly, these patriotic citizens felt that they were better able to handle the war effort that the Tsar and his bureaucrats, to say nothing of the unpopular (German) Empress with her strange sidekick Rasputin.

The Brusilov Offensive, 1916

The patriotic citizens were right. The War–Industrial committees and the Special Conference on National Defense did more than line industrialists' pockets. They began to transform the Russian Empire from an industrializing agrarian polity into a modern, technocratic mobilization state. The Special Conference, in particular, "began as an engine for utilization of free enterprise," as a classic historical treatment had it. "It ended by inaugurating the Soviet economy."[3] This embryonic warfare state rebuilt the armed forces, now increasingly equipped with what they needed.

This buildup enabled General Aleksei Brusilov to successfully attack Austrian forces in the period June to September 1916. The offensive showed what could be done if military professionals, supported by the necessary hardware, were allowed to do their job without interference by indecisive monarchs, lickspittles, and holy men. The Russian Empire, it turned out, could be a match for the Central Powers' military machine, a lesson too many Germans and Austrians forgot at their own peril soon afterwards. They were reminded after 1943, and by some of the same men who had been commanders under Brusilov. By then, the tentative beginnings of the Russian warfare state had transmogrified into the Soviet military-industrial behemoth led by Iosif Stalin.

Welfare

The strains of war mobilized state and society for warfare, but at the same time also increased the demands for welfare. Committees to assist soldiers' families formed all over the country, growing the nongovernmental sector. Public organizations and charities became entangled with the Ministry of the Interior, with local government, and with charities run by members of the imperial family. Professional organizations provided assistance to a variety of constituencies and were financed in this quest by the state. Local self-government (*zemstvo*), now organized in an All-Russian Union, became involved in running food banks, hospitals, and washing and disinfection stations for soldiers and refugees, as well as caring for war disabled. Funding was provided by the central government. Likewise, aid to the families of soldiers and war dead was in the hands of a Supreme Council for the Care of Soldiers' Families, which united government bureaucracies with voluntary associations. A similar combination of state and society characterized the Special Council for the Organization of Refugees, which tried to grapple with the enormous refugee crisis caused by the Great Retreat, combining welfare provision with mobilization to work.

Dual Polarization

Slowly but surely, then, a peculiar kind of state developed as a compact of nongovernment and state organizations. It allowed industrial, political, and military professionals to solve the problems of wartime in new and creative ways: mobilization of human and other resources, production and distribution of armaments and ammunition, healthcare and the provision of welfare to the population. For the time being, however, these efforts were thwarted by the Tsar, his wife, and the nonentities they had surrounded themselves with. Brusilov's victory was turned into defeat by the timidity of his fellow generals, "silly idiots" in the Tsar's uncharacteristically insightful judgment.[4]

Elsewhere, he showed less vision. Unable to comprehend the demands of modern warfare, Nicholas II clung stubbornly to his claim to absolute rule. His wife, Aleksandra, became more and more enthralled by her spiritual advisor, the over-sexed holy man Rasputin, always ready to scandalize public opinion. By late 1916, the gulf between educated society and the regime had grown so wide that a liberal leader, intent upon winning the war, saw only two options for explaining the state of affairs: the Tsar's men were either stupid or treasonous.

As the war went on, the second void of prewar society also reopened: the rift between educated society and the mass of workers and peasants. The lives of proletarians had been precarious as the best of times. Now, they became dramatically worse. The growth of the urban labor force fueled by the wartime production boom was not matched by housing construction. Labor conditions in the expanding industries declined. Costs of living increased and wages by no means matched inflation. Already long workdays lengthened even further, as did the queues in front of the bread stores. The working-class quarters became restless again.

When the Russian Empire faced a re-play of the drama of an unsuccessful war touching off domestic revolution, it played out on a quite different stage to that of 1905. An assertive liberal society – clustered around the Duma, the voluntary organizations, and the new institutions of the emerging warfare state – was ready to take over the war effort from the incompetent and corrupt Tsarist regime; the army, much bigger than its predecessor during the Russo-Japanese war, already showed signs of strain and the garrisoned units in the cities were unwilling to either go to the front or put down domestic unrest; the working class had become more female, more peasant, more youthful, and more unsettled; as state authority and established social and economic ties crumbled under the strains of war, violence and crime increased, adding to the overall volatility; the ongoing population displacement ensured that revolutionary moods circulated quickly throughout the country; and the Tsar, his authority already seriously battered by 1905 and its aftermath, took command of the army at the height of the Great Retreat, thereby both removing himself from Petrograd politics and making himself personally responsible for the military disasters he presided over. The country increasingly resembled a revolutionary powder keg ready to ignite.

Urban Revolutions in Russia (1): February 1917

The spark flew in Petrograd on International Women's Day 1917 (February 23/March 8). Antiwar demonstrations by women workers who were worried about the food shortage soon grew into city-wide proletarian unrest. Calls were heard for the overthrow of Tsarism and an end to the war. By February 25 the city was effectively shut down by a general strike. Soldiers increasingly refused to follow orders to disperse the revolutionary crowds. When confronted by demonstrating women asking them to join "the people," many did, taking their rifles with them. Even elite Cossack units began to waver, sometimes defending the crowds from attacking police. The state's monopoly of force began to dissipate.

Soon, the mutiny of its soldiers convinced the military leaders that rebellion against the Tsar was the only option, should they desire to continue the war. Faced with the threat of losing control over their men, the top brass, joining civilian politicians, pressured Nicholas II to resign. He relented on March 2, ending over 300 years of Romanov rule.

The February uprising and the resulting abdication of the Tsar began what is usually referred to as the "Russian Revolution." A better term would be "revolutions in the Russian empire" (*Rossiiskie revoliutsii* rather than *Russkaia revoliutsiia*), as the upheaval was not one event, but a cluster of revolutions, revolts, wars, and civil wars. This process took place in the context of World War I; it stretched, at the very least, from 1916 to 1923; it encompassed not just "Russia," but engulfed all the lands which, by 1914, were part of the Russian Empire; it included urban and rural revolutions, national, anti-imperial movements, as well as interstate wars, border conflicts, ethnic and social confrontations; and all of these violent political processes were entangled with each other as well as with a military mutiny against the war.

Urban Revolutions in Russia (2): October 1917

In a centralized state, what happened in the capital was crucial. After the Tsar's fall in early March, two entities took over, a transfiguration of the twin political innovations of the 1905 revolution. The Duma supplied the politicians to staff

29

the caretaker government, which was to hold power only until a Constituent Assembly could be elected and democratically decide over the new order, land redistribution, and all other questions of political reform. The Provisional Government was initially supported by the Petrograd Soviet of Workers' and Soldiers' Deputies, which had been formed in late February following the model of the city's Soviet of 1905. It served as a representation of the revolutionary proletariat and the military garrison of the capital. Originally, it was dominated by moderate socialists, but their inability to find a clear language to express the discontent of the urban lower orders marginalized them more and more. Throughout 1917 the Soviet drifted further and further to the left, where much more radical communists agitated for an end to the war, the distribution of land, and "all power to the Soviets." These were the successful slogans of Lenin's Bolsheviks, originally a splinter party of the Russian Social Democrats, but increasingly a power to be reckoned with. Lenin had not even been in the country when the February revolution broke out, but only made it back from Swiss exile with the help of the Germans who provided a "sealed train" through their territory. (The fiction was that by declaring the train extraterritorial, Lenin did not collude with Russia's enemy). When he arrived, his slogans seemed out of touch with reality. By the end of the year, the increasingly radicalized Petrograd Soviet had become one of the mainstays of Lenin's power.

A major reason for this leftward drift was the war, which, despite the revolution, continued. At first, many had hoped that the revolution would reinvigorate a Russia now armed to the teeth and a real match to the Germans. And indeed, in a new effort in the summer of 1917, German defenses quickly crumbled under the unheard of pounding they now received by Russian artillery. The Russian army, however, had already disintegrated so far that the new superiority could no longer be exploited. The so-called Kerensky-offensive degenerated into revolutionary chatter, followed by mutiny. Counter attacks led to headlong flight. The Germans and Austrians won the day, despite their numerical inferiority. Russia lost all that had been gained with so much blood during the Brusilov offensive of 1916. Only on the Ottoman front did the revolutionary state continue to fight and win.

The war now went from bad to worse. The army began to wither away, as more and more men left for home to take part in the anticipated revolutionary distribution of land. In the cities, support for moderate socialists dissipated as the strength of Bolshevism grew. The simple slogans of Vladimir Lenin's party – peace, bread, land, all power to the Soviets – appealed to an increasingly exhausted, angry, and hungry proletariat. What was left of the army dissolved into armed gangs led by charismatic warlords. Deserters and bandits further contributed to the atmosphere of violence, fear, and terror. If a state is an organization with a monopoly over the legitimate use of violence in a given territory, then there was no "state" in Russia in much of 1917.

By the summer of that year, then, the hope that the Provisional Government could continue the war and institute orderly political and social reforms after victory was no longer realistic. The choice instead was between military dictatorship from the right, and revolutionary dictatorship from the left. The threat of the former reared its head in August, when Lavr Georgievich Kornilov (1870–1918), one of the early warlords, tried to take control. It was neutralized by an alliance between the government and the Petrograd Soviet, now in control of the capital's military forces. When Lenin's Bolsheviks, whose support in the Soviet had become overwhelming, decided to take power in October, the provisional government no longer had anyone to back it up. The October uprising, far from the heroic military struggle it would be depicted as later, amounted to picking up power not defended by anyone.

Subsequently, there was some fighting, which marked the start of the war between the Bolshevik "Reds" and those who opposed them. Drawing on the history of the French revolution, the anti-Bolshevik forces were quickly dubbed the "Whites." This color-coding, which implies that all enemies of the Bolsheviks were counter-revolutionaries, obscures a much more complex reality, as we shall see. Nevertheless, it became a useful shorthand to reduce the complexity of the convoluted story of the "Russian Civil War," which is often depicted as a two-way struggle between "Reds" and "Whites." At first, the Reds won the day. In Petrograd, officer cadets rose against the Bolsheviks, but were defeated with relative ease. Outside the capital, General Petr Krasnov led a force of Cossacks against quickly mobilized Bolshevik militias, the "Red Guards." The anti-Bolshevik forces lost, and Krasnov retreated to fight another day, this time from the Cossack territories of the Don. In Moscow, street fighting erupted and continued for several days. Again, the Reds won the struggle. Other skirmishes developed between General Kornilov's Tekintsy, his personal troops, about 400 strong, whom he tried to take with him after he left his detention in Bykhov and marched south to Novocherkassk. Harassed by Red Guards in superior numbers, the Tekintsy eventually gave up and changed sides. Kornilov continued alone and eventually made it to anti-Bolshevik territory, from where he continued the struggle.

With military challenges beaten back, the Bolsheviks faced one other obstacle to keeping power: the ballot box. Elections to the long-awaited Constituent Assembly finally took place in late November but failed to deliver the Bolsheviks a democratic mandate to rule. While securing significant support among proletarians and soldiers, Lenin's urban party was out-polled by the agrarian Socialist Revolutionaries (SRs), who had a much wider constituency in this peasant country. Hence, Lenin's men dissolved the annoying body after only 13 hours of proceedings in January 1918. They would not hold another democratic election until 1989 (see Chapter 9).

Rural Revolutions in 1917

However compelling the political drama unfolding in Petrograd, much of the unrest in 1917 took place in the countryside, where the majority of the population still lived. The revolution received much of its wrath from the accumulated resentments of rural dwellers: Russian and Ukrainian peasants lusting for the lands of crown, church, nobility; Muslim nomads rebelling against military conscription and the incursion of Christian, Slavic settlers on their pastures; Finnish farmers bracing themselves against a potential takeover of power by urban proletarians; etc. While the details thus varied by region and by culture and circumstance, what we can discern in the countryside in 1917 is a large-scale revolt of rural folk against rule by outsiders.

Lenin, not a fan of what Karl Marx had dubbed the "idiocy of rural life," for tactical reasons empowered them to revolt. Among the first decrees his government issued after taking power was the decree on land. It gave peasants carte blanche to do what they wanted, and had in many places already done throughout 1917: to take the lands controlled by gentry, state, and church. The resulting spontaneous distribution of land not only neutralized the countryside; it also further disintegrated the army, as nobody wanted to be left out in this free-for-all.

Central Asia, 1916–1918

The rural revolution differed by region. In Turkestan the struggle had begun in 1916 when Central Asians rose against newly introduced conscription. Their uprising was met with unbelievable brutality from both armed Slavic settlers and Russian troops sent in to put the rebellion down. The violence continued into 1917. In Central Asia, that is, the Steppe and Turkestan Governor-Generalships, then, the events of that year only further fueled, but did not initially cause, a confrontation about war and colonialism, a struggle between town and country, between colonizers and colonized, settlers and nomads, Christians and Muslims.

This civil war developed its own dynamic. In the words of one historian, Turkestan had "for all intents and purposes become independent" from Russia after February. "Events in that pivotal year transpired with little involvement of the imperial center."[5] This was an unequal struggle. The Europeans were much better armed than the indigenous peoples, who also suffered from a terrible famine caused partially by bad weather and partially by the breakdown of railroad communications due to the strains of war and the chaos of revolution.

The Central Asian civil war was a multisided struggle. In the northern regions of the Steppe, indigenous liberals formed the *Alash Orda* government, which demanded territorial autonomy within the continuing imperial framework. This government was tolerated by Slavic settlers and the emerging White movement of Cossacks, with strongholds in Orenburg and Uralsk. In the west of the Steppe, by contrast, newly established Soviets united Russian working class and Kazakh poor with Socialist Revolutionary Party (SR) or Bolshevik leanings to challenge the *Alash Orda*'s authority.

Further south, in the cotton producing regions of Turkestan, ethnic relations were much more fraught. Here, Russian and Ukrainian workers, soldiers, settlers, and officials often sided with "the Bolsheviks," who became a stand-in for colonial rule by Slavs. The Muslim majority was represented by the Turkestan Muslim Central Council, organized in April 1917, while the Tashkent Soviet represented the Russian and European minority, mostly workers and soldiers. The Soviet had risen against the Provisional Government before the Petrograd uprising, but this coup was suppressed by a punitive military expedition. The second attempt succeeded and the Soviet took power in Tashkent in the wake of Petrograd's Red October. Other regional cities followed a similar path and by the year's end Soviet rule was formally established with the Turkestan Council of People's Commissars (*Turksovnarkom*) mirroring the new Russian government (*Sovnarkom*), where "ministers" were called "People's Commissars" to stress their revolutionary credentials.

Less revolutionary was the relationship of *Turksovnarkom* with the Muslim majority. Like colonial masters of old, the communists refused to admit the native population into government positions. The Central Council responded by organizing a counter-government based in Kokand, in what is today Uzbekistan. It united Muslim and Russian opposition to Bolshevism. The Kokand Autonomy did not last, however. By February 1918, the Bolsheviks liquidated it with incredible brutality. Cut off from the revolutionary mainland by White forces to its north, the region remained isolated to September 1919, descending even further into its own civil war, to which we return in Chapter 3.

This complex and incredibly violent struggle, fed by class as much as ethnicity, also had an international aspect, fueled by the geopolitics of World War I. British troops were intent on protecting their empire's approaches to India from German and Turkish incursions. The small expeditionary force sent towards Tashkent, however, was not only outmanned by Bolshevik forces, it was also hampered by its inability to mobilize the local populations. To stir Muslim nationalism would have alienated the White forces further north, in Siberia, the only hope to re-establish a second front against Germany. The interventionists fought some battles alongside White and Turkmen troops, but could not make a major difference locally. They evacuated in early 1919.

Further Cracks in the Empire, 1917

Central Asia was not the only region cut off from the imperial center. After two-and-a-half years of fighting, Poland, parts of the western Baltics, and sections of Belarus were occupied by the enemy. By the time the revolution broke out in Petrograd, they were thus removed from the revolutionary political process and subject to imperial policies of Germany. In what was left of the empire, cracks began to appear, caused partially by the war, partially by the revolution, partially by the entanglements between the two.

The provisional government abolished legislation restricting the civil rights of non-Russians and minority religions. The administrations of the Caucasus and Ukraine passed into the hand of locals rather than centrally appointed governors. Borders were redrawn along ethnic lines in the Baltics, transforming the province of Estland into an enlarged, and self-governing Estonia – as it turned out, an essential step in the emergence of modern Estonia, Latvia, and Lithuania from Russia's Baltic provinces (Estland, Livland, and Courland). Finland, its constitution restored, acquired a coalition government with a social-democratic majority intent upon leaving the Russian Empire. This aspiration put the country at loggerheads with the government in Petrograd for the rest of the year. In addition to these changes from above came pressures from below. In the context of 1917, when several centers of state power competed and expression of political views was as free as never before, national self-affirmation reached heights even unseen in the 1905 revolution.

Ukraine and Belarus in 1917

Ukraine was a case in point. The Central Council (*Ukrains'ka Tsentral'na Rada*) had originally been formed as an entity loyal to the Provisional Government in Petrograd, but acquired more and more authority in lock-step with the decline of central power. It was led by a prolific historian of Ukraine, at that point of his career not only a nationalist but also a moderate socialist and a democrat: Mykhailo Hrushevsky (1866–1934). Under his leadership, the Rada called, first, for autonomy within a federal republic, then, by the year's end, for independence along the lines promised to Finland and Poland. Such affirmation was driven in part by a national movement at the frontline, where Ukrainian soldiers first demanded, then formed national units, which could become the basis for a Ukrainian national army. Ukrainian peasants had no intention of sharing the rich black earth lands they hoped to take from church, state, and nobility. Hence the aspiration for autonomy, even independence, also in the village.

By June, the Rada had taken up these demands and presented a proposal for autonomy and the integration of predominantly Ukrainian populated areas into one administrative unit to the Provisional Government. The latter stalled, as always citing the elusive Constituent Assembly as the proper place to discuss such matters. The Rada reacted by declaring autonomy unilaterally. The Petrograd government, in turn, could do little else than grant administrative powers to the Rada, which in effect became a government organ in an increasingly federalizing state.

In neighboring Belarus, the nationalist movement was much weaker. Inspired by events in Ukraine, however, a Great Belarusian Rada was formed in the summer of 1917, which also took control of the organizations of Belarusian soldiers at the frontline, which ran through the country. The Russian units, meanwhile, fell increasingly under Bolshevik influence.

The Caucasus in 1917–1918

Outside the European regions of the empire, the lines of confrontation often ran between local Bolsheviks or other socialists who predominantly organized Russian or other European soldiers and workers in the cities, and native politicians who organized the locals. Take the immensely complex history of the northern Caucasus in the Russian revolution. In the region around Vladikavkaz the Terek Cossacks, relatively wealthy agriculturalists, faced a variety of mountain peoples, some of them poor and landless, as well as Russian, Georgian, and Armenian city dwellers (workers, merchants, officials). In March, the Cossacks formed a government to defend their interests, while the city dwellers found their organization in the urban Soviets. In neighboring Chechnya and Dagestan, local fundamentalists began a religious war against Christians and liberal Muslims alike, which drew on a long tradition of resistance against the Russian Empire. They were opposed by more educated and more Europeanized local nationalists who formed the Union of Mountain Peoples. It merged at year's end with the Cossack government to form the Terek-Dagestan Government.

In December 1917, fighting erupted between Chechen and Ingush and the landholding Terek Cossacks. It became so brutal that the Terek-Dagestan Government crumbled under the pressure. As the mountain peoples attacked the cities as well, the three-way struggle between Cossacks, city dwellers, and mountain peoples simplified for a while into a war of Russians against Muslims. It bound the territory closer to Leninist Russia, as returning soldiers with Bolshevik allegiance organized much of the Russian defense. For the time being, the Bolshevik-led coalition government of the Terek People's Republic managed to survive a return of the Cossack threat between June and September.

Further north, in the Cossack lands of the Don and Kuban, the newly formed Bolshevik forces won their first major victories. The Reds took Orenburg, Rostov, and Novocherkassk in January and February 1918. Kornilov, who after the loss of his Tekintsy had been recruiting a small Volunteer Army in Rostov, was forced to leave a city in revolutionary turmoil. What followed was a desperate fighting retreat towards Ekaterinodar, known as the "Ice March" or the "First Kuban Campaign." Constantly harassed by Red troops in superior numbers, the Volunteers fought for sheer survival only to find the city in Bolshevik hands once they reached it in April. Kornilov was killed during the ensuing battle. His successor, Denikin, retreated to rest and re-equip his army.

The Fallout of Red October in the West: Finland, Ukraine, Belarus in late 1917 and early 1918

Other parts of the empire broke away. Finland declared independence, and received it by a revolutionary regime that thought that, surely, this was only a temporary concession. Soon, world revolution would break out and would unite all the toilers of the world. Alas, world revolution existed in the same realm of wishful thinking as much of Lenin's other optimistic predictions of 1917, such as the idea that with revolution the state would wither away, presumably together with other annoyances of the past, such as money, exploitation, wife beating, religion, drunkenness, or housework. World revolution did not come, housework continued, and Finland remained apart, descending into one of the most lethal civil wars of European history. Despite lasting only three-and-a-half months (late January through mid-May 1918), it cost the lives of about 1% of the population, a bloodbath won by the counter-revolutionaries.

In Ukraine and Belarus, meanwhile, Red forces initially held the advantage. When news of the Bolshevik uprising in Petrograd reached Kyiv on October 25, 1917, three political groups were in a position to take power: the Central Rada, the Bolsheviks, and the Russian army still loyal to the Provisional Government. In this three-way struggle, the Central Rada eventually prevailed in Kyiv, while the Bolsheviks established a rival government in Kharkiv further to the East. The anarchist Nestor Makhno declared much of the south a "Free Territory." Soon, the Rada and the Bolsheviks were at war and Red forces – many of them Russian proletarians – advanced towards the Ukrainian capital. They had little trouble with most cities on the way, which fell to Bolshevism on their own (most city dwellers spoke Russian and did not identify as "Ukrainian"). On January 26 they took Kyiv after a terribly bloody assault on the city. The Rada fled to Zhytomyr, while its diplomats in Brest-Litovsk tried to save the day by signing a treaty with the Central Powers. Further south, in Crimea, the Bolsheviks took the port city of Sevastopol, while the elected Tatar Constituent Assembly (*Kurultai*) claimed authority over the peninsula as a whole.

In neighboring Belarus, the struggle was between the Central Belarusian Rada, now renamed the Great Belarusian Rada, and the Bolsheviks, who controlled much of the army at the frontline. Urged on by their comrades in Petrograd, the Bolsheviks declared themselves in charge, a claim to power that was strengthened by a victory at the ballot box during the November elections to the Constituent Assembly. In sharp contrast to the empire as a whole where the Bolsheviks were a minority party, in Belarus they gained 67% of the vote, largely due to their support among frontline troops (the battle zone continued to run through the country). Notwithstanding such popularity, in December 1917 Belarusian nationalists declared independence, but in contrast to Ukraine they had nothing to back up this claim to power – until the Germans arrived.

Brest-Litovsk, March 1918

It was the German army, then, which spoiled the initial successes of the Bolsheviks in the empire's western regions. These were considerable. With strong working-class backing in the industrial centers Lenin's followers had managed to spread their influence through the network of Soviets across the Russian heartland. Controlling many of the armaments held there, they beat back military challenges to their position in both Moscow and Petrograd and managed to reconquer much of Ukraine and the Cossack lands. With the land decree they neutralized the vast countryside. Once peasants rebelled against the new requisitioning policies, introduced in an attempt to solve the food crisis the Bolsheviks had inherited, they used force to subdue them. With the dissolution of the Constituent Assembly they destroyed the one competing locus of legitimate political power. And by allying themselves with local Slavs, they could also claim "Soviet power" in Central Asia, although in reality Tashkent was cut off.

Meanwhile, the German army remained at the frontline. Intent upon exploiting Russia's sudden weakness and Lenin's clear determination to end the war, the Germans accepted a cease-fire on December 2/15 and began negotiations with the new Bolshevik government on December 9/22 in the destroyed city of Brest-Litovsk. The Central Powers' position hardened when newly independent Ukraine signed a separate peace on January 27/February 9, the day after Bolshevik forces had taken Kyiv. This "first Brest-Litovsk" treaty would ease food shortages in Austria and hence lessen the pressure to find a quick settlement. The diplomatically inexperienced Bolsheviks, hopeful for a revolution in Germany, stalled the process when Germany demanded independence for the occupied countries.

Eventually, negotiations with the Bolsheviks broke down and the Germans set their armies in motion again. Attacking empty trenches – the Russian army had withered away as peasant recruits scrambled to reach their villages in anticipation of land distribution – the Germans had no trouble in returning to a war of movement. Largely unopposed, they took to the railroad lines and captured one station after another. While the Bolsheviks struggled for a response, the Germans swallowed up the rest of Livland and added Estonia to their occupations. They swept across Belarus and Ukraine, taking Minsk in late February and entering Red Kyiv on March 1. Lenin's Petrograd government, whose embryonic militias were able to rout disorganized nationalists but not regular German soldiers, faced the choice of accepting a punishing peace, or dying heroically resisting an overwhelming enemy. Realistic as ever, Lenin took the former path and revolutionary Russia signed the Treaty of Brest-Litovsk on March 3, 1918.

The Treaty saved Lenin's revolution, but it did not end the war. In Ukraine, March 1918 was just a moment in a violent continuum. German troops, who had taken Kyiv just days before the Treaty was signed, now also took possession of the regions promised to them. Fighting thus continued with local Bolshevik forces. The Germans had little trouble subduing them, however, taking Kharkiv on April 8, Luhansk on April 29, Sevastopol on the Crimean peninsula on May 1, and Rostov a week later. By now, they also occupied the Baltics, Poland, western Belarus, and parts of the North Caucasus.

The Treaty's stipulations were painful. Bolshevik Russia lost Poland, the Baltics, Ukraine, Finland, and the Kars province in the Trans-Caucasus – or 26% of the empire's prewar population and the most important centers of industry (73% of the steel industry, 75% of coal mines) as well as agricultural production (27% of agricultural land, including the empire's bread basket, Ukraine). The Trans-Caucasus was to remain independent, which really meant submission to the Central Powers.

The Trans-Caucasus after Brest-Litovsk

This status did not go down well with the leaders of what would become Armenia, Azerbaijan, and Georgia. Here, a Special Transcaucasian Committee had taken over the government in March 1917, but had to contend, like the provisional government in Petrograd, with local Soviets. After October, an anti-Bolshevik government – the Transcaucasian Commissariat –came into existence and was strengthened when deputies to the dissolved Constituent Assembly returned home. In order to avoid the stipulation of the treaty of Brest-Litovsk, this government declared independence in April 1918: the Trans-Caucasus Democratic Federative Republic came into existence and continued the war with the Ottomans.

Overlapping partially with the Trans-Caucasus Federation, partially with independent Azerbaijan was the short-lived "Baku Commune" (April to July 1918). The history of this Bolshevik interlude is a complex tangle of ethnic, social, and political animosities within the setting of an ongoing world war. At its birth stood tragedy: several days of fighting between the city's Muslims and the city's Soviet (which included mostly Russians and Armenians), which degenerated into a massacre of the city's Muslims (the "March Days"). The Commune ended in farce when non-Bolshevik socialists invited British forces from Persia to defend the city against advancing Turkish-Azeri forces. The British came, saw how bad things were, and made a run for it, leaving what was now the "Centrocaspian Dictatorship" at the mercy of the Muslim army. It took the city in September, prompting the Armenian population – the social base of both the Commune and the Dictatorship – to flee from the terrible retribution for the March days.

Thus Baku became the capital of newly independent Azerbaijan, one of three successors of the Trans-Caucasus Federation, which fell apart under the Ottoman onslaught. After German meddling, Georgia had declared independence at the end of May, followed swiftly by its neighbors Azerbaijan and Armenia. By November, the end of World War I saw Turkey retreat from the region, and British troops back in Baku and in neighboring Georgia who stayed until the second half of 1919. The three Trans-Caucasus republics were swallowed up by the Soviets shortly thereafter, in 1920 and 1921.

German Occupation, 1918

1918, thus, became the year of imperial breakdown. Finland and Poland, the Baltic States, Ukraine, and the Trans-Caucasus republics were among the most prominent of the new states. But the Bolsheviks also lost control to competing Russian governments – known as the Whites – who took over much of the East and South of the old empire. The success of the Whites also cut off Central Asia, which descended even further into its own civil war, from which it would emerge only in 1923. The Bolsheviks, meanwhile, were reduced more or less to the territory of Russia before Peter the Great had begun imperial expansion in the seventeenth century.

The breakdown of the old empire allowed new nations to make first steps at statehood, although under often crippling conditions. The Germans ruled the Baltic states and Belarus with the iron fist of a military dictatorship. Ukraine, newly independent, soon lost its embryonic freedom when the Rada was disinclined to help the Germans collect grain from the peasantry. It was dissolved by the occupiers, who helped a self-fashioned "Hetman," fundamentally dependent upon German bayonets, into power. The dictatorship of the former tsarist general Pavlo Petrovych Skoropadskyi (1873–1945) was once routinely denounced as a mere puppet regime of the Germans. Recently, it has been re-evaluated as a time of stability within the larger period of upheaval, of some economic growth, and of nation and institution building. Under the Hetman's leadership, two Ukrainian universities were founded along with the Ukrainian Academy of Sciences. He also took more care in building an administration than his predecessors of the Rada, a legacy he would pass on to his successors after he was toppled by yet another coup. As long as he allowed grain requisitions, the Germans left him more or less alone, as their goal in Ukraine was not to build a colony, but to create a stable nation state as a buffer against Bolshevik Russia. What Skoropadskyi did not manage was to build a regular, functioning, and effective army. Like the Rada before him, he relied on German bayonets for both internal and external security. Once they disappeared, his regime quickly collapsed.

German occupation was far from benign, but given what followed later many would remember it as such by the late 1930s. With not enough soldiers on the ground to actually control a region several times the size of Germany, the Kaiser's troops reverted to food requisitioning squads, punitive battalions, hostage shoot-ings, and public hangings. As in the Bolshevik hinterland, peasants resisted the extraction of food from the Ukrainian and Belarusian countryside. Their parti-san war cost tens of thousands of lives, while the deposed SRs began a terrorist campaign against the occupiers, killing the German commander-in-chief in Ukraine in July 1918. Given that much of the west of what would become the Soviet Union was under German occupation until November 1918, it makes little sense to end World War I before that date. Indeed, the entire first year of what is usually categorized as the "Russian Civil War" – from November 1917 to November 1918 – still took place in the context of the war in the West: nei-ther the military interventions of the Allies nor the choices the Bolsheviks and their enemies made are understandable outside this context.

Anti-Bolshevik Successes in the South in 1918

After the Trans-Caucasus had resisted Bolshevization, the Finnish civil war had taken this northern country out of the empire, and the treaty of Brest-Litovsk had chopped off the western borderlands, more and more of the empire's remains were taken over by anti-Bolshevik forces. The Reds might have been successful in the Cossack lands initially, but their reign of terror in the region triggered a popular uprising in March. By May the town of Novocherkassk had become the center of the rebellion. In April General Krasnov, who after his defeat outside Petrograd had made his way south, was elected Ataman (leader) of the Don Cossacks intent on defending their way of life. He soon made a deal with the

Germans advancing from the west. The Cossacks provided food and coal in exchange for weapons. Thus equipped, they had managed to eject the Reds from their lands by the middle of August.

In June, Denikin, too, was back on the campaign trail in the south, and after determined battles took Ekaterinodar in August. More battles followed, bleeding the Volunteer Army white, but also ensuring victory. In the same month Krasnov's Don Cossacks began harassing Tsaritsyn, an armament producing city on the Volga, until October under the brutal command of Lenin's right-hand man Iosif Stalin. They did not manage to take this vital rail junction, and the city became known as "Red Verdun" well before it became world famous as Stalingrad in World War II.

Red Whites in 1918

Elsewhere, too, the enemies of Bolshevism were on the march, although often "Red" and "White" (labels from the French Revolution, denoting revolutionaries and monarchists, respectively) did not properly describe the complex nature of the politics involved. On July 6, 1918, the left SRs rebelled in Moscow and Yaroslavl, some 160 miles further north-east. These were bona fide revolutionaries, who had left the Bolshevik government after the disappointment of Brest-Litovsk. After Mensheviks had been arrested in June, they were the only leftists still able to oppose Lenin's party within Bolshevik-controlled territory. Their uprising was put down: Reds fighting Reds. The Bolsheviks won; SRs were banned from the Soviets; another step towards the one-party state had been taken. In response, the SRs intensified their terrorism. Skilled in such "direct action" from the days of the Romanovs, they took the Petrograd Secret Police (Cheka) chief's life on August 30. Later the same day, an assassin likely with an SR background shot Lenin, but failed to kill him. The Bolsheviks, in their turn, shot hostages by the hundreds in retaliation.

In the North of Russia, likewise, strange opponents and even stranger allies emerged. After British landings at Murmansk (on invitation of the local Soviet and the Bolshevik government in Moscow) and incursions of Finnish Whites into northern Russia, Red and British forces initially fought together: the war against Germany was conducted here by proxy. Soon, however, Brest-Litovsk put the Moscow government on the side of the Germans. The Murmansk Soviet, chaired by an anarchist, meanwhile continued to welcome the British as security against the Finns (and hence the Germans) and as a source of supplies.

After heated exchanges between Murmansk and Moscow, it came to a break in early July (just as further south-west the left SRs were subdued brutally, first in Moscow, then in Yaroslavl). The Bolsheviks severed telegraph lines and blew up railroad bridges, while the Murmansk Soviet signed an agreement with the foreign interventionists. Skirmishes between British and Bolshevik forces were won by the former.

Shortly thereafter, in August, after the arrival of a Franco-British flotilla, the Bolshevik authorities were toppled in neighboring Archangel and a coalition of SRs and other moderate Socialists took over. Their goal was to march on Moscow, eliminate the Bolshevik government, and renew the war against Germany – hence the support they got from the Allies, who now landed in force. Amazingly, but somewhat in line with this unpopular program to renew the war effort, they also proceeded to dissolve local Soviets, including the anti-Bolshevik one in Murmansk, locking up their leaders in newly created concentration camps.

Within two months, however, their government fell in turn. In a pattern that would repeat itself elsewhere on non-Bolshevik territory, the original socialist government of the Supreme Administration of the Northern Region was succeeded by liberals and conservatives, who in their turn would make way for a military dictator: a steady march to the right.

The Anti-Bolshevik East in 1918

The Volga region and Siberia followed this pattern closely. Here, too the labels "Red" and "White" were initially misleading. In July, the Tsar and his family were executed by Bolsheviks in Ekaterinburg, in order to prevent their liberation by "whites." The forces pressing down on the city in the Urals, however, while anti-Bolshevik, were indeed quite "red." KOMUCH was a government formed by members of the Socialist Revolutionaries in Samara. It derived its claim to legitimacy from the Constituent Assembly (the acronym stood for "Committee of Members of the Constituent Assembly"), flew a red flag, proclaimed a radical agricultural program, and was committed to defending the February revolution from the October insurrection. That this body could form and consolidate itself in Siberia was due to the Czech legion, a corps of former Austro-Hungarian citizens who had volunteered themselves to the Provisional Government to fight their former masters.

They had seen action against the Kaiser's troops in Ukraine in February 1918, trying to stop the German occupation side-by-side with Red troops. After their temporary allies had made peace with the enemy at Brest-Litovsk, they tried to exit the country along the rail line to the east, to Vladivostok, in order to continue fighting on the side of the Allies. Fearing extradition to the Central Powers (and hence the firing squad), the 40,000 strong force rebelled when Bolsheviks tried to disarm them. The Legion took control of the Bolshevik towns along the Trans-Siberian railway, all denuded of Red troops busy further east making short work of Grigorii Semenov's Whites. Aided by Japanese intervention troops and some White forces under Ataman Ivan Kalmykov advancing from the Pacific, by September the Czechs controlled the rails all the way to Vladivostok. For the time being, Bolshevism was history in Siberia.

The counter-revolutionary Whites, meanwhile, had been confined to the stretch of the Russian controlled Chinese Eastern Railway through Manchuria. Only a small group under Semenov had fought on Bolshevik territory, but had been all but defeated by the time of the Czech revolt, while Admiral Alexander Kolchak had been forced to leave Harbin for Tokyo, a victim of intrigues between various White factions stuck in an international game involving the Chinese, Japanese, and US governments. Kalmykov's murderous gang, likewise, completely depended on its Japanese sponsors.

Without the Czechs, thus, Soviet power would have been secure in Siberia. The sympathies of most of these foreign fighters were with their own cause of national liberation, which they hoped to achieve as a prize of allied victory. Many also had socialist sympathies, which drew them to the SRs. When both the Allies and the SRs asked the Czechs to remain in Siberia and establish a front against Bolshevism, they complied. This decision makes sense if seen less in the framework of the Russian Civil War but in the context in which the Czechs thought themselves: the ongoing world war. They attempted to establish a new eastern front against Germany. The Bolsheviks just happened to be in the way.

If events in the Volga region and Siberia were structured by the ongoing war between the Central Powers and the western Allies, the backdrop of ongoing hostilities in the west also defined the possible for Bolshevik Russia. The loss of Siberia and the north to anti-Bolshevik forces supported by the Allies destroyed the option to retreat into the depth of Asia, should the Germans resume their attack on Moscow. Given the poor state of the Red Army, threatened by internal enemies in the east, north, and south, the Bolsheviks were pushed to make even more concessions to Germany. A new treaty was signed in in August 1918, after which Lenin could risk transferring troops from the western front (facing the Germans) to the east (facing KOMUCH).

The Fall of KOMUCH: September to November 1918

The Czech legion was thus outmanned by a resurgent Red Army, which won the battle of Kazan in September, the first major military defeat for KOMUCH and the start of its path into historical obscurity. A few days later, Simbirsk fell to the Red Army, followed by Samara in early October. But the Czechs were also neutralized by politics. A second government had been established in Siberia, further east in the city of Omsk: the Provisional Government of Siberia, or PSG.

Much further to the right than KOMUCH, it refused to unite its troops, and in particular its many officers, with the SR forces. Thus, when the Red Army began its offensive in early September, KOMUCH had little to hold against it. The resulting military setbacks, in turn, had political consequences: KOMUCH had to give up its independence and united with PSG and a dozen of other small Siberian "governments" into a polity known as the Directory. As it was seated in Omsk, this new entity in effect meant a takeover of KOMUCH by PSG. Yet, the majority of the Directory – three out of five members – were still SRs and the others were not monarchists but regionalists and liberal "Kadets." These "Whites" were still fairly "Red."

Eventually, the socialist phase of the eastern front against Bolshevism came to an end. The Directory was only the beginning of a slide to the right. About a week after the Kaiser fell in the November revolution in Germany and a few days after the armistice ended World War I on the western front, a coup of officers in Omsk, supported by British intervention troops, deposed the Directory in the night of November 17/18 and put Admiral Kolchak, back from Japan, in power.

A military man with academic credentials, an Arctic explorer and veteran of the Russo-Japanese war as well as World War I, Kolchak had resisted the demands of his revolutionized sailors in February 1917, theatrically throwing his sword over board from his vessel. After the October Revolution, he attempted to assemble anti-Bolshevik forces in China, but failed to negotiate the complex politics involved. He returned to Russia to serve as a minister in the Directory. Now, he began to rule under the title of "Supreme Ruler of All the Russias," claiming dictatorial power of the entirety of the Tsar's former domains. Given that the strategically and economically essential center of the country was in Bolshevik hands and imminent German retreat in the western borderlands left these basically ungoverned, these claims were from the outset spurious.

The Allies were of limited help. Britain, China, Japan, France, and the United States had troops in Vladivostok and elsewhere in the Far East and Siberia. The Japanese intervention was the largest and was fueled by the hope to once and for all neutralize Russia in Japan's backyard. The other foreign troops saw little or no action, however. Their main contribution was to instill in the young Bolshevik state a permanent fear of foreign encirclement. This Red xenophobia relied on a fair share of historical amnesia: After all, Lenin would not have made it back to Russia without a German "sealed train"; much of the fighting force of the early Bolshevik state was made up of revolutionized German and Austro-Hungarian prisoners of war ("internationals"), including the ever-present Czechs; and fighting the "counter-revolution" was only possible by appeasing Germany. The "Russian" civil war was an international affair on all sides of the frontlines.

War, Revolution, Civil War, 1914–1918

By the time the German war effort collapsed in October 1918 and the Kaiser fell in the German revolution in November, the White forces in the South, led by Kornilov, Denikin, and Wrangel, were on the ascendancy. By early 1919, the Terek People's Republic was history and the northern Caucasus had been conquered by Denikin's forces. Meanwhile, the civil war in Central Asia continued independently. The Trans-Caucasus also remained apart. In Siberia, Kolchak had taken control, suppressed opposition to his rule with outstanding brutality, and prepared his troops for an assault on the Red heart of Russia.

The Bolshevik heartland of the old empire, hungry and freezing, braced itself for the onslaught with grim determination. Since Brest-Litovsk, when the left SRs had resigned in protest from Lenin's government, Bolshevik Russia was ruled by a one-party dictatorship. Throughout 1918, Lenin tightened his reins within the ruling party itself. His personal power increased. Discussions of controversial issues became less frequent. The experience of facing regular German army units early in the year also killed, once and for all, the dream of democratically led armed forces. Instead of revolutionary militias, the Bolsheviks now built a regular, highly disciplined army.

German surrender thus did not end the war in the "shatter-zone" of the Romanov Empire, where "the First World War failed to end."[6] Instead, the world war had transformed into a multiplicity of civil wars. Some historians blame the Bolsheviks for this transformation, others their opponents, and a third group argue that the violence was inevitable, given the destructive impact of the world war, the extent of the political breakdown, and the depth of both the social divisions in society and the ideological differences between the camps. Like in the discussion about the brutalization of Bolshevism (Chapter 4), with which this dispute is intimately entangled, it is hard to see how one could remove the Bolshevik leadership from responsibility. Lenin and his men actively sought civil war, believed it was historically necessary, and made no attempts to stop escalation in 1917–1918. "The only correct proletarian slogan," wrote Lenin in 1914, "is to transform the present imperialist war into a civil war."[7] By the end of 1918, he had succeeded in this quest.

Notes

1 Peter Holquist, *Making War, Forging Revolution. Russia's Continuum of Crisis, 1914–1921* (Cambridge, MA and London: Harvard University Press, 2002).

2 Joshua A. Sanborn, *Imperial Apocalypse. The Great War and the Destruction of the Russian Empire* (Oxford: Oxford University Press, 2014).

3 Norman Stone, *The Eastern Front 1914–1917* (London: Penguin, 1998), 201.

4 Letter of Nicholas to his wife, 22 June 1916, http://www.alexanderpalace.org/letters/june16.html, accessed December 28, 2017.

5 Abdeed Khalid, *Making Uzbekistan. Nation, Empire, and Revolution in the Early USSR* (Ithaca, NY and London: Cornell University Press, 2015), 70–1.

6 Robert Gerwarth, *The Vanquished. Why the First World War Failed to End, 1917–1923* (London: Penguin, 2016).

7 V.I. Lenin, *1914–1017*, https://www.marxists.org/archive/lenin/works/1914/sep/00.htm, accessed December 28, 2017.

Bibliography

Acton, Edward, Vladimir Cherniaev, and William Rosenberg. *Critical Companion to the Russian Revolution 1914–1921* (London: Arnold, 1997).

Beyrau, Dietrich. "Brutalization Revisited: The Case of Russia," *Journal of Contemporary History* 50, no. 1 (January 1, 2015): 15–37.

Bisher, Jamie. *White Terror. Cossack Warlords of the Trans-Siberian* (London and New York: Routledge, 2005).

du Quenoy, Paul. "The Skoropads'ky Hetmanate and the Ukrainian National Idea," *The Ukrainian Quarterly* LVI, no. 3 (2000): 245–71.

Engelstein, Laura. *Russia in Flames. War, Revolution, Civil War, 1914–1921* (Oxford: Oxford University Press, 2017).

Figes, Orlando. *A People's Tragedy. The Russian Revolution: 1891–1924* (New York: Penguin Books, 1996).

Fitzpatrick, Sheila. *The Russian Revolution*, 4th edition (Oxford: Oxford University Press, 2017).

Gatrell, Peter. *Russia's First World War. A Social and Economic History* (London: Pearson Longman, 2005).

Gatrell, Peter. *A Whole Empire Walking. Refugees in Russia during World War I* (Bloomington: Indiana University Press, 2005).

Haapala, Pertti, and Marko Tikka. "Revolution, Civil War, and Terror in Finland in 1918," in: *War in Peace. Paramilitary Violence in Europe after the Great War*, ed. Robert Gerwarth and John Horne (Oxford: Oxford University Press, 2013), 72–84.

Hoffmann, David L. *Cultivating the Masses. Modern State Practices and Soviet Socialism, 1914–1939* (Ithaca, NY and London: Cornell University Press, 2011).

Jahn, Hubertus. *Patriotic Culture in Russia during World War I* (Ithaca, NY and London: Cornell University Press, 1995).

Jones, David R. "Imperial Russia's Forces at War," in: *Military Effectiveness. Volume 1: The First World War*, new edition, ed. Allan R. Millet and Williamson Murray (Cambridge: Cambridge University Press, 2010), 249–328.

Liber, George O. *Total Wars and the Making of Modern Ukraine, 1914–1954* (Toronto: University of Toronto Press, 2016).

Lohr, Eric. *Nationalizing the Russian Empire. The Campaign against Enemy Aliens during World War I* (Cambridge, MA: Harvard University Press, 2003).

Lohr, Eric, "War and revolution, 1914–1917," in: *The Cambridge History of Russia. Volume II: Imperial Russia, 1689–1917* ed. Dominic Lieven (Cambridge: Cambridge University Press, 2006), 655–69.

Lieven, Dominic. *Russia and the Origins of the First World War* (London: Macmillan, 1983).

Lieven, Dominic. *Towards the Flame. Empire, War and the End of Tsarist Russia* (London: Penguin, 2015).

Lincoln, W. Bruce. *Passage through Armageddon. The Russians in War and Revolution 1914–1918* (New York: Simon and Schuster, 1986).

Liulevicius, Vejas Gabriel. *War Land on the Eastern Front. Culture, National Identity and German Occupation in World War I* (Cambridge: Cambridge University Press, 2000).

Norris, Stephen M. *A War of Images. Russian Popular Prints, Wartime Culture, and National Identity 1812–1945* (DeKalb: Northern Illinois University Press, 2006).

Petrone, Karen. *The Great War in Russian Memory* (Bloomington: Indiana University Press, 2011).

Pipes, Richard. *The Russian Revolution 1899–1919* (London: Fontana Press, 1990).

Pipes, Richard. *A Concise History of the Russian Revolution* (New York: Vintage Books, 1996).

Pipes, Richard. *The Formation of the Soviet Union. Communism and Nationalism, 1917–1923* (Cambridge, MA: Harvard University Press, 1997).

Plokhy, Serhii. *Unmaking Imperial Russia; Mykhailo Hrushevsky and the Writing of Ukrainian History* (Toronto: University of Toronto Press, 2005).

Rabinowitch, Alexander. *The Bolsheviks Come to Power: The Revolution of 1917 in Petrograd* (Chicago: Haymarket Books, 2004).

Rabinowitch, Alexander. *The Bolsheviks in Power: The First Year of Soviet Rule in Petrograd* (Bloomington: Indiana University Press, 2007).

Radkey, Oliver H. *Russia Goes to the Polls. The Election to the All-Russian Constituent Assembly, 1917* (Ithaca, NY and London: Cornell University Press, 1989).

Read, Christopher. *War and Revolution in Russia, 1914–22. The Collapse of Tsarism and the Establishment of Soviet Power* (Basingstoke: Palgrave Macmillan, 2013)

Reynolds, Michael A. *Shattering Empires. The Clash and Collapse of the Ottoman and Russian Empires 1908–1918* (Cambridge: Cambridge University Press, 2011).

Sanborn, Joshua. "The Mobilization of 1914 and the Question of the Russian Nation: A Reexamination," *Slavic Review* 59, no. 2 (2000): 267–89.

Sanborn, Joshua A. *Drafting the Russian Nation. Military Conscription, Total War, and Mass Politics, 1905–1925* (DeKalb, Illinois: Northern Illinois University Press, 2003).

Sanborn, Joshua A. "Russian Imperialism, 1914–2014: Annexationist, Adventurist, or Anxious?" *Revolutionary Russia* 27, no. 2 (2014): 92–108.

Smele, Jonathan D. *The "Russian" Civil Wars, 1916–1926. Ten Years That Shook the World* (Oxford: Oxford University Press, 2015).

Smith, S. A. *The Russian Revolution. A Very Short Introduction* (Oxford: Oxford University Press, 2002).

Smith, S. A. *Russia in Revolution. An Empire in Crisis, 1890–1928* (Oxford: Oxford University Press, 2017).

Steinberg, Mark D., and Vladimir M. Khrustalev, *The Fall of the Romanovs. Political Dreams and Personal Struggles in a Time of Revolution* (New Haven, CT and London: Yale University Press, 1995).

Suny, Ronald G. *The Baku Commune, 1917–1918: Class and Nationality in the Russian Revolution* (Princeton, NJ: Princeton University Press, 1972).

Suny, Ronald G. ed. "National Revolutions and Civil War in Russia," in: *The Revenge of the Past. Nationalism, Revolution, and the Collapse of the Soviet Union* (Stanford, CA: Stanford University Press, 1993), 20–82.

Tepora, Tuomas, and Aapo Roselius, eds. *The Finnish Civil War 1918. History, Memory, Legacy* (Leiden: Brill, 2014).

von Hagen, Mark. "The Great War and the Mobilization of Ethnicity in the Russian Empire," in: *Post-Soviet Political Order: Conflict and State-Building*, ed. Barnett Rubin and Jack Snyder (London: Routledge, 1998), 32–53.

von Hagen, Mark. *War in a European Borderland. Occupations and Occupation Plans in Galicia and Ukraine 1914–1918* (Seattle and London: University of Washington Press, 2007).

Wildman, Allan K. *The End of the Russian Imperial Army*, 2 vols. (Princeton, NJ: Princeton University Press, 1980–1987).

3

Regathering the Empire (1918–1923)

By the time the German war effort collapsed in the west in late October 1918 the former Minister of the Interior Petr Durnovo's worst nightmare had become reality (see Chapter 1). The emperor had seen fit to go to war against Germany. The Germans had won. The empire had broken apart into warring splinter states. What was left of the central state was reduced to the size of early modern Russia. It was ruled by the kind of political criminals he had fought as a minister. His tsar had been executed along with the royal family. German jackboots strutted all over Ukraine and the Baltics. Finland and the Trans-Caucasus had broken away. Siberia, freed from the Reds, was descending into a nightmarish regime of theft and terror by White warlords: Ivan Kalmykov in Khabarovsk, Grigorii Semenov in Chita (both supported by Japanese intervention troops), and soon, from November 18, Aleksander Kolchak in Omsk (supported by the British). Durnovo should have felt both vindicated and depressed. Fate, however, had been kind. The former Minister of the Interior did not have to experience the descent of the empire into the "hopeless anarchy" of the civil war he had predicted. He had died in September 1915.

As we shall see in this chapter, however, the Bolsheviks eventually reined in the anarchy and regathered a good deal of the late tsar's domain, inadvertently turning from internationalist revolutionaries into Red imperialists. We can distinguish two phases of this process: one shorter one encompassing a bit more than the year 1919, and a longer one from the spring of 1920.

During the first period of imperial reconquest (November 1918 to Spring 1920, or "the year of 1919," for short) the main enemies of Moscow were various "White" forces. The Bolsheviks, after serious setbacks and interrupted by periods

The Soviet Union: A Short History, First Edition. Mark Edele.
© 2019 John Wiley & Sons, Inc. Published 2019 by John Wiley & Sons, Inc.

of retreat and retrenchment, consolidated their position and reconquered much of the old empire: from the Germans in Ukraine and Belarus, then from their "White" enemies in the south, east, and north, but also from "Green" peasant rebels. This period saw the bulk of the regathering of the late tsar's domain under Bolshevik rule. The Whites were defeated in Siberia in the east, in Ukraine in the west, outside Petrograd in the north, and in south Russia as well. The story is convoluted, as the Red Army swept back and forth over vast territories, advanced, was beaten back, advanced again. Overall, however, this long year saw the emergence of the Red phoenix from the tsarist ashes.

In the second period from the spring of 1920, Bolshevik expansion was completed in the south with the reconquest of the Caucasus and Trans-Caucasus. Further east, the defeat of the Whites had re-established communications with Central Asia in 1919. The Red Army could now join its local allies – urban Slavic settlers – in their civil war against their Muslim and nomadic adversaries. This struggle would continue until 1923 and in some places 1926, only to re-ignite later. Meanwhile, in 1920 and 1921, the Bolsheviks had to pacify their hinterland, where revolutionary uprisings of sailors and peasants were drowned in blood. And in the west, a major war with the young Polish state (1920–1921) ended in military defeat of the Red Army, checking further expansion into Eastern Europe for the time being.

The reconstruction of empire came at terrible cost, as we shall see in Chapter 4.

At the same time, there were constructive aspects nested within the destruction. The Bolsheviks created some of the basic pillars of the emerging warfare state: the Red Army as the most important institution, the secret police terrorizing real and imagined enemies, the Bolshevik party shadowing the new state structure, and a command economy geared towards extracting resources to pay for warfare. In effect, these Marxist revolutionaries, who expected the state to "wither away" after the class war was won and for imperialism to melt into thin air once its capitalist underpinnings were removed, created a warfare state ruling an empire able to withstand the shocks of the twentieth century.

Organizing the Means of Violence

The center of this new empire and the basis for its success against its competitors included the Red Army on the one hand and the Extraordinary Commission for the Fight against Counter-Revolution and Sabotage, or Cheka, on the other. The Bolsheviks had not been idle while their enemies gathered their forces and had begun to build an army of their own. The sorry performance of the paramilitary Red Guards in Ukraine in 1918, who turned out to be useless even against second-grade German infantry, convinced the leadership to abandon revolutionary dreams of worker militias recruited from radical workers and led by elected officers. Instead, revolutionary Russia would embrace the established practice of a standing army. Both officers ("commanders") and men were drafted, subject to severe discipline, and expected to follow orders without backchat. The death penalty, once abolished during the revolution, was reinstated for deserters. A remarkable military renaissance followed.

The first steps towards building this Red Army were thus taken not as part of a civil war against internal enemies but within the continuing war with Germany in early 1918. This was a crucial context, as it ensured the initial collaboration of many military specialists. The army, built under the revolutionary commissar of military affairs, Leon Trotsky (1879–1940), to defend the most radical socialist revolution thus far, would be commanded by tsarist officers, led by a military administration taken over from the old regime, and armed with the weapons the bourgeoisie and bureaucracy of the late empire had produced during World War I. Together, these factors explain why the Reds were able to equip an army several times the size of all opposing forces of the civil war combined.

If many officers initially volunteered to serve the Bolsheviks in order to defend Mother Russia against the Germans, they soon found themselves fighting internal enemies of Bolshevism, often led by colleagues with whom they had more in common than with the unwashed revolutionary soldiery they commanded. Defections to the Whites, often with entire units and even of very high-ranking commanders were thus frequent early in the civil war. The problem was solved with a three-pronged tactic. Supplies for military personnel and their families were superior to those of civilians. In the context of the severe shortages of the civil war years this fact often made the difference between a hard life and a slow death from starvation. Second, the families of defectors and deserters were punished for the deeds of their family member, a system of hostage taking that re-emerged in World War II. Third, commanders were shadowed by "commissars," Bolshevik party officials charged with ensuring that the "military specialists" did their job and would not sabotage revolutionary war making.

The rank and file of this new army also were no longer just "conscious proletarians," as in the early Red Guards of revolutionary days, but conscripted peasants. They were held in line with a similar combination of welfare and repression. Blocking detachments, charged with arresting deserters and those retreating without orders, were placed behind their lines, a practice to reappear in the war against Germany two decades later. Deserters were shot and their families deprived of land in the village. Red Army men who served loyally, meanwhile, were rewarded with preference in land distribution.

The first time the Red Army showed its mettle was in September 1918, when Kazan was taken back from the Whites after the Bolshevik appeasement of Germany had given them the ability to move their forces from the western front, facing Germany, to the east (see Chapter 2). A string of victories followed, bringing Uralsk, Orenburg, Ufa, Izhevsk, and Votinsk into Bolshevik hands by early 1919. If the new military machine of the emerging Red Empire was born in World War I's storms of steel, then, it was tempered in the fires of the civil war.

The second arm of the new Bolshevik regime was the Cheka, tasked with finding and eliminating enemies and terrorizing the population into submission. The Red Army and Cheka formed the center of the developing state, which focused on two basic operations: extract people and resources and mobilize them to fight. This crude and brutal warfare state, later called "War Communism," formed the institutional base of the Bolshevik regime.

With Lenin as the CEO, the Council of People's Commissars (Sovnarkom) with its ministries (renamed "Commissariats") at its head, and the Red Army and Cheka as the center of operations, this state focused on fighting for the survival of "the revolution." The Bolshevized executive organs of local Soviets were quickly transformed from directing organs of revolutionary "democracy" into a governing structure at the province level. Like the prerevolutionary personnel ("bourgeois specialists") who ran much of the commissariats and other parts of the overall system, the local Soviets were controlled and directed by the growing apparatus of the Bolshevik Party, which functioned, from the middle of 1918, without competing parties even from the socialist camp.

Holding on to political power and building an army was not enough. The Red Army needed to be equipped and fed, and all resources of the new state were geared to that end. Ideological commitments against market mechanisms and private property went hand in hand with the experience of the warfare states built in both Germany and Russia during World War I. One plank of the Bolshevik economic order was forced grain requisitioning from the peasantry; another was nationalization of industry, by late 1920 even of very small enterprises; a third was the reckless use of the printing press to pay for the war, leading to galloping inflation (which some saw as a good sign: in Communism, after all, there would be no money); and finally there was labor conscription shadowing the conscription to fight. The economic results of these policies were catastrophic, and the civilian population only survived (insofar as it did) because of the efforts of black market traders, the so-called "bag-men" who transported scarce goods to the cities.

Ukraine in 1919

Soon, the Bolshevik warfare state and its Red Army would be put to the test in the west as well. In November 1918, the Germans, defeated on the western front and rocked by revolution at home, began to retreat in panic and disorder from Ukraine and Belarus. The latter, with no established nationalist movement, was quickly occupied by the Red Army and became the Belarusian Soviet Republic, which in February 1919 swallowed Lithuania. This new Bolshevik stronghold, however, did not last. It was occupied by Poland later in the year.

In Ukraine, things were more complicated, although here, too, no one White Army rose to replace the Germans and oppose the Reds. The disappearance of the German bayonets upon which the Hetmanate of Skoropadskyi had rested allowed an uprising against his regime. Ukraine was now ruled by a "Directory" of five men who hoped to maintain national independence while also promoting socialism. Their most prominent leader was Simon Petliura (1879–1926), a journalist who had served as secretary for military affairs under the Central Rada in 1917. He would become the Soviets' most hated exponent of Ukraine's struggle for independence but is also remembered for the anti-Semitic violence that flourished under his rule. Further west, in Eastern Galicia, an independent Western Ukrainian state was proclaimed and merged, in January 1919, with the Ukrainian mainland. The Ukrainian state founded in 1917 was thus reborn: the Ukrainian People's Republic, now stronger for the institutions Skoropadskyi had built.

Nevertheless, the Directory ruled little beyond the borders of Kyiv. Instead, a peasant insurrection plunged large sections of Ukraine into anarchy throughout 1919; driven by their local concerns and led by a variety of warlords, including the most famous of them, the anarchist Nestor Makhno, the insurgents formed disconnected bands which plundered and staged pogroms, but did not organize a competing government to the Directory.

In this situation of powerlessness the new Ukrainian state found itself under attack from the Red Army, which quickly routed Ukrainian resistance. Kyiv fell in February 1919. The newly independent Poland, liberated from Russian dominance by the Germans and now from German occupation by their defeat, attacked from the north-west shortly thereafter. Eastern Galicia was annexed before the year was out, and would remain Polish until World War II. What was left of the Directory was squashed into a tiny strip between Poland and Red Ukraine.

It was Denikin's army, now filled by drafted recruits and renamed the Armed Forces of South Russia, which saved the remains of non-Bolshevik Ukraine from compete annihilation. The former Volunteer Army began a comprehensive offensive against the Red lands in March, pushing the Red Army out of central and eastern Ukraine. By the dawn of the year 1920, however, the Red tide had washed back across Ukraine, evicting Denikin's Whites with the aid of Makhno's anarchists. Showing the usual combination of pragmatic flexibility with long-term intolerance to any alternative kind of socialism, the Bolsheviks then turned against Makhno, ending this episode of anarchism. Only Crimea remained anti-Bolshevik for the time being. It would become the final staging ground of the forces of the last of the White generals: Petr Nikolaevich Wrangel (Vrangel, 1878–1928).

White Armies in the South and East

Ukraine's fate, then, was decided by the three-way struggle between "Red" and "White" Russia, and independent Poland. In January, Krasnov's Cossacks were beaten once again outside Tsaritsyn and forced to retreat. Krasnov resigned and transferred his troops to the unloved Denikin. The new leader would soon be supplied substantially by Britain and had widened his personnel base by introducing conscription. Thus strengthened, he had conquered the northern Caucasus in the winter of 1918/1919, then, after taking over Krasnov's forces, turned north. In March 1919, his troops began to advance into the Bolshevik heartland from the south while Kolchak attacked from the east. At first they were successful. A Cossack uprising at its rear (provoked by the Bolshevik policy of "merciless mass terror"[1]) engulfed the Red Army in the region in a two-front war, and Denikin's troops advanced deep into Bolshevik territory. Aided by freshly delivered British tanks, Cossacks commanded by Wrangel even took Tsaritsyn this time. By mid-October, the Armed Forces of South Russia had taken Chernigov, Kursk, and Orel. The Whites now stood 240 miles from Moscow. The Red capital seemed within reach.

On Kolchak's front, meanwhile, things had not gone so well. The Admiral had never controlled his hinterland beyond Lake Baikal, where rival warlords and intervention troops jostled for command of the Trans-Siberian railroad – the life-line for the Omsk government. A growing Red partisan movement in their rear added to the woes of the Siberian Whites, whose brutality, graft, and corruption furnished a constant stream of recruits to the enemy. After initial successes in March and April, a massive counter-attack by the Red Army drove the White forces back in May. By June, Kolchak's advance had ended in defeat, and the Red counter-strikes continued. From now on, the Whites would be in continuous retreat on this front. The Red Army took Perm on July 1, Zlatoust two weeks later, and Cheliabinsk by the end of the month. By the middle of August, Kolchak had lost the Urals – a natural line of defense and the only industrial region in the White east. After a final counter-attack was beaten back in September, the Red Army marched into Kolchak's capital Omsk on November 14.

Assault from the Baltics: Iudenich (October to November 1919)

While Kolchak retreated from the blows of the Red Army in the east, Estonia became the staging ground for yet another anti-Bolshevik front in the north-west: the assault on Red Petrograd in early October 1919 by General Iudenich, at the same time as Denikin's troops aimed at the heart of Bolshevik Russia: Moscow (which had taken over as capital from the more exposed Petrograd in March 1918).

After short but bloody civil wars, the former German satellites in the Baltics had become independent, anti-Bolshevik states. The Red Army had marched into Latvia in January 1919 and helped set up a Bolshevik government in Riga. It soon faced stiff competition from German "Free Corps" (Freikorps) units: paramilitaries formed from the former occupation forces and volunteers from both Germany and the local Baltic German community. They took Riga in May 1919, the beginning of the end of the short Bolshevik phase of Latvia's history. Further south, in Lithuania, the civil war was more confused, with the nationalists fighting a complex three-way war against the Red Army, a German Freikorps disguised as the "West Russian Volunteer Army", as well as the Polish army. Vilnius changed hands repeatedly, and it would take until the end of 1920 until the borders of the new state were fixed. In the northern Baltics, finally, Estonia fought a short but victorious war against invading Bolshevik Russia between December 1918 and March 1919. In 1920, all three Baltic republics signed peace treaties with the Russian Soviet Republic (RSFSR, that is, Bolshevik Russia). They would remain outside the sphere of Bolshevik control until World War II.

Originally formed under the tutelage of the occupying Germans in Pskov and, after relocation to Estonia, also somewhat reluctantly supported by British tanks and other supplies, Iudenich's army became a major threat to the birth place of the Russian Revolution, despite the numerical superiority of the Reds. After the Northwestern Army had established a bridgehead in Soviet territory in May and June 1919, Iudenich took control of this front in October. His attack was supported by Estonian troops, but not as he had hoped by the Finns. By late October, the Whites had reached Petrograd's suburbs, and Trotsky armed the city's workers for self-defense. Reinforcements were also sent from other fronts. In parallel, Lenin's government undermined Iudenich's rear by peace negotiations with Estonia. Once Trotsky's superior numbers were brought to bear in a counter-attack, Iudenich called off the siege and retreated towards Estonia. The Estonians disarmed his troops at the border, before being thanked for this betrayal by Red attacks, which ceased only in January 1920.

The disunity of the various enemies of Bolshevism was one of Lenin's assets during this period, which ended in Bolshevik victories on all fronts: after Kolchak's retreat in May and June 1919 and Iudenich's in October, Denikin's thrust for Moscow was stopped when Orel was taken back by the Red Army on October 20. The second asset was the superior numbers in men and materiel the Reds could mobilize. Third came the lack of attention White warlords gave to institution building and the creation of a constituency. Denikin's absent agrarian program and his Russocentrism were as much responsible for his defeat as was the Red Army. Nestor Makhno's Ukrainian peasant anarchists liberated large swathes of countryside in Denikin's rear and peasants also rose elsewhere. Dagestan was in revolt. As a result, Denikin now fought a three-front war: against the Red Army in the north, against Makhno in the east, and against the mountain peoples in the South.

White Defeat in South and North

When the Bolsheviks set the newly formed Red cavalry under Semen Mikhailovich Budennyi (1883–1973) against Denikin's northern front in October, the latter quickly crumbled. The fall of Voronezh on October 24 marked the beginning of the rout of the White Army in the south and west. The Reds took Kyiv on December 16. By the start of 1920, Rostov was back in Bolshevik hands. By February, the Whites had been pushed back to the Kuban river. In late March, their remnants evacuated to Crimea. In April, Denikin went into exile and Wrangel took command of what was left of the Whites in the south.

In early 1920, the Red Army occupied the north Caucasus, which had already been freed from White forces by the local mountaineers. The occupiers were welcomed with red flags by a population who mistook the Red enemy of their White enemy as a friend. And indeed, in April the Reds expelled about 9,000 Cossacks and handed their land over to the local Ingush. However, the honeymoon between mountaineers and Bolsheviks was short lived. The arrogant behavior of the Russian occupiers, who began to requisition food and fodder, forced locals into the Red Army, attacked patriarchal traditions, and outlawed trade, led to a quick change in local mood. In August, a bloody uprising broke out in Chechnya and Dagestan. Pitting the Muslim population against the Russian Bolsheviks, it lasted almost a year. This forgotten war was "particularly fierce," as a classical account has it. "No compromises were possible between the adversaries; no prisoners were taken and the losses suffered by the Red Army were high."[2]

By the summer of 1921 the rebel country lay completely in ruins. However, pacification had been achieved not only by military means but also by a parallel process of allowing mountaineers to expropriate their neighbors, the Terek Cossacks, with whom they had been locked in a vicious civil war ever since the revolution. After a lull following the initial expulsions in April, from October 1920 and lasting until January 1921 approximately 30,000 people, or a quarter of the Cossack population of the Terek, were expelled from their homes as a punishment for their support for the Whites and a recent anti-Soviet rebellion. Chechens, Ingush, and Ossetians took over their land and property, in the process often kidnapping or killing remaining inhabitants, as if to prove that in conditions of civil war the line between victim and perpetrator is constantly shifting.

The victorious Bolsheviks, in collaboration with moderate local nationalists, established the Mountaineer Autonomous Soviet Socialist Republic as part of the RSFSR in January 1921. It existed until 1924, when it was carved up into several administrative units. The northern Caucasus remained a thorn in the Bolshevik side, however, and fighting erupted again in 1925, during Stalin's first revolution from above at the start of the 1930s, and during World War II.

Further north, the Murmansk and Arkhangelsk strongpoints also fell to the Bolsheviks after the Allies had withdrawn in the fall of 1919. By March 1920, the north was Red.

Endgame in the East

After Kolchak had to evacuate Omsk in November 1919, the fate of the Whites in the east was sealed. The Red Army pushed them out of central Siberia, another nightmarish "Ice March." Kolchak was captured by the Czech Legion, which had long withdrawn from fighting but continued to be a major player in the struggle for control of the railroad from Lake Baikal to Vladivostok. They handed him over to revolutionaries (Mensheviks, SRs, and Bolsheviks), who had taken power in Irkutsk. Kolchak was interrogated, then shot on February 7, 1920. The pathetic remainders of his White forces passed by the city shortly thereafter and continued east, followed closely by the Red Army, which took over Irkutsk on March 5. Bringing one chapter of the international history of this civil war to an end by September, the Czechs withdrew to Vladivostok and evacuated from there, along with most of the intervention forces except the Japanese.

Meanwhile, the leadership of what was left of the White movement in the east had passed to Ataman Semenov, a particularly bloodthirsty warlord who, with the backing of the Japanese intervention troops had long claimed command over the Cossacks of Siberia and the Far East. His hold over the Trans-Baikal region had always been tenuous, however, and a growing partisan movement had taken over large segments of the Amur region. Only Vladivostok, Khabarovsk, Chita, and the Chinese Eastern railroad through Manchuria remained "White." While the Red Army advanced from the west along the railroad towards Irkutsk, Red partisans tightened the noose in the hinterland. Khabarovsk fell to the Red insurgents on February 16. Eventually, the Japanese cut their losses, retreated from the Trans-Baikal and consented to the establishment of a nominally independent Far Eastern Republic. This entity, which came increasingly under Bolshevik control and would be absorbed into the RSFSR in November 1922, stretched from the eastern shores of Lake Baikal to the Pacific. Vladivostok, technically under a White administration, remained occupied by Japan until 1922, northern Sakhalin even until 1925.

Once the Japanese retreated from the Trans-Baikal region, Semenov's forces quickly collapsed. What followed was one of the most bizarre episodes of the White war effort. The Austrian born Baltic-German Baron Roman von Ungern-Sternberg, an unhinged lieutenant of Semenov's, crossed with his band into Outer Mongolia, in order to regroup. He took Urga (Ulan-Bator) in February 1921. The Red Army pursued the "bloody Baron," took Urga, but let Ungern escape, who in July began raiding Soviet territory. Eventually, his war-weary troops mutinied and tried to assassinate the Baron, who managed to escape but was soon captured by the Red Army. After a show trial, he was executed in September. Mongolia, meanwhile, was Bolshevized, the only region that had not been part of the Tsarist's empire to suffer such a fate in the civil war. It became the first Soviet satellite, a site of an important battle at the beginning of World War II in Asia (Chapter 6), and the model for Soviet imperialism in other regions after 1945 (Chapter 7).

Fixing the Border in the West: The Bolshevik–Polish War

While the Red Empire thus acquired its first satellite in the south-east, in the west its expansion was curtailed by its newly independent neighbor Poland (which since 1919 had occupied parts of Lithuania and Belarus). After the collapse of the White armies in Ukraine under the combined onslaught of the Red Army and Makhno's anarchists, the Ukrainian People's Republic again faced imminent extinction. In desperation, Petliura made common cause with Poland. This unlikely friend joined the Ukrainian nationalists in an attack on Kyiv, which they captured from the Reds on May 7, 1920. The counter-attacking Red Army not only took back Kyiv but pressed on to the gates of Warsaw. Their eventual defeat outside the Polish capital by combined Polish and Ukrainian forces fixed the Soviet–Polish border until 1939 and for the time being ended hopes that Red bayonets could carry the revolution into Germany.

Poland gained western Ukraine in the Treaty of Riga (March 18, 1921) and would only lose it again in 1939. At the same time, however, it abandoned eastern Ukraine to the Soviets. Ukraine would remain part of the Soviet Union until its end, interrupted only by German occupation during World War II. As a result of its misadventure in Ukraine, Poland evacuated Belarus as well, which became a Soviet Republic again in August 1920, while Lithuania, also liberated from Polish occupation, retained its independence until World War II, a period of national self-determination it shared with the two other Baltic republics: Estonia and Latvia. The ultimate losers of 1920–1921 in the west, meanwhile, were the Ukrainian nationalists who, after years of fighting gained nothing but Stalin's continuing suspicion. Ukraine became one of the major republics within the Soviet Union, but independence had to wait until 1991.

Revolutionaries against Bolshevism

While the Red Army thus reconstructed the old empire in a new form, Bolshevik power was challenged internally, when peasants, workers, and sailors – once all central to Bolshevik success after October – rebelled. The Bolsheviks had fought the peasantry over grain requisitioning ever since 1918. Once his initial attempts to deal with the urban food shortage by increasing exchange between the city and the countryside had failed, Lenin sent squads of urban communists, each 75 men strong and armed with machine guns as well as hand grenades, to take by force what the peasants were not willing to give voluntarily. Their low-level counter-insurgency in the Bolshevik hinterland triggered numerous rebellions – 200 by the summer of 1918. In August 1920 this nagging war with the peasantry exploded into a full-scale uprising in the Russian heartland: in Tambov province, some 300 miles southeast of Moscow. By year's end well above 20,000 armed partisans fought against the government, calling for a Constituent Assembly and an end to grain confiscations. Lenin sent a punitive expedition, which put down the insurgency with outrageous brutality. At the same time, the Soviet government gave in to part of the demands: grain requisitioning was ended in a decree of February 2, 1921, which replaced it with a tax. This change would become one of the central pillars of the New Economic Policy, inaugurated on the Tenth Party Congress.

Peasants, who also rose in the Volga region and Western Siberia after these had been cleared of the Whites, had always been problematic "petty bourgeois" characters in Bolshevik minds. More worrisome was the loss of control over core constituencies: workers and radicalized soldiers, the kinds of people who had made the urban revolution in October 1917. In the winter of 1920/1921, strikes erupted in Moscow and Petrograd, and in March the naval base of Kronstadt, within striking distance of the birthplace of the Bolshevik revolution, descended into mutiny. Like many of the early "Whites" in 1918, and like their striking proletarian comrades, these were not counter-revolutionaries, although the Bolsheviks proclaimed them as such. Their demands included free and secret ballots to elections in the Soviets, freedom of press, speech, and assembly for "the democracy" (that is, workers, peasants, anarchists, and all leftist parties), freedom of association for worker and peasant unions, and an abolition of privileges for the Bolshevik party and its members. These were indeed radical leftist demands. They did not even ask for the reinstatement of the Constituent Assembly, as

KOMUCH and other anti-Bolshevik Reds had done before. Much further to the left, they wanted a return to what they conceived as the "original" October: "Soviet democracy." Lenin had them gunned down mercilessly by specially selected troops.

Crimea and the Trans-Caucasus

While Bolshevik rule was thus increasingly experienced as counter-revolutionary by Lenin's original constituents, to non-Russian peoples it began to present itself as a new form of imperialism. This imperialism was Red rather than Russian, as the conquest of Crimea from General Wrangel suggested. After fierce fighting beginning in June, Wrangel evacuated the remnants of his forces in the middle of November 1920 and the peninsula became part of the Bolshevik state. The Hungarian Communist Béla Kun (1886–1938), one of the many Austro-Hungarian POWs who had become Bolsheviks during the heady days of the Revolution, was back in Bolshevik lands after a failed revolutionary excursion to Hungary. He oversaw mass shootings, which prompted armed resistance by Crimean Tatars. Eventually, mass terror was replaced with limited concessions in a "Crimean Autonomous Soviet Socialist Republic" (October 1921).

In parallel with this campaign and overlapping also with the Soviet–Polish war (February 1920 to March 1921) went the reincorporation of the Trans-Caucasus, another of the Tsarist domains that had been temporarily lost. Reconquest began in April 1920 when the Red Army took advantage of the distraction of a border war between Armenia and Azerbaijan and annexed the latter without much trouble. Once Moscow had recovered from fighting against Poland and the conquest of Crimea, Armenia followed in November 1920, in the wake of a failed uprising and a Turkish invasion. Turkey and Moscow made peace over the corpse of Armenian independence: the Soviets dominated the Trans-Caucasus, and the Turks received disputed territories west of Armenia. The last of the non-Bolshevik republics beyond the Caucasus, Georgia, was swallowed up in February 1921.

These were takeovers of an oil rich region, which had been part of the Russian Empire for a bit over a century, and whose weak governments were unable to offer effective resistance. The annexations were at times cloaked in Red rags by local communists requesting military assistance from Moscow – usually when troops were already on the march or while indeed marching with them. There was military resistance in both Azerbaijan and in Georgia, where the Red Army had to fight for Tiflis. Local uprisings followed in Azerbaijan later in the year and in Armenia at the start of 1921. Georgia followed suit in 1924. All these attempts were suppressed and the three countries would remain part of the Red Empire until the 1990s, first as the "Trans-Caucasian SFSR," then, from 1936, as three republics within the Soviet Union.

Central Asia

By the middle of 1921, then, the European part of the former Russian Empire had been pacified under several new states: Poland, Latvia, Lithuania, and Finland, as well as Bolshevik Russia, which had also reconquered Belarus and Ukraine as well as Georgia, Armenia, and Azerbaijan. It further controlled the nominally independent Far Eastern Republic and the Mongolian satellite. Meanwhile, the south-eastern periphery continued to bleed. As discussed in Chapter 2, local Bolsheviks had taken power in Tashkent and other cities early on, establishing the Turksovnarkom, which eliminated competitors by force. Central Asia had descended into its own civil war, cut off until 1919 from the Bolshevik mainland by the rule of the Whites in the Volga region and Siberia.

Local Muslims had already risen against Russian domination in 1916, and were not easily subdued by city-based communists. An attempt by the Tashkent Bolsheviks to make short work of the Emirate of Bukhara failed miserably in February and March 1918. At the same time, the maltreatment of the countryside led to growing Muslim resistance against the Red masters. Soon, the entire country was embroiled in a guerrilla war, known as the Basmachi movement. Another headache for the Bolsheviks was the Transcaspian government Russian railroad workers had set up in Ashkhabad after an uprising in July 1918. With British support they held out for 18 months.

In September 1919, with the defeat of Kolchak, connection to the Bolshevik heartland was finally re-established. The Red Army spent much of the winter of 1919/1920 mopping up the remainders of various White Cossack units (some of whom eventually escaped to Persia) in the steppes of today's Kazakhstan. Once that was accomplished, it turned its attention to the Transcaspians. Bereft of foreign help – British troops had pulled out early in 1919 – the railroad-workers' polity was unable to resist and was liquidated in February 1920. At the same time, the Muslim state of Khiva was also taken over by the Reds, followed by Bukhara in September.

Meanwhile, the Muslim insurgency of the Basmachi, which had simmered ever since 1918, moved into higher gear. In 1921, Enver Pasha (1881–1922) arrived. This hero of the Young Turk Revolution, the Balkan war and world war, former Ottoman Minister for War and perpetrator of the Armenian genocide had been sent by Lenin to help put down the Basmachi. Instead, he changed sides and reorganized the guerrilla gangs into a proper army with command hierarchies, titles, medals, and uniforms. The Basmachi now took control over larger and larger areas of Central Asia, but were eventually defeated by the Red

Army in 1923, Enver fell in battle in 1922. Returning to insurgency tactics and moving back and forth across the border with Afghanistan, the Muslim guerrillas continued to harass Bolshevik forces well into 1926. The last of these resisters was only eliminated in 1934.

Red imperialism in Central Asia, as in Crimea and elsewhere, then, was marked by military conquest and often severe brutality. But the Red imperialists had also learned over the years of fighting that terror alone would not do. They developed a second policy plank, attempting to appease the Muslims now under their control. In a prefiguration of what would become the New Economic Policy (NEP), Bazaars were reopened in Turkestan in 1920 and small-scale trade was permitted to native populations (but not to other, Slavic, residents). Food distribution favored them as well, and priority was given to recruitment into the Bolshevik party. The NEP, inaugurated in 1921, aided pacification here as elsewhere. In addition, in 1922, Muslim religious schools and sharia courts were re-established. The Central Asian territories also received special status within the emerging Soviet Union. In the neighboring Kirghiz Autonomous Soviet Socialist Republic (today's Kazakhstan), a land reform was meant to alleviate the tensions between local Kazakhs and Slavic settlers, although in practice it deteriorated into mass expulsions of the former by the latter.

Red Imperialism

The history of how the Romanov state became the Red Empire leaves us with a paradox: Red imperialism. The Bolsheviks were anticapitalist internationalists who were devoted to ending imperial repression – "the highest stage of capitalism," to quote Lenin's 1917 pamphlet.[3] With the abolition of capitalism came the withering away of not only ethnic particularism, but also of states, money, and other annoyances of modern life, among them imperialism. This blissful state would come into being by an international upheaval: world revolution. Given this ideological background, one would not have predicted what eventually happened. Why did a group of revolutionary internationalists, devoted to the abolition of capitalism, and with it of imperialism, end up resurrecting a poor-man's version of the Romanov Empire?

Part of the answer lies in the culture of empire. The major players on the Bolshevik side (Lenin, Trotsky, Stalin, Kamenev, Bukharin, Zinoviev, Kalinin, Molotov) had grown up as subjects of this empire. They might have consciously been internationalists, Marxists, communists. Yet their mental world inevitably revolved around the polity they learned their politics in. "Everything was dear and familiar," wrote Lenin's wife, Nadezhda Krupskaya (1869–1939) about entering Finland from Sweden in early 1917, "The rickety old third-class carriages, the Russian soldiers. It made you feel good." Finland, in her experience, was Russian.[4] Nor was such cultural imperialism restricted to Russians. The Bolsheviks were, like the empire they emerged from, a multinational party. Much has been made of the role of Jews in this anti-anti-Semitic party, Trotsky among the most prominent. But the leadership also included men like the Georgian Stalin or the Pole and Cheka founder Feliks Dzierżyński (Dzerzhinsky), "men of the borderlands," who as non-Russians might well have been drawn to separatism. The universalist creed of revolutionary Marxism they embraced, instead, pulled them away from such localism. Even more than the cosmopolitan intellectuals like Krupskaya or Lenin, their lives and thoughts revolved around the geography of the empire, which they would reconstruct in proletarian form. It was in the large spaces of the empire where they worked illegally, were arrested, shipped to Siberia, escaped only to be arrested again. This geography left its mark on their outlook.[5]

Moreover, universalist communism went quite well with imperialism. Both were trans-nationalist ideologies, which preferred higher-order organization over ethnic or local particularisms. In a situation where the expected world revolution failed to materialize, the reconstruction of empire was the second best option. What else should the Bolsheviks have done? Pack up, give in, and accept that their entire revolution had been based on false premises? Become nationalists and restrict themselves to the ethnically Russian heartland? Or fight like hell to extend Bolshevik power over as much of the old empire as possible, to build a bridgehead for the world revolution to come? Should we be surprised that they chose the latter path, which transformed them from revolutionary internationalist into red imperialists?

There were also the hard facts of the economy, which pushed the Marxist revolutionaries to become statist imperialists. Tsarism had developed a regional division of labor: Petersburg/Petrograd was the center of heavy industry; the Donbass produced coal, iron, and steel as well as engineering products; northern and central Ukraine, western Siberia, and the northern Caucasus produced the grain to feed the population and to create capital by exporting to the world markets; Central Asia also provided grain, but more importantly the cotton, which would be spun in the textile mills of Moscow; Baku provided the oil for kerosene lamps, stoves, and heaters, as well as for powering the growing fleet of combustion engine driven cars, trucks, and tanks then also used in the world and civil wars; a system of railroad lines, running on its own imperial gage, held the entire edifice together and the ports at the shores of the Black Sea, the Baltics, and the Pacific allowed connections to the world markets. If the Bolsheviks wanted to take over the industrial system of late Tsarist capitalism, they had to take over the Tsarist empire as well. If they needed to build "socialism in one country" (and that was all they could do, given that the world's proletarians had not made a global revolution), this country needed to be an empire.[6]

A History of Violence

The process of transforming the Romanov Empire into the USSR was painful and violent. The world war was a terrible carnage, often conducted with poor supplies and terrible leadership. The civil war was fought in a variety of theaters by a huge array of forces, both domestic and international. In many ways, it makes more sense to see it not as one conflict, but as the wars of the succession of the Russian Empire. These wars, however, did have uniting characteristics.

The most outstanding of these shared traits was an unbelievable brutality. Enemies were shot or hanged, of course, but that was the least of it. Often they were tortured, mutilated, blinded, drowned, thrown down mine shafts, or buried alive. Hands, feet, and genitals were cut off, and the latter sometimes stuffed in the dead foe's mouth. The repertoire of graphic violence all sides used also included dousing enemies with water and letting them freeze to death in the winter. Quarter was seldom given, although the Red Army was more likely than others to discriminate on class grounds, killing only officers and letting the ranks live, particularly if they would change sides.

Historians are divided about how to best explain this violence. Some note the brutalizing influence of years of warfare since 1914, which had cheapened life considerably and had got men used to taking what they wanted by force of arms. The Finnish example, however, shows that exceptional brutality can emerge without wartime brutalization. Finland was neither a frontline zone nor did its sons have to fight in the tsarist army (they paid taxes instead). What the war did do was to weaken established imperial authority and then state authority in general, accompanied by a war-induced cycle of economic boom and bust. The national government that took over in 1917 collapsed quickly and by the end of the year there was effectively no state in Finland. The war also increased the availability of weapons, a dangerous situation under conditions of state collapse and increased social tensions. Prewar social and ideological divisions were thus both exacerbated and armed and soon opposing political groups tried to fill the power vacuum by force. The country spiraled quickly into one of the most lethal civil wars of the century.

Moreover, postwar violence was the exception rather than the rule among the combatant nations of World War I. This oft-forgotten fact points to the centrality of state breakdown, rather than war, in the genesis of civil war brutality. Groups of armed men (and some women) stepped into the void left by a disintegrating state. These groups were weak, minorities operating in an often hostile or indifferent environment. None of them was supported by a functioning administration or managed to enforce its own monopoly of power. Thus, violence became a pragmatic necessity, independent of the ideologies involved. It was used to frighten the enemy into submission, no matter if it was inflicted by German occupation troops in Ukraine, by White forces in the South or the east, by SR execution squats operating on German or Bolshevik held territories, or by the Bolsheviks in the center. Lethal, extrajudicial violence also served "to shake up our own ranks," as Trotsky explained the utility of the Romanov executions: once the own hands were bloodied, "there was no turning back." Ahead lay "either complete victory or complete ruin."[7]

Ideology also played a role, in particular on the Bolshevik side. Historians have long debated if Lenin's men had been "brutalized" by the experience of the civil war, or if their ideology predetermined their brutality. Both sides of the argument can marshal strong evidence in support of their position. It is easy to find Lenin quotations before and during the October revolution that advocate extreme violence against enemies. The ruling classes, he reasoned not illogically, would resist the confiscation of their privileges and the theft of their property, which were at the center of a socialist revolution. This resistance had to be broken by force, or else the revolution would fail. Civil war was necessary, thought Lenin, and he actively sought it.

The counter-argument points to the clear increase in the level of violence from relatively small beginnings immediately after the October insurrection through their escalation in the war against peasant rebels to the orgy of Red Terror that occurred after the attempt at Lenin's life in mid-year. This escalation was not just rational and ideological, but also irrational and emotional: resentment and revenge played as much a part as ideological conviction. Others have pointed out that we do not need to choose one or the other explanation. Resentment and ideology can reinforce each other, and civil war is unlikely to lead to restraint. It is indeed hard to see how the brutality of the civil war would remain without consequences on people who had gone through it. To many Bolsheviks, both of the old guard and of the younger proletarians who entered the Party while serving in the Red Army or Cheka, this war was a formative experience, but one "for which their past and thoughts had prepared them."[8]

A similar escalation of a pre-existing readiness for violence can be observed in violence against Jews, mostly by "White" armies, but also by Makhno's guerrillas and occasionally even the Red Army. Anti-Semitism was, of course not new, and terrible pogroms had broken out in 1881 and then again during the 1905 revolution. During World War I, anti-Jewish violence became partially legitimized by the state, with the army treating Jews as potential German spies. The Tsarist army became well-known for its anti-Semitic excesses, in particular in Galicia. This "normalization" of the pogrom seeped over into the civil war, and became a major factor in pushing many Jews towards the anti-anti-Semitic Bolsheviks, even if by class background many might have been less than inclined to support them. More tragically in the long run, they made the German occupiers in 1918 seem the lesser of two evils, a judgment with a deadly afterlife from 1939, and in particular 1941.

Why did the Bolsheviks Win?

It was only once a group of armed men managed to subdue their opponents that new states could enforce a new monopoly of violence and thus pacify the empire. Among the successor states of the Romanov Empire the largest is the subject to the rest of this book: the Union of Soviet Socialist Republics. Why did the Bolsheviks, a minority party with many enemies, win over their challengers? Explanations of Bolshevik success can be divided into military and political. Militarily, the Bolsheviks had the advantage that they controlled the center of the old empire, the Russian heartland with Moscow and Petrograd as the most important cities. This geographic fact had serious military implications: it allowed moving forces relatively swiftly by railway from one front to the other. Meanwhile, their opponents, divided by huge distances impossible to overcome, had both to march and to strike separately. With the industrial center the Bolsheviks also controlled much of the armaments industry the tsarist warfare state had built during World War I (see chapter 2), as well as significant reserves of weapons and ammunition. And they could draw on a much larger pool of human resources than their enemies. With a population of 60 million and a territory approaching a million square miles, the rump territory the Bolsheviks controlled was still the largest and most populous state in Europe – *after* the amputation of Finland, the Baltics, Belarus and Ukraine, the Don and Kuban, the Trans-Caucasus, the Urals and the Volga, the Arctic coast and Siberia. Their opponents, meanwhile, had to make do with whatever men and materiel they could find outside of the industrial heartland. While receiving substantial aid from the Allies (in particular Britain and the US), these shipments were hampered by extremely long supply lines.

As important were political factors. The breaking away of much of the outlying regions had the unintended consequence that it Russianized the Bolshevik territories: The RSFSR in 1918/1919 was as close to a nation state of Russians as Russia would ever be. Meanwhile, many of the simmering ethnic conflicts were concentrated in White territories. Political contests added to the divisions among anti-Bolsheviks. Mensheviks, SRs, Left SRs, and anarchists could never find common ground. In the Volga region, the Mensheviks opposed armed resistance against Bolshevism, undermining KOMUCH's ability to mobilize the working class. Both here and elsewhere, anti-Bolshevik socialists never saw eye-to-eye with the military men who would have to lead the fighting, but who invariably toppled socialist and even liberal governments. In the Cossack lands of south Russia the liberal politicians who had come to fight Bolshevism from there, understood neither their Cossack hosts who were to lead this fight, nor the dispossessed urban and rural masses. The early leader of the White Army – Mikhail Vasilevich Alekseev (1857–1918) – was despised by the most charismatic of his comrades in arms – Kornilov – whom he had arrested just months earlier when defending Aleksandr Kerensky's Provisional Government against the general's coup (Chapter 2). Meanwhile, Krasnov hated Denikin. Krasnov's Cossacks were ready to fight for the liberation of their lands but not – as Kornilov's volunteers – for the resurrection of the Russian Empire. The Provisional Government of Siberia was locked in a struggle with KOMUCH until it managed to absorb it. In the north-east, Iudenich was betrayed by his Baltic allies and not helped by the Finns. When the Finns did try to assist a Murmansk-based British-Russian attack towards Petrozavodsk in May 1919, they in turn were snubbed as an ally of the former German enemy.

Further examples abound, but the point should be clear: "the Whites" were not a unified movement. Personalities and ideology (from socialism on the left to monarchism and proto-Fascism on the right), nationalism, imperialism, and anticolonial desires divided the foes of Bolshevism. There was no lack of personal hostilities among the leading Bolsheviks either, but they were united by a shared ideology (a version of revolutionary Marxism), a leader with very high authority (Lenin), and party discipline. These traits made them a superior warring party.

All sides used coercion to extract food and fodder, and men and equipment from their surroundings. All sides alienated the peasantry by forced food requisitioning. However, the Bolsheviks – whose leadership was made up of civilian politicians, not military men – added carrots to the stick. They promised servicemen and their families land as well as other benefits, while denying both to deserters and draft dodgers. They played the imperial card well, proclaiming their support for national self-determination while in practice undermining it. They promised to defend the gains of the revolution: land to the peasants and control over the factories to the proletariat. Even when forced to drown military or peasant rebellions in blood to hold on to power, they also made concessions: an end to War Communism, and special support for demobilized servicemen. They also knew where they were going in the long run – towards Communism – and had an ideology to offer, which in many ways resembled a secular, millenarian religion. More importantly maybe was their clear short-term goal: to take back the lands of the tsar from the counter-revolution, unite them under Bolshevik leadership, and wait for world revolution.

Meanwhile, the Whites, divided politically and ideologically, temporized. Unable to find common ground, they continued the disastrous tactic of 1917 of declaring that all political questions would be resolved after the end of hostilities by an elected constituent assembly. They had little to offer to the broad mass of peasants and proletarians, either in terms of real concessions or in terms of worldview. During the first phase of the civil war (examined in Chapter 2) they even continued to proclaim that Russia would remain in the war against the Central Powers, a position that had already doomed the Provisional Government. Their Russocentrism alienated the peoples of the non-Russian periphery, while the Bolsheviks promised autonomy and national liberation.

That these promises turned out to be hollow once the war was won mattered little while the fighting raged. Alliances between White Russians and anti-Bolshevik Finns, Lithuanians, Estonians, Ukrainians, or Poles would at best be tactical, and support from Jews was more or less impossible given the widespread violent anti-Semitism. The Greens, meanwhile, had such a local focus on peasant demands that they could barely see beyond their own district; and the nationalists were not only divided internally but also often competed over territory with each other. The divisions and conflicts between Bolshevism's various enemies played into Lenin's hands.

Finally, the entities that survived the imperial apocalypse – Finland, Poland, the Baltic republics, and the Bolshevik Empire – all managed to build functioning states in the process of war and revolution. The defeated opponents of Bolshevism were unsuccessful in developing an institutional base, and in many instances did not even try to do so. Instead, they lived by the law of the gun: warlordism. Others, such as Skoropadskyi in Ukraine, focused on the "wrong" institutions in the circumstances. Universities or academies might help build a nation, but what was needed first of all was an efficient army to win and defend independence. The Bolsheviks understood this simple fact of life in the ruins of empire. They built a crude and inefficient, but ultimately effective, warfare state focused on the means of violence necessary to win and keep power. Everything else was subordinated to the core institutions: the Red Army and the Cheka.

The Bolsheviks, then, won because they were both ruthless and pragmatic politicians, state builders with a clear vision and a sense of the own historical mission and righteousness. In the final analysis, it is no surprise that poorly armed, politically and geographically divided movements, often devoid of a mass base and without a shared goal other than the defeat of Bolshevism, would lose against ideological warriors with flexible tactics, large supplies of weapons, a united territory, a strong social base in the cities, growing institutional backing in a developing warfare state, and a clear vision of the future. Nevertheless, this outcome was far from obvious to anybody involved at the time, as the overview of the convoluted fighting in this and the previous chapter made clear. These were desperate years for the Bolsheviks and their enemies, and they would deeply shape the societies that emerged from the ashes of the Tsarist empire: the Union of Soviet Socialist Republics, Poland, Latvia, Lithuania, Estonia, and Finland.

Notes

1 Orgburo circular on terror against Cossacks, January 24, 1919, as quoted in Shane O'Rourke, *The Cossacks* (Manchester: Manchester University Press, 2007), 247.
2 Marie Bennigsen Broxup, "The Last Ghazawat. The 1920–1921 Uprising," in: *The North Caucasus Barrier: The Russian Advance Towards the Muslim World*, ed. Marie Bennigsen Broxup (London: Hurst & Company, 1992), 112–45, here: 114.

3   *Vladimir Ilyich Lenin: Imperialism, the Highest Stage of Capitalism*, https://www.marxists. org/archive/lenin/works/1916/imp-hsc/, accessed December 28, 2017.

4   N. K. Krupskaya, *Reminiscences of Lenin* (1933) https://www.marxistsfr.org/archive/ krupskaya/works/rol/rol21.htm, accessed December 28, 2017.

5   Alfred J. Rieber, "Stalin, Man of the Borderlands," *The American Historical Review* 106, no. 5 (2001): 1651–91.

6   The classical formulation is Stalin's December 1924 essay "The October Revolution and the Tactics of the Russian Communists," https://www.marxists.org/reference/ archive/stalin/works/1924/12.htm, accessed January 6, 2017.

7   W. Bruce Lincoln, *Red Victory. A History of the Russian Civil War 1918–1921* (New York: Simon & Schuster, 1989), 155.

8   Sheila Fitzpatrick, "The Civil War as a Formative Experience," in: *Bolshevik Culture: Experience and Order in the Russian Revolution*, ed. Abbott Gleason, Peter Kenez and Richard Stites (Bloomington: Indiana University Press, 1985), 57–76, here: 74.

Bibliography

Acton, Edward, Vladimir Cherniaev, and William Rosenberg. *Critical Companion to the Russian Revolution 1914–1921* (London: Arnold, 1997).

Argenbright, Robert. "Red Tsaritsyn: Precursor of Stalinist Terror," *Revolutionary Russia* 4, no. 2 (1991): 157–83.

Avrich, Paul, *Kronstadt 1921* (Princeton, NJ: Princeton University Press, 1970).

Babel, Isaac, *Konarmiia. Red Cavalry* (London: Bristol Classical Press, 1994).

Babel, Isaac, *The Complete Works of Isaac Babel*, ed. Nathalie Babel (New York: W.W. Norton, 2002).

Ballis, William. "The Political Evolution of a Soviet Satellite: The Mongolian People's Republic," *The Western Political Quarterly* 9, no. 2 (June 1956): 293–328.

Barany, Zoltan. "Soviet Takeovers: The Role of Advisers in Mongolia in the 1920s and in Eastern Europe after World War II," *East European Quarterly* 28, no. 4 (1995): 409–33.

Bartov, Omer. "Genocide in a Multiethnic Town. Event, Origins, Aftermath," in: *Totalitarian Dictatorship: New Histories*, ed. Daniela Baratieri, Mark Edele, and Giuseppe Finaldi (London: Routledge, 2013), 212–31.

Beyrau, Dietrich, "Brutalization Revisited: The Case of Russia," *Journal of Contemporary History* 50, no. 1 (January 1, 2015): 15–37.

Bisher, Jamie. *White Terror. Cossack Warlords of the Trans-Siberian* (London and New York: Routledge, 2005).

Brovkin, Vladimir, *Behind the Front Lines of the Civil War: Political Parties and Social Movements in Russia, 1918–1922* (Princeton, NJ: Princeton University Press, 1994).

Daly, Jonathan and Leonid Trofimov, eds. *Russia in War and Revolution, 1914–1922. A Documentary History* (Indianapolis: Hackett Publishing, 2009).

Davies, Norman, *White Eagle. Red Star. The Polish–Soviet War 1919–1920 and "the Miracle on the Vistula"* (London: Random House, 2003).

du Quenoy, Paul. "Warlordism a La Russe: Baron Von Ungern–Sternberg's Anti–Bolshevik Crusade, 1917–21." *Revolutionary Russia* 16, no. 2 (2003): 1–27.

Edele, Mark, and Robert Gerwarth. "The Limits of Demobilization: Global Perspectives on the Aftermath of the Great War." *Journal of Contemporary History* 50, no. 1 (January 1, 2015): 3–14.

Engelstein, Laura. *Russia in Flames. War, Revolution, Civil War, 1914–1921* (Oxford: Oxford University Press, 2017).

Figes, Orlando. *A People's Tragedy. The Russian Revolution: 1891–1924* (New York: Penguin Books, 1996).

Fitzpatrick, Sheila. "Vengeance and Ressentiment in the Russian Revolution." *French Historical Studies* 24, no. 4 (2001): 579–88.

Fitzpatrick, Sheila. *The Russian Revolution*, 4th edition (Oxford: Oxford University Press, 2017).

Gerwarth, Robert. *The Vanquished. Why the First World War Failed to End, 1917–1923* (London: Allen Lane, 2016).

Graziosi, Andrea. *The Great Soviet Peasant War: Bolsheviks and Peasants, 1917–1933* (Cambridge: Ukrainian Research Institute, 1996).

Hessler, Julie. *A Social History of Soviet Trade. Trade Policy, Retail Practices, and Consumption, 1917–1953* (Princeton, NJ and Oxford: Princeton University Press, 2004).

Kenez, Peter, *Civil War in South Russia, 1918: The First Year of the Volunteer Army* (Berkeley: University of California Press, 1971).

Kenez, Peter, *Civil War in South Russia, 1919–1920: The Defeat of the Whites* (Berkeley: University of California Press, 1977).

Koenker, Diane, William G. Rosenberg, and Ronald G. Suny, eds. *Party, State, and Society in the Russian Civil War. Explorations in Social History* (Bloomington and Indianapolis: Indiana University Press, 1989).

Landis, Eric C. *Bandits and Partisans. The Antonov Movement in the Russian Civil War* (Pittsburgh: University of Pittsburgh Press, 2008).

Liber, George O. *Total Wars and the Making of Modern Ukraine, 1914–1954* (Toronto: University of Toronto Press, 2016).

Lincoln, W. Bruce. *Red Victory. A History of the Russian Civil War 1918–1921* (New York: Simon & Schuster, 1989).

Marshall, Alex. *The Caucasus under Soviet Rule* (London: Routledge, 2010).

Mawdsley, Evan. *The Russian Civil War* (New York: Pegasus Books, 2005).

Mayer, Arno J. *The Furies. Violence and Terror in the French and Russian Revolutions* (Princeton, NJ: Princeton University Press, 2000).

O'Rourke, Shane. "Trial Run: The Deportation of the Terek Cossacks 1920," in: *Removing Peoples. Forced Removal in the Modern World*, ed. Richard Bessel and Claudia B. Haake (Oxford: Oxford University Press, 2009), 255–79.

Palmer, James. *The Bloody White Baron* (London: Faber and Faber, 2008).

Pipes, Richard. *The Formation of the Soviet Union. Communism and Nationalism, 1917–1923*, revised edition (Cambridge, MA: Harvard University Press, 1997).

Raleigh, Donald J. *Experiencing Russia's Civil War. Politics, Society, and Revolutionary Culture in Saratov, 1917–1922* (Princeton, NJ and Oxford: Princeton University Press, 2002).

Read, Christopher, *War and Revolution in Russia, 1914–22. The Collapse of Tsarism and the Establishment of Soviet Power* (Basingstoke: Palgrave Macmillan, 2013).

Ritter, William S. "The Final Phase in the Liquidation of Anti–Soviet Resistance in Tadzhikistan: Ibrahim Bek and the Basmachi, 1924–31," *Soviet Studies* 37, no. 4 (1985): 484–93.

Sanborn, Joshua. "The Genesis of Russian Warlordism: Violence and Governance During the First World War and the Civil War," *Contemporary European History* 19, no. 3 (2010): 195–213.

Smele, Jonathan D. *Historical Dictionary of the Russian Civil Wars, 1916–1926*, 2 vols (Lanham: Rowman & Littlefield, 2015).

Smele, Jonathan D. *The "Russian" Civil Wars, 1916–1926. Ten Years That Shook the World* (Oxford: Oxford University Press, 2015).

Smith, S. A. *Russia in Revolution. An Empire in Crisis, 1890–1928* (Oxford: Oxford University Press, 2017).

Sunderland, Willard. "Baron Ungern. Toxic Cosmopolitan," *Ab Imperio* 3 (2005): 285–98.

Sunderland, Willard. *The Baron's Cloak: A History of the Russian Empire in War and Revolution* (Ithaca, NY: Cornell University Press, 2014).

von Hagen, Mark. *Soldiers in the Proletarian Dictatorship. The Red Army and the Soviet Socialist State, 1917–1930.* (Ithaca, NY and London: Cornell University Press, 1990).

Part II

The Interwar Years

4

Consolidating the Empire (1921–1928)

The period between 1904 and 1924 forms one historical unit. As the first three chapters of this book have shown, this was a period when the Tsarist empire was first violently unmade, then reconstituted as a Red empire. Given that this empire would again descend into violent chaos in 1930s and 1940s, we can call this the first and the later period of 1937 to 1947 the second "epoch of violence."[1]

Such a perspective has gained ground among historians since the fall of the Soviet Union made the October Revolution of 1917 less central to understanding the long sweep of Soviet history: no longer the foundational moment of a sovereign state, it became an episode in the transformation of international war into civil war, one step in the violent transfiguration of empire. At the same time, World War I and the civil war became more prominent as moments where the "new," post-Soviet states of the western periphery in particular made their debuts.

As Chapters 2 and 3 have shown, then, what used to be called the "Russian Civil War" is better understood as a period of breakdown and reconstitution of empire. An easy way to remember its periods is by year: 1914, the year World War I broke out; 1915, the year of military catastrophe; 1916, the start of revolt against the empire in Central Asia; 1917, the year of revolution; 1918, the year of imperial breakdown; 1919, the war between the Bolsheviks and the Whites; 1920, the year of consolidation and containment of Bolshevism.

The Russian Empire's civil wars ended in most regions in 1921. In Ukraine and Belarus, the Treaty of Riga in March and Nestor Makhno's flight abroad in August mark the end of the fighting, and in Russia the defeat of the Kronstadt

The Soviet Union: A Short History, First Edition. Mark Edele.
© 2019 John Wiley & Sons, Inc. Published 2019 by John Wiley & Sons, Inc.

and Tambov uprisings in March and June are similar landmarks. The reconquest of the Trans-Caucasus was completed with the fall of Tbilisi in February and the borders with Turkey were fixed in the Treaty of Kars in October. The Georgian uprising of August 1924 could provide another end-point in this region, but it is probably better understood as an aftershock. In the Far East, the Japanese evacuation of Vladivostok in 1922 marks the final end of the civil wars, and in Central Asia the majority of the Basmachi were defeated in 1923, although fighting continued in some areas until 1926. Despite such complications, a convenient endpoint of imperial reconstruction is 1924, when a new constitution formalized the makeup of the Red Empire. Elsewhere, however, pacification had been concluded earlier and postwar reconstruction begun. The Tenth Congress of the Bolshevik Party in 1921, which announced what came to be known as the New Economic Policy (NEP), marks the start of this process.

From here on, this book switches from dealing with all territories of the disintegrating Romanov Empire to focus on the largest of the successor states: the Soviet Union. Once it emerged from the cauldron of war, revolution, and civil war, this new, Red empire was remarkably continuous with its predecessor. The overall losses (Finland, Baltics, Bessarabia, Poland, and parts of the Trans-Caucasus) constituted only 2% of the territory held in 1914. Many borders – with Persia (Iran), Afghanistan, China, and Japan – remained intact and Mongolia became a de facto satellite in 1921, the only territorial acquisition after 1914.

While Bolshevik success in imperial reconstruction was impressive and Lenin's men ruled over what continued to be the world's largest territorial state, the losses were painful as well. The newly independent successor states of the Romanovs included Finland, a territory of nearly 126,000 square miles and a population of 3.3 million; Estonia (16,000 square miles and 1.8 million people); Lithuania (23,000 square miles and 2.3 million inhabitants); Latvia (27,000 square miles and 2.5 million humans); former Tsarist areas of Poland, Ukraine and Belarus, which went to the newly independent Poland (96,000 square miles and 16 million subjects); Bessarabia, annexed by Romania (17,000 square miles and 2.5 million residents); and territories in Trans-Caucasia ceded to Turkey (8,000 square miles and about half-a-million citizens).

Exhaustion

More crippling than the shrinking of the empire was demographic breakdown within the borders of what was left. Current estimates for population losses for the regions that would form the Soviet Union range from 16 to 25 million – a tally just below the Soviet excess deaths in World War II (25–27 million). The largest cause of population decline was increased mortality from hunger and disease, followed by military action, death from terror, pogroms, and crime. Between 1.5 and 2.5 million people emigrated, often from the former privileged classes. Emigration thus contributed to the process of social leveling that the revolution had engendered, but also deprived the new regime of some of the best-educated members of society.

The economy was in shambles. In 1913 the Russian Empire had produced 29 million tons of coal, by 1920 this output had dropped to 9 million and by 1923 had only recovered to less than 13 million. Iron ore production went from 9.2 million tons in 1913 to only 100,000 tons in 1921. In 1923 only 100 cars and 11 tractors were produced. The industrial working class had dropped from 3.6 million in 1917 to 1.5 million in 1920 – a catastrophic development for a regime that considered itself to be "proletarian." With deindustrialization came de-urbanization, as many proletarians fled the hungry cities or entered the Red Army. By the early 1920s, grass grew on Petrograd's Nevski Prospekt, once the proud promenade for the most sophisticated of late Tsarist urbanities.

The villages too were hungry. A shortage of labor and draft animals, the destruction and confiscation of agricultural implements and tools, and the ruthless grain requisitioning policies of "war communism" all contributed to an agricultural crisis shadowing the industrial one. In 1921–1922, millions suffered from famine and about one million peasants died as a result of it. Hunger further swelled the ranks of homeless children and youth produced by the dislocations and destructions of war, revolution, and civil war. They joined a larger stream of hundreds of thousands fleeing the hungry regions in search of food and survival.

Market Socialism

The Bolsheviks were thus in serious danger of losing the peace after winning the war. Something needed to be done, and quickly. The way forward first appeared in direct reaction to pacification efforts both at the periphery and the center of the empire. In 1920, the native population of Turkestan received the right to small-scale trade, while in the wake of the Tambov uprising, the defeated rebels were also offered some concessions, in particular the replacement of grain requisitioning by a tax (Chapter 3).

What emerged, then, was a tactical retreat. The warfare state of the civil war years was wound back. What was termed "war communism" in retrospect had been a system of forced grain collections, central allocation of resources (at least in theory), food rationing, military and labor conscription, and an inflationary increase of the amount of money in circulation. It was replaced by a hybrid system of state-led socialism with elements of legal markets, dubbed the "New Economic Policy" (NEP).

The NEP was inaugurated at the Tenth Congress of the Bolshevik Party in March 1921. With the backdrop of the Kronstadt rising, Lenin's party extended the deals that had been struck with the Turkestan and Tambov rebels to the entire empire: in return for peace in the countryside, the Bolsheviks replaced grain requisitioning with a tax in kind (eventually replaced by a money tax). Grain surpluses could be sold on the market. Other elements of the new economic system were put in place one by one: rationing was abolished and food distribution reversed from the state to the market; small-scale enterprises producing, likewise, on the basis of demand and supply became legal again; compulsory labor service in industry was replaced by contractual work obligations, payments in kind (rations) by wage payments linked to skill and productivity; state-owned enterprises producing consumer goods were to be guided by the market in setting the prices for their products; fiscal policy was used to influence the price of industrial goods; and eventually, the currency was stabilized by putting the ruble on the gold standard. Within this market-driven system existed enclaves of state-directed and centrally planned heavy industry, which functioned irrespective of market forces and was already very much in line with what would emerge for the economy as a whole in the 1930s.

The reintroduction of market elements and the management of the economy by fiscal policy had dramatic results. By the mid-1920s a similar percentage of the empire's population lived in cities as before the war. The working class recovered its share in the population at the end of the decade. By 1927, both agricultural and industrial production had returned to their pre-World War I levels of output, as had the number of workers employed in industry. National income followed suit in 1928.

Experiments in Culture and Life

The economic dynamism of the 1920s was shadowed by a bustling cultural scene. Several intellectual currents fought each other, all with roots in the late Tsarist era. There were those artists who felt they owed their allegiance to Russia rather than the revolution, and who continued to produce art and literature, which their critics labeled "bourgeois." In the non-Russian republics, the policy of promoting indigenous cultures led to the development of national literatures, or a flowering thereof, where it already existed, such as in Ukraine. Such efforts were opposed by so-called "proletarian" writers and artists producing agitprop, as well as by what has been described as the "caffeinated avant garde" of futurists like Vladimir Mayakovsky. The latter tried to break away from what they saw as obsolete cultural forms, merge culture and life, and thus create a new mentality adequate for the Socialist epoch.[2]

Few understood such art, and both officials and proletarians were mostly puzzled by it. More popular were novels that prefigured what would become "Socialist Realism" under Stalin: romantic depictions of reality not how it was, but how it ought to be. The civil war was a favorite topic of this emerging school. This multiplicity of voices was tolerated by the Bolshevik Party, which temporarily stood aside.

Besides literature, cinema flourished the most. Embraced as a modern form of communication with "the masses," the movies became so central to Bolshevik cultural identity that the Russian film industry of the late Tsarist period was all but forgotten and only rediscovered by scholars in the 1990s. Some of the most memorable movies of the Soviet epoch were shot in these years, including *Battleship Potemkin* (1925) or *Man with a Movie Camera* (1929).

In practice, the possibilities of building a new, communist life were limited. In the cities, communal living became the norm when the big apartments of the former ruling classes were divided up among proletarians. Building on the prerevolutionary tradition of living and working cooperatives (*artel'*), during the civil war such arrangements sometimes became communes with shared kitchens and detailed rules about how to live and work. In the 1920s, such experiments continued among students and workers, sometimes with more, sometimes with less success. More frequent were simply communities of need, ruled by vigilant house committees.

Most peasants, meanwhile, continued to prefer the family household. In Russia, the revolution had strengthened the village commune as the organization of individual peasant families and as a local self-governing body, which also redistributed land to the households. It functioned alongside the local Soviet, supposedly the representative of central power in the village, but indeed usually coopted by local communities for their own needs. In Ukraine and Belarus the revolution had strengthened the individual households themselves, who directly held land. Nowhere had it led to large-scale, modern and effective agricultural collectives, the daydream of many socialists. Landless peasants and returning veterans sometimes organized collectives, but these were above all survival groups. Most fell apart as the economy recovered in the first half of the 1920s. There were some attempts at collectivization, but they were a minority concern. Enthusiastic foreigners – Americans, Czechs, Austrians, Australians – also tried their hand at agricultural communism in Ukraine and on the Don. Jarringly to the atheist Bolsheviks, some of the most successful agricultural communes, meanwhile, were religious. In particular Tolstoyans, Christian pacifists and vegetarians, created thriving agricultural communities, which came under attack at the end of the decade. One of them, the "Life and Labor Commune" managed to survive after resettlement to Siberia into the 1930s.

A distinct subculture developed within the Bolshevik Party, now overwhelmingly made up of people who had joined since the October

Revolution. These new members, who constituted 97% of the Party in 1922, were much more proletarian and less educated, more militaristic and more male than the old Bolsheviks of the prewar vintage had been. Together with the "Old Bolsheviks" they formed a somewhat beleaguered, militant minority in the Soviet Empire: in 1922, only 0.3% of the population were members of the Bolsheviks. The communist youth organization (Komsomol) had a somewhat broader reach, organizing about 2% of the eligible youth in 1920. Among communist true believers, new rituals were trialed, in order to displace religious ones in a new, atheist age. "Octobering" replaced baptism, and little communists were named "Marks," "Engelina," or "Stalina," some unfortunates even "Barrikada" and "Giotin" (Guillotine). On the next stage of the life cycle, "red weddings" included the singing of the Internationale and vows of fidelity to both the partner and Communism. Everyday living was ascetic, focused on self-improvement and mastery of Marxism-Leninism. Clothing was militant: the commissar's leather coat was the favorite garment for male and female communists alike.

Meanwhile, escapism and easy living became a preoccupation of many more, particularly in the big cities. The boulevard culture of late Tsarism survived into the NEP years, when very much the same songs were performed in the reopened cafes and restaurants as had been in the decadent years of the Romanovs. Youth, dressed in suits and fashionable dresses rather than leather coats, were in the thrall of a dancing craze. The foxtrot threatened bourgeois contamination of the young. Cocaine could be bought with relative ease and was consumed frequently, as was, of course, alcohol. A limited version of prohibition had been introduced by the Tsarist government at the beginning of World War I. In order to keep the army sober, the sale of hard liquor was restricted to restaurants. The Bolshevik regime continued these restrictions, as the proletariat had "no need of intoxication," as Lenin wrote optimistically. Its "strongest stimulant" was class struggle itself, for which it needed "clarity, clarity, and once again – clarity." In reality, the unavailability of vodka only led to substitution: moonshine (*samogon*) was consumed widely, as was eau de cologne, "a drink for intellectuals."[3] Prohibition was lifted in 1924 and a state monopoly over vodka production and distribution reinstated in 1925, chiefly in order to raise money. This policy was successful: by the late 1920s, 12% of state revenue was derived from alcohol sales.

Drugs were not the only way to escape a bleak postwar reality. Sex preoccupied many and promiscuity was encouraged by the most liberal divorce laws in the world. A popular theory stated that sexual desire was like thirst, and should be fought in the same way: by giving in. This "glass of water" theory, often falsely ascribed to the Bolshevik feminist Aleksandra Mikhailovna Kollontai (1872–1952), scandalized Bolshevik puritans, but was quite popular, in particular among young men.

Religion and Atheism

While many youth thus seemed to fall into decadence, austere communist believers in an atheist future also faced the mass of the population still enthralled with superstition, religion, and general lack of enlightenment. Despite all efforts of the "League of the Militant Godless" to mock, bully, or sometimes even educate the peasantry out of backwardness, the young atheists faced the same stubborn hostility their intelligentsia forebears had encountered when "going to the people" in the nineteenth century.

Such culture clashes were even more pronounced in the Muslim areas of the Red Empire, where the absence of a proletariat, the apparent reign of patriarchy, an incomprehensible religion, and oriental dress codes combined to entice the European revolutionaries and their local allies to see women as a "surrogate proletariat."[4] A campaign to "unveil" the indigenous culminated in 1927, when thousands of enlightened women tore off the offending cloth and burned it in public. This symbolic attack, however, backfired spectacularly. While for some young radicals the link to the Bolshevik modernizers paved a way out of patriarchy, for many others the onslaught on local custom appeared as a colonial attack on propriety. The veil, as a result, became more popular and more widespread, as Muslim society closed ranks against the infidel outsiders and their local allies (who were often pushed back into line by threats of physical and sexual violence). Moreover, the concentration on the symbolism of unveiling also hindered attempts to emancipate women from patriarchal custom in Muslim regions such as Turkmenistan, where the veil was not customary.

The 1920s, then, was an anxious period for communist true believers, for whom the color, diversity, and hubbub of the Soviet "roaring twenties" evoked negative reactions. Was this, they asked, what so many comrades had fought and died for since 1917? Foxtrotting youth, cocaine and sex addicts, petty bourgeois "NEP-men" who made their money in trade and spent their evenings sipping cocktails with ladies of ill repute: was this "socialism"? Or had capitalism returned? Had the revolution been defeated not by the louse, as Lenin had worried in 1919, but by *embourgeoisement*? Had the village, full of uncultured, samogon-brewing, hard-fisted peasants intent on running their own affairs been the real victor of the revolution? Did the peasants, in particular the rich among them, who seemed to dominate village society, hold the proletariat by the throat by not marketing their grain? And what about the workers? By 1923, in this "worker state," over 600,000 were registered as unemployed. By 1924, this number had risen to 1.3 million, only to increase further to 1.7 million by 1929 (many of them women and adolescents who had been pushed out of work by returning Red Army veterans). In socialism there should be no unemployment. Did these numbers show that capitalism was back? Why was nothing done about this? Why was there no renewed socialist offensive?

The Persistence of the Warfare State

The activists were only partially right in their anger towards NEP. The new economic policy was a major retreat from the attempt at complete state control of the economy; it was a concession to market forces; it was a compromise with the peasantry, which did not necessarily benefit the working class. However, it was not a complete marketization, even if it appeared to many as such. What the Bolsheviks called the "commanding heights" of the economy – banking, major industry, foreign trade – remained state owned and operated, although now within a market environment. The stock market did not reappear. The economy remained, to a significant extent, not only regulated, but controlled and owned by the state. The NEP, then, was a combination of a limited market with the persistence of the state economy, which had emerged during the prolonged period of warfare since 1914. The Bolshevik warfare state was only partially demobilized in the context of peace; it merely adapted to the demands of an interwar period.

Why this continuity? War communism was not only a reaction to the exigencies of war, but also conformed to fundamental traits of Bolshevik ideology. As Marxists, Lenin's men were deeply suspicious of market forces, social self-organization, and the "anarchy" of supply and demand. The warfare state provided an alternative to liberal economics by collecting and allocating resources centrally – an apparently more "rational" organization of the economy. Thus, the persistence of major elements of the warfare state into the peacetime of NEP had ideological roots.

Within this general ideological framework, however, economic pressures also asserted themselves, which militated against a free rein of the market. The initial attempt to let supply and demand take care of the price of consumer goods failed miserably in the "scissors crisis" of 1923: the prices of consumer goods outran the prices of agricultural goods, lowering incentives to market grain, and hence threatening the entire edifice of NEP. Indirect measures failed to remedy the situation. Given that grain needed to be extracted from the countryside, both to feed the cities and in order to export it to raise capital, price regulation became inevitable to a leadership unwilling to just meekly follow market forces if they led into crisis.

The continued Bolshevik embrace of the state is harder to explain in ideological terms. To Marx, the state was a fundamentally coercive entity, in existence only in order to suppress the exploited classes and bolster the rule of the property-owning minority over the majority. In socialism, then, no state would be necessary: the exploiting capitalists would have been expropriated; classes would cease to exist; class war would end; and no state was needed, as nobody was left to repress. It would "wither away," in Lenin's optimistic prediction of 1917.

The opposite happened: the Bolshevik state became stronger, more intrusive, and more repressive than its Tsarist predecessor. This persistence had several reasons. One cause was considerable domestic opposition to Bolshevik rule. For one, there were rival socialists, liberals, and monarchists who, while defeated during the civil war could be considered dormant at best. Even more threatening from a Marxist point of view was a considerable "class opposition." While the "exploiters" might have been "expropriated," many of them were still around and were unlikely to harbor tender feelings towards those who had stolen their property, taken over their homes, and thrown them into destitution. Thus, a state was still necessary to suppress these remnants of the old order. Eventually, Stalin would make sense of this fundamental paradox by arguing that class war was likely to increase as society moved towards Socialism – an ideologically consistent way to make sense of reality.

Domestic opposition also included anti-imperial forces within the multinational empire. On the southern frontier, the civil war did not end in 1921, but guerrilla fighting continued well into 1926. The northern Caucasus saw a major rebellion in the period 1920 to 1922 and enough rebel forces remained in the mountains thereafter that a pacification operation of army and police in the summer of 1925 included over 7,000 troops, several bomber planes, and artillery. There were uprisings in Karelia (1921–1922), Georgia (1924), Yakutia (1924–1925, 1927–1928), Ajiristan (1927, 1929), and Karbadinia (1928). Ukraine remained a major center for "political banditism" in the middle of the decade. In Central Asia, Basmachi operating from Afghanistan also kept Soviet forces busy into the early 1930s. Historians thus speak of "almost continuous armed resistance to Soviet power" in the borderlands.[5]

Opposition to Bolshevik rule also had an international component. Not only were many of the two or so million émigrés, who had left the empire as a result of the Bolshevik takeover hostile to the regime that had forced them to leave; many of them were also actively organizing efforts to continue fighting the civil war they had lost. The countries surrounding the Bolsheviks were opposed to this revolutionary state and could be expected to eventually fight it. Here, a real-life threat was further increased by the ideological conviction that capitalism would necessarily lead to war and that it was through war-turned-civil-war that world socialism would be triumphant. It had become abundantly clear since 1914 that in order to beat the mass armies of capitalist states a regular army was required. And to equip and supply such an army, a state was necessary.

It was for these reasons, then, that major aspects of the warfare state continued into the postwar years: an ideological opposition to market forces and domestic as well as international threats to Bolshevik rule. In real-life terms ("objectively speaking," as Marxists would say), the state was also the only real source of power the Bolsheviks had: Popular uprisings at the end of the civil war had made it clear that Lenin's men were an embattled minority in a hostile environment and the working class in whose name they claimed to rule had all but "withered away" as a result of the destruction of war and civil war. The flowering of all kinds of "petty bourgeois" ways of life in the wake of the NEP did little to dispel this sense of isolation. Police reports, of the time, about life in the countryside were full of lurid detail of corruption, violence, banditism, and anti-Soviet utterances. The village seemed hostile territory to the urban rulers in the Kremlin.

Hence, unless they wanted to give up power, the Bolsheviks needed to make peace with the state. Eventually, they did so with the aid of a double psychological move. For one, Stalin found an ideologically consistent justification for the persistence of the state. Expanding on a distinction playing a relatively minor role in Marxist thought until then, he reinforced the difference between "socialism" and "communism." The state would continue to exist during socialism and only wither away once full communism was reached somewhere behind the horizon. Second, Bolsheviks also remained consistent with the original revolutionary hostility to state organization by transposing it to anger at "bureaucracy," a cultural trait uniting the years of war communism with NEP and the years of Stalinism to follow. While "the state" was a good thing for the time being (during socialism), "bureaucracy" was not. The basic truth that one cannot have the one without the other mattered less in this perception of the world than the ability to blame all red tape, heartlessness, and detached decision making to "bureaucrats" while the Soviet state could be said to "care" about the population.

The Nascent Welfare State

This "care" expressed itself in a second aspect of the Soviet state, which came to the fore in the 1920s. While during war communism all efforts had been concentrated on war making, this warfare state was supplemented after 1921 with a growing field of welfare for the "deserving" classes of workers and poor peasants. Such concern with the laboring masses was ideologically unproblematic. After all, the revolution of 1917 had been a revolution for the betterment of the working classes. Its goal was "communism" – a state of affairs where working people would no longer be exploited, would live a dignified life without want, and would run their own affairs. All would contribute to the best of their abilities to the common good and would receive according to need in return. Those who refused to work would not eat (as paragraph 18 of the 1918 constitution stated), but those who worked would eat their fill.

To be sure, the idea that the state – or a compact of state and public organizations – should care for the welfare of the population, was neither new nor inherently socialist. As discussed in Chapters 1 and 2, the building of a welfare state had begun in the final prewar years and the field of both government and non-government provision of welfare grew massively during World War I. The Provisional Government continued this tradition and introduced Ministries of State Care, Labor, and Food Supply, "institutional expressions of the ideal that the state was obligated to look after the welfare of its citizens," as one historian has it.[6] The establishment of these ministries marked a further centralization and state control of the various welfare efforts, which had emerged since the outbreak of the war. At the same time, the provisions of the 1912 legislation for victims of war were extended in new, more generous pensions and the food aid for soldiers' families also increased. In parallel, the 1912 worker's insurance legislation also received serious government attention. The Provisional Government, then, built upon and expanded the field of state welfare it had inherited from its predecessor.

After October, the Bolsheviks merely continued this practice, often employing the same professionals as the old regime had and further centralizing the resources of voluntary societies in state hands. A new "Commissariat of Social Welfare" now took control of this expanding field of state action. It took its place next to the Commissariats of Public Health, and of Education. Thus, 3 of the 18 People's Commissars (that is, ministers) listed in the 1918 constitution of the RSFSR (section 43) were tasked with various aspects of welfare, elevating these concerns to a similar level as foreign affairs, policing, defense, or economic management. Building on the legal work of the Provisional Government, the newly created People's Commissariat of Labor announced in 1917 that all toilers would be insured against accident, sickness, and disability and would receive healthcare. Maternity leave and widow's pensions would also be available. All these benefits would be financed by an insurance scheme underwritten completely by employers' contributions. These grandiose plans came to naught, as in the economic apocalypse of the civil war they could not be financed. However, the precedent had been set: the new workers' state would provide welfare to the proletariat.

Bolshevik welfare, however, came with the ideological twist that only deserving classes (soldiers, poor peasants, and proletarians) had a right to state help, while "enemy" or "former" classes were discriminated against. In reality, of course, even the "good" classes could not count on many benefits beyond basic food rations. The new state was unable to provide the same level of care as the voluntary associations it had gobbled up.

Welfare thus became a stated goal rather than a practice during the Civil War. Disease, poor hygiene, bad nutrition, terrible living quarters, and generalized poverty made life miserable for most. Illiteracy and poor education hampered not only the advancement of the state but also the extent to which life could become better for the individual proletarian. The country swarmed with homeless children, cast adrift by the storms of collective violence of the previous decade.

Public health improved in the 1920s, partially through investment in personnel and infrastructure, partially by campaigns for personal hygiene, vaccination, and preventative care. Literacy also grew by a concerted effort to "liquidate illiteracy." Physical culture was promoted as part of the general push for personal betterment. Both the proletarians of the Russian heartland and the nomads of the non-Russian borderlands were exhorted to brush their teeth and thus demonstrate their level of "culturedness." The new soviet person, no matter his or her ethnicity, would be healthy, literate, disciplined, and fit.

The efforts to build a socialist welfare state were hampered by the poverty of the state. The Commissariat of Social Security did not have enough funds to actually administer the many programs it ran on paper. Welfare targeting women and children was cut to save money. Day-care centers and kindergartens organized by factories during the years of the civil war closed down. With the end of rationing in 1921, cafeterias, which had fed much of what was left of the urban proletariat, began to disappear. This decline of communal eateries made it harder for working mothers to feed the family. The number of libraries and reading rooms declined early in the decade, also due to lack of money. Disabled workers with savings were denied pension payments.

Severe budgetary constraints enforced creativity. The housing problem was largely dealt with by expropriations of existing housing stock and its redistribution to poorer sections of the population. Few new houses were built, unless on private initiative. After initial revolutionary hostility towards the family as a seat of patriarchal power, the emerging Soviet state began to draft kinship back into the provision of welfare. While legally registered marriages could be divorced with unparalleled ease, inheritance law for "personal property" (including the peasant hut) strengthened the family as a unit, which was also held responsible for looking after its old and young members, who otherwise would have become wards of the state. Adoption, outlawed after the revolution, became not only legal in 1925, but was encouraged as part of the fight against child homelessness.

While much of welfare provision was de facto left to the family and other forms of social self-organization, the fields the Bolshevik state began to focus on tended to be connected in one form or another to warfare. Education and healthcare – the greatest fields of achievement of the nascent Soviet welfare state – were directly linked to defense: soldiers and workers needed to be healthy to sustain a modern war effort, and literacy was increasingly necessary to perform well in modern, industrialized warfare. Benefits to disabled veterans and other victims of war had clear implications for mobilization and loyal service in future wars. Hence, care for war invalids and the families of serving soldiers became the major preoccupation of the Commissariat of Social Security, often to the detriment of other groups. Nevertheless, as the economy recovered throughout NEP, so did welfare expenditure. At the same time, however, growing unemployment put additional strain on resources. By the end of the NEP, the socialist welfare state remained a revolutionary dream like many others.

Dictatorship

Neither the economic liberalization, nor the cultural experiments, nor the growing field of welfare implied democratization. To drive home the point, the Soviets had forced the dissolution of the Mensheviks and arrested 5,000 of them in early 1921. In 1922, they organized a show trial of 12 leading Socialist Revolutionaries (SRs), once the Bolsheviks' most popular rivals on the left. All 12 accused were sentenced to death and although the sentences were commuted to life imprisonment, the message was clear: the partial retreat in economic matters was not to be accompanied by a political thaw. A group of 160 leading "bourgeois" intellectuals who had not voluntarily gone into exile were expelled from the Soviet Union later in the year.

The dictatorship became stronger just when the economic reins were somewhat slackened. The Tenth Party Congress in 1921, which had introduced the NEP, also decided on a major change within the party itself. Until then, Party members were free to organize factions and to use them to lobby for policy positions, as long as they toed the party line once a decision was reached. The resolution "On Party Unity" now warned that "every person who voices criticism must be mindful of the party's situation in the midst of enemy encirclement." It instructed the Party's leadership "to carry out the complete destruction of all manner of factionalism," and ordered "the immediate dissolution, without exception, of all groups that have been formed on the basis of some platform or other." It threatened that failure to comply would result in "unconditional and immediate expulsion from the party."[7]

The ban on factions accelerated a process within the Bolshevik Party, which is sometimes described as the move from Leninism to Stalinism. The difference can be over-stressed. Lenin was certainly no democrat in any reasonable meaning of the word. Like Stalin he supported terror toward enemies. On August 11, 1918, for example, Lenin instructed his comrades in Penza province to "mercilessly" suppress a peasant rebellion, which he blamed on the rich farmers, the "kulaks." "The interests of the *entire* revolution require this," he wrote "because now 'the last decisive battle' with the kulaks is under way *everywhere*." In order to establish an example, the comrades should hang "*no fewer than one hundred* known kulaks, rich men, bloodsuckers," then publish their names and seize their grain. Hostages were also to be taken. "Do it in such a way," he explained the reasoning behind such brutality "that for hundreds of versts around the people will see, tremble, know, shout: *they are strangling* and will strangle to death the bloodsucking kulaks." In a postscript he added: "Find some truly hard people."[8] Soon, more and more of the Bolshevik ranks were made up of these Leninist "hard people."

Unlike Stalin, however, Lenin conceived the enemies to be exterminated as a threat external to the Party, which itself could be kept pure by internal mechanisms such as the party purge that excluded (but did not kill) "foreign elements" from its ranks. Long before the term acquired its lethal connotation, the Party had "purged" close to a quarter of its members in 1921. Within his party of true believers, Lenin ruled not by terror, but by persuasion and backroom politics backed by his considerable authority. Under Lenin, government was a team effort led by a strong, authoritarian but not dictatorial leader. This style was different from the way the last tsar had run his empire (Nicholas had refused any encroachment on his autocratic authority by any team of ministers and instead met with each of them one on one), but it was also different from what Stalin would do later.

The ban on factions was an essential step in Stalin's march to power. Factions, of course, continued to be there: given that no political problem ever has only one possible solution, and given that interests vary between social and institutional groupings, a ban on factions only meant that whoever lost the struggle found themselves in the position of illegality. In this system, the winners took it all. It was only under Stalin in the 1930s, in conditions of terror within and against the Party, that factions did indeed disappear.

For the time being, the ban on factions only raised the stakes of factional politics. With a strong and undisputed leader like Lenin at the helm, this might have led to a unification of the party, as whatever position Lenin took was clearly the "party line." However, Lenin's powers were dwindling. Already increasingly sick, he suffered a stroke in early 1922, which forced him into a somewhat ungracefully suffered retirement. A second stroke followed in December and a third in March 1923. Lenin died on January 21, 1924.

There was no mechanism for succession in the Bolshevik party. A power struggle was thus inevitable. The most likely contender to take over leadership was the arrogant, brilliant, and popular Leon Trotsky, builder of the Red Army and passionate orator. This first round of the post-Lenin power struggle began in 1923 in the context of the "scissors crisis" and the backdrop of a failed revolution in Germany as well as a fight over federalism within the emerging Soviet Union.

Once Lenin was dead, the leadership struggle exploded and continued to the end of the decade, with changing alliances among the top Bolsheviks. Trotsky was defeated in 1924 by the triumvirate of Zinoviev, Kamenev, and Stalin; in 1925, Stalin broke with the former two and teamed up with Bukharin to defend the NEP against Zinoviev and Kamenev; and in 1926 the winners joined up yet again with Rykov and Tomsky to defeat the "united opposition" of Trotsky, Zinoviev, and Kamenev. The fight against the "left opposition" ended in 1927 with Trotsky's expulsion from the Bolshevik Party and his 1928 exile to Alma Ata (and from there abroad).

A new grain procurement crisis in 1927 and 1928 saw Stalin change course. Once a defender of the NEP he now became one of its opponents, attacking the "right opposition" of the NEP supporters around his old comrade Bukharin. Stalin's faction won again and by early 1929 "team Stalin" was in charge of the Soviet Union.[9]

The factional fights were about personal power: given the ban on factions, the winner would be able to sideline his "illegal" opponents. But they were also about options about the political and economic future of the Red Empire. They were, thus, about ideology in practice: how to build Socialism, now that the war against the counter-revolution was won, but world revolution had not ensued. As discussed in more detail in Chapter 5, there were two basic options within the parameters of Bolshevik ideology (which all participant both shared and took for granted): a continuation of the NEP, including relatively low levels of growth of heavy industry and a dependence on foreign loans; or a return to war communism, that is a full takeover of the economy by the state and an antagonistic relationship with the countryside.

During the 1920s, most protagonists argued for courses of action somewhere in-between these extremes. Trotsky's program of 1923, for example, had three prongs. He supported in basic outlines the continuation of NEP insofar as it left agriculture largely to market mechanisms. The way to increase productivity of agriculture was to create economic incentives to sell grain. These incentives would come in the form of cheap industrial products. In order to lessen the prices of industrial production, Trotsky proposed a comprehensive system of planning of the state-owned sector. The official response to the "scissors crisis," likewise, combined market and state elements, including an amalgamation of small factories to gain economies of scale, price controls, the expansion of state-trade in manufactured goods in the countryside, and fiscal measures all designed to lower industrial prices, while leaving agriculture to the market.

Other options were not discussed, because they were outside the parameters of Bolshevik ideology: democratization of the country, a complete privatization of the economy, or a full reintegration into the capitalist world system were all impossibilities both individually and in combination. Nevertheless, it is remarkable to what extent the party leadership of the 1920s, including Stalin, embraced liberal economic thought in running the economy. Everybody in the leadership stressed the importance of the gold standard and a balanced budget, neither of them the usual preoccupation of revolutionary Marxism. This did not mean that the Bolsheviks had ditched their ideology. On the contrary: Bolshevism was a self-consciously flexible form of Marxism and in the 1920s the leadership erred on the side of pragmatism.

Empire

The new state, then, was neither simply a welfare nor a warfare state. It combined aspects of market economics with state control of industry, economic liberalization, and relative cultural diversity with a dictatorial government, repression of dissent and discrimination against "class aliens" with social welfare for deserving classes. Like its Tsarist predecessor it was also a multinational empire.

The 1918 constitution had already noted that the "Russian Soviet Republic is organized on the basis of a free union of free nations, as a federation of soviet national republics" (section 2). At the time this claim to multinationality was fairly tentative, as one non-Russian region after the other was breaking away. Soon, the Bolsheviks controlled largely Russian areas. The aspiration expressed in the constitution was that of the leading Bolsheviks: to gather the old Tsarist empire under the red flag. In 1918, these hopes were squashed, but in the period 1919 to 1923 much of the old empire had been reunited with Bolshevik Russia.

Officially, the regathering of "Russian" lands did not constitute imperialism. Quite the opposite: It was an anti-imperial liberation. The 1918 constitution already affirmed "the full independence of Finland," disengagement in Persia, and "the right of Armenia to self-determination" (section 6). It declared that there would be no discrimination on the basis of race or nationality (section 22). Favoritism was to be extended to individuals solely on the basis of social class or service to the regime.[10]

The 1924 constitution made this claim to national liberation a central pillar of the socialist order. The preamble proclaimed:

> Since the foundation of the Soviet Republics, the states of the world have been divided into two camps: the camp of Capitalism and the camp of Socialism. There, in the camp of Capitalism: national hate and inequality, colonial slavery and chauvinism, national oppression and massacres, brutalities and imperialistic wars. Here, in the camp of Socialism: reciprocal confidence and peace, national liberty and equality, the pacific co-existence and fraternal collaboration of peoples.[11]

By the time these grandiose lines were written, the Red Army had regathered Ukraine and Belarus, the Trans-Caucasus, Siberia, and Central Asia. Until the proclamation of the Soviet Union in December 1922, the legal fiction was that these territories formed their own states, bound to the RSFSR only through a system of bilateral treaties. Now, the Socialist Soviet Republic of Ukraine, the Socialist Soviet Republic of Belarus, the Socialist Soviet Republic of Transcaucasia (itself a rather involuntary union of the Socialist Republics of Azerbaijan, Georgia, and Armenia) had joined the RSFSR in a new, formally federal state: "The Union of Socialist Soviet Republics." The Central Asian republics were at this stage not "union republics" but subdivisions of the RSFSR. They would be elevated to nominally independent constituent republics of the USSR between 1925 and 1936. Technically, they had the right "to freely withdraw from the Union," as article 4 of the 1924 constitution proclaimed. In practice, this right would only become a reality in 1991.

Why did the Bolsheviks build an at least formally federalist state? After all, these were Marxists, revolutionaries, and anti-nationalists. They were committed to dictatorship and centralism until communism's arrival would make both unnecessary. The reasons for this paradox are complex. There were aspects of ideology: nationalism was seen as a stage in the historical development, which would wither away like other annoyances, once communism emerged. Until such a time, it needed to be tactically accommodated, in order to blunt its potential for "misleading" the proletariat. The republics would be nationalist in "form" and socialist "in content." The new state, likewise, was federalist in structure but dictatorial in reality. Second, there was resistance from Bolsheviks in the borderlands to a full takeover of their regions by Russia. Third, there were international political ramifications. Many of the borderlands had established diplomatic relations and signed treaties with the outside world. These relationships could only continue if there was a pretense of federalism rather than outright annexation. And looking towards the future, which still seemed to promise revolution in other countries, it would be easier to integrate emerging socialist states in both Europe and Asia if the new state was a "Union of Soviet Socialist Republics" rather than an enlarged "Bolshevik Russia."

Within the USSR, Russia was dominant. According to the 1926 census, the RSFSR had a population of 100.9 million people, followed by Ukraine with 29 million, the Trans-Caucasian republic with 5.8 million, Uzbekistan with 5.3 million, and Belarus with 5 million. The capital of the Union was Moscow, the heart of pre-Petrine Russia. The members of the ruling Communist Party of the Soviet Union were in their vast majority (72% in 1922) Russian. Ukrainians came second with only 6% followed by Jews with 5%. It was this Russian party – centralized and controlled from the top down – which held the new state together and transformed the formal federalism into a de facto dictatorship ruled from Moscow. The shadow-structure of the Party also paralleled the administrative hierarchy, allowing control of a state still relying to a large degree on specialists from the old regime. The Party was also central to transforming the local soviets, once hotbeds of revolutionary democratism, into disciplined executive organs of the dictatorship. (This process was not complete in the 1920s, in particularly with regards to village soviets, which continued to be run by the locals).

The predominance of Russians in the Communist Party was partially balanced by determined policies of indigenization (*korenizatsiia*) in the non-Russian republics. This policy had some successes. By 1927, Ukrainians made up the majority of members of the Ukrainian Communist Party, up from less than a quarter in 1922. By 1930 their share was also dominant among state bureaucrats in Ukraine. Affirmative action policies also led to a growth of educated elites in all non-Russian republics, and extended well beyond the titular nationality of the non-Russian republics. National cultures and languages were developed aggressively. This policy was intended to weaken the appeal of nationalism, but in fact it led to further nation building, in extreme cases even the invention of a nation where no such idea had previously existed. Minority nationalities in the borderlands – such as Germans or Poles in Ukraine, Finns in Karelia, or Koreans in the Far East – received special privileges, in order to project a positive image outwards and entice their national brethren across the border to make revolution and join the Union.

The affirmation of minority rights within a dictatorial regime led by an overwhelmingly Russian party formed one of the fundamental contradictions in Soviet practice right to the end of this state in 1991: between Red imperialism, which forced non-Russian areas under Soviet (and, indeed, Russian) rule on the one hand, and the "affirmative action empire," which tried to develop and advance minority nationalities on the other.[12] This contradiction emerged for very convoluted historical reasons, as this and previous chapters have shown. It led to the paradox that this socialist state "promoted ethnic particularism."[13] In the long run, indeed, the "purely formal feature" of federalism became "one of the most consequential aspects of the formation of the Soviet Union," as a visionary historian had written in 1954.[14] In 1991, in fact, the Soviet Union broke apart along the fault lines drawn up by the boundaries between union republics, now national in content rather than mere form.

For the time being, however, the new union was remarkably stable, although not without tensions. The rule of Russian communists over the non-Russian periphery was recognized as a problem by the Bolsheviks, and concerted efforts were made to lessen, maybe even eradicate "Great Russian chauvinism," while helping non-Russian cadres along. Red imperialism was a fact of life, but it was certainly not the intention of the Bolshevik leadership. In a way, the Russian rule over non-Russian peripheries was only one expression of the rule of the city over the countryside in a regime which considered itself "proletarian" and hence city based. In the 1920s, the vast majority of the population (well over 80%) still lived in villages. The Communist Party, by contrast, was overwhelmingly urban, with above 90% of its members living in towns. Urbanity, meanwhile, was located overwhelmingly in the Russian republic, which contained 64% of all towns and cities in 1926. The tensions created by an urban regime nested uncomfortably within a peasant society exploded at the end of the decade.

Notes

1   Peter Holquist, "Violent Russia, Deadly Marxism? Russia in the Epoch of Violence, 1905–21," *Kritika: Explorations in Russian and Eurasian History* 4, no. 3 (2003): 627–52.

2   Iva Glisic, "Caffeinated Avant-Garde: Futurism During the Russian Civil War 1917–1921," *Australian Journal of Politics & History* 58, no. 3 (2012): 353–66.

3   Stephen White, *Russia Goes Dry. Alcohol, State and Society* (Cambridge, New York, Melbourne: Cambridge University Press, 1996), 16, 18.

4   Gregory J. Massell, *The Surrogate Proletariat: Moslem Women and Revolutionary Strategies in Soviet Central Asia, 1919–1929* (Princeton, NJ: Princeton University Press, 1974).

5   Jeffrey Burds, "The Soviet War against 'Fifth Columnists': The Case of Chechnya, 1942–4," *Journal of Contemporary History* 42, no. 2 (2007): 267–314, here: 282.

6   David L. Hoffmann, *Cultivating the Masses. Modern State Practices and Soviet Socialism, 1914–1939* (Ithaca, NY and London: Cornell University Press, 2011), 46.

7   *On Party Unity*, https://www.marxists.org/history/ussr/government/party-congress/10th/16.htm, accessed December 28, 2017.

8   Lenin, letter to Penza comrades, August 11, 1918, reprinted in: *The Unknown Lenin. From the Secret Archive*, ed. Richard Pipes, David Brandenberger, and Catherine A. Fitzpatrick (New Haven, CT: Yale University Press, 1996), 50. A verst is 0.6629 of a mile.

9   Stephen G. Wheatcroft, "From Team-Stalin to Degenerate Tyranny," *The Nature of Stalin's Dictatorship. The Politburo, 1924–1953*, ed. E. A. Rees (Basingstoke: Palgrave Macmillan, 2004), 79–107.

10 *1918 Constitution* https://www.marxists.org/history/ussr/government/constitution/1918/, accessed December 28, 2017.

11 Robert V. Daniels (ed.), *A Documentary History of Communism in Russia: From Lenin to Gorbachev* (Burlington: University of Vermont Press, 1993).

12 Terry Martin, *The Affirmative Action Empire. Nations and Nationalism in the Soviet Union, 1923–1939* (Ithaca, NY and London: Cornell University Press, 2001).

13 Slezkine, Yuri. "The Soviet Union as a Communal Apartment, or How a Socialist State Promoted Ethnic Particularism." *Slavic Review* 53, no. 2 (1994): 415–52.

14 Richard Pipes, *The Formation of the Soviet Union. Communism and Nationalism. 1917–1923* (Cambridge, MA: Harvard University Press, 1954), 286.

Bibliography

Alexopoulos, Golfo. *Stalin's Outcasts: Aliens, Citizens, and the Soviet State, 1926–1936* (Ithaca, NY: Cornell University Press, 2003).

Ball, Alan M. *And Now My Soul Is Hardened. Abandoned Children in Soviet Russia, 1918–1930* (Berkeley, Los Angeles, London: University of California Press, 1994).

Clark, Katerina. *Petersburg, Crucible of Cultural Revolution* (Cambridge, MA and London: Harvard University Press, 1995).

David-Fox, Michael. *Revolution of the Mind: Higher Learning among the Bolsheviks, 1918–1929* (Ithaca, NY: Cornell University Press, 1997).

Edgar, Adrienne Lynn. "Emancipation of the Unveiled: Turkmen Women under Soviet Rule, 1924–29." *The Russian Review* 62, no. 1 (2003): 132–49.

Edgerton, William, ed. *Memoirs of Peasant Tolstoyans in Soviet Russia* (Bloomington and Indianapolis: Indiana University Press, 1993).

Fitzpatrick, Sheila. *The Cultural Front. Power and Culture in Revolutionary Russia* (Ithaca and London: Cornell University Press, 1992).

Fitzpatrick, Sheila. *On Stalin's Team. The Years of Living Dangerously in Soviet Politics* (Melbourne: Melbourne University Press, 2015).

Fitzpatrick, Sheila. *The Russian Revolution*, 4th edition (Oxford: Oxford University Press, 2017).

Fitzpatrick, Sheila, Alexander Rabinowitch, and Richard Stites, eds. *Russia in the Era of NEP* (Bloomington and Indianapolis: Indiana University Press, 1991).

Glisic, Iva. *The Futurist Files: Avant-Garde, Politics, and Ideology in Russia, 1905–1930* (DeKalb: Northern Illinois University Press, 2018).

Goldman, Wendy. *Women, the State, and Revolution: Soviet Family Policy and Social Life, 1917–1936* (Cambridge: Cambridge University Press, 1993).

Gorsuch, Anne E. *Youth in Revolutionary Russia. Enthusiasts, Bohemians, Delinquents* (Bloomington and Indianapolis: Indiana University Press, 2000).

Heinzen, James. *Inventing a Soviet Countryside. State Power and the Transformation of Rural Russia, 1917–1929* (Pittsburgh, PA.: University of Pittsburgh Press, 2004).

Hoffmann, David L. *Cultivating the Masses. Modern State Practices and Soviet Socialism, 1914–1939* (Ithaca, NY and London: Cornell University Press, 2011).

Jahn, Hubertus F. "The Housing Revolution in Petrograd 1917–1920," *Jahrbücher für Geschichte Osteuropas* 38, no. 2 (1990): 212–27.

Khlevniuk, Oleg. *Stalin. New Biography of a Dictator* (New Haven, CT and London: Yale University Press, 2015).

Kolakowski, Leszek. "Marxist Roots of Stalinism," in: *Stalinism. Essays in Historical Interpretation*, ed. Robert C. Tucker (New York: W. W. Norton, 1977), 283–98.

Kotsonis, Yanni. *States of Obligation. Taxes and Citizenship in the Russian Empire and Early Soviet Republic* (Toronto: University of Toronto Press, 2014).

Martin, Terry. *The Affirmative Action Empire. Nations and Nationalism in the Soviet Union, 1923–1939* (Ithaca, NY and London: Cornell University Press, 2001).

Massell, Gregory J. *The Surrogate Proletariat: Moslem Women and Revolutionary Strategies in Soviet Central Asia, 1919–1929* (Princeton, NJ: Princeton University Press, 1974).

McDonald, Tracy. *Face to the Village. The Riazan Countryside under Soviet Rule, 1921–1930* (Toronto: University of Toronto Press, 2011).

Naiman, Eric. *Sex in Public. The Incarnation of Early Soviet Ideology* (Princeton, NJ: Princeton University Press, 1997).

Northrop, Douglas. *Veiled Empire. Gender & Power in Stalinist Central Asia* (Ithaca, NY and London: Cornell University Press, 2004).

Nove, Alec. *An Economic History of the USSR 1917–1991*, new and final edition (London: Penguin, 1992).

Phillips, Laura. *Bolsheviks and the Bottle. Drink and Worker Culture in St. Petersburg, 1900–1929* (DeKalb: Northern Illinois University Press, 2000).

Pipes, Richard, *The Formation of the Soviet Union. Communism and Nationalism, 1917–1923*, revised edition (Cambridge, MA: Harvard University Press, 1997).

Pipes, Richard, David Brandenberger, and Catherine A. Fitzpatrick, eds. *The Unknown Lenin. From the Secret Archive*, ed. (New Haven, CT: Yale University Press, 1996).

Sanchez-Sibony, Oscar. "Depression Stalinism: The Great Break Reconsidered," *Kritika: Explorations in Russian and Eurasian History* 15, no. 1 (2014): 23–49.

Sanchez-Sibony, Oscar, *Red Globalization: The Political Economy of the Soviet Cold War from Stalin to Khrushchev* (Cambridge: Cambridge University Press, 2014).

Siegelbaum, Lewis H. *Soviet State and Society between Revolutions, 1918–1929* (Cambridge: Cambridge University Press, 1992).

Siegelbaum, Lewis H., and Ronald Grigor Suny, eds. *Making Workers Soviet. Power Class and Identity* (Ithaca, NY and London: Cornell University Press, 1994).

Slezkine, Yuri. "The Soviet Union as a Communal Apartment, or How a Socialist State Promoted Ethnic Particularism," *Slavic Review* 53, no. 2 (1994): 415–52. Reprinted in: *Stalinism. New Directions*, ed. Sheila Fitzpatrick (London and New York: Routledge, 2000), 348–67.

Smith, Douglas. *Former People. The Last Days of the Russian Aristocracy* (London: Pan Books, 2013).

Stites, Richard. *Revolutionary Dreams. Utopian Vision and Experimental Life in the Russian Revolution* (New York and Oxford: Oxford University Press, 1989).

Steinberg, Mark D. *Proletarian Imagination. Self, Modernity, and the Sacred in Russia, 1910–1925* (Ithaca, NY and London: Cornell University Press, 2002).

van Ree, Eric. *The Political Thought of Joseph Stalin. A Study in Twentieth-Century Revolutionary Patriotism* (London and New York: Routledge Curzon, 2002).

van Ree, Eric. "Stalin as Marxist: The Western Roots of Stalin's Russification of Marxism," in: *Stalin. A New History*, ed. Sarah Davies and James R. Harris. (Cambridge: Cambridge University Press, 2005), 159–80.

von Geldern, James, and Richard Stites, eds. *Mass Culture in Soviet Russia. Tales, Poems, Songs, Movies, Plays, and Folklore. 1917–1953* (Bloomington and Indianapolis: Indiana University Press, 1995).

Wood, Elizabeth A. *The Baba and the Comrade. Gender and Politics in Revolutionary Russia* (Bloomington and Indianapolis: Indiana University Press, 1997).

Youngblood, Denise J. *Movies for the Masses: Popular Cinema and Soviet Society in the 1920s* (Cambridge: Cambridge University Press, 1992).

Part III

The Second Age of Violence

5

Building the Warfare State
(1928–1938)

At the end of the 1920s, the Soviet Empire, now headed by Stalin's men, embarked on a new round of upheaval, revolution, and internal colonization. In many ways this "Revolution from Above" looked like a civil war: The Bolsheviks against the population, indeed eventually against their own party. This revolution remade the Soviet Union from a backward agrarian country ruled by authoritarian socialists into a totalitarian warfare state ready to take on its international enemies. This transformation came in two stages: 1928 to 1932 and 1937 to 1938.

The first revolution from above (1928–1932) targeted the peasantry in particular, as well as other remnants of the old order. It was made up of three parallel processes: a "cultural revolution" (1928–1931), that attempted to destroy the old elites and their culture and replace them by "proletarian" alternatives; the economic revolution of the First Five-Year Plan (1929–1932) that attempted to force the country into the industrial age; and a rural revolution in the form of forced collectivization (from 1929), which was meant to pulverize peasant resistance to the extraction of grain that was needed to pay for the building of new industries. The first revolution from above resulted in untold hardship, social and geographic dislocation of unprecedented scale, a growing archipelago of camps and special settlements (the "Gulag," run by the successor of the Cheka, now called NKVD), plummeting living standards, terribly low consumption levels, an increasingly hierarchical society, and a disastrous famine in the period 1932 to 1933 that killed millions. But it also laid the groundwork for the country that would be able to withstand the German storm from 1941. If in the 1914 to 1917 it was the victory of the western Allies that ultimately

The Soviet Union: A Short History, First Edition. Mark Edele.
© 2019 John Wiley & Sons, Inc. Published 2019 by John Wiley & Sons, Inc.

saved the lands of the Russian Empire from German occupation, in 1941 to 1945 it was the Soviet Empire that saved Europe from the Nazis.

It is harder to see any redeeming aspects in the second revolution from above (1937–1938), although it followed the same logic of turning the country into an armed camp headed by an undisputed dictator. This second revolution is better known as the "Great Terror" or the "Great Purges." Stalin, whose faction had won the war against the peasantry, and who had forced the country into a strange kind of primitive industrialism, where underfed workers built tanks and airplanes but lived in dugouts and barracks, now turned his attention to eliminate opponents within. Some of these enemies were real, others imagined, but they all were supposed to be exterminated in order to unite the country in preparation for war.

This perverse logic first focused on the Communist Party itself, a major tactical innovation, as until the mid-1930s "terror" was something Bolsheviks did to their enemies, not to themselves. Soon, however, targets outside the party came back into focus, a shift of attention to the wider society accounting for the largest number of victims. These were defined either as social others, who were targeted in NKVD Order 00447 of July 1937 (former rich peasants, former Tsarist officials, White Army officers, and members of political parties other than the Bolsheviks, former peasant insurgents from civil war days, clergy, people who had lost their civil rights, criminals, beggars, and other "socially harmful elements") or as national enemies (diaspora nationalities with potential links to foreign governments, such as Poles, Germans, Koreans, Latvians, or Finns). Finally, potential opponents in the military were executed in a bloody purge of the officer corps in 1937 and 1938, to prevent any possible attempt at "Bonapartism."

The result of the second revolution from above was a country where nobody dared to stick his or her head out too far. Opposition to Stalin's regime, let alone resistance to it, had been pulverized. Even his closest associates trembled before the totalitarian dictator. Now, it seemed, Stalin could lead his empire into war, which he believed to be inevitable. There would be no repeat of the imperial apocalypse of World War I. However, it would soon transpire that one could not effectively wage war without experienced officers, with an army fearing initiative, and with political associates waiting to be told what to do by "the boss." Moreover, every elimination of enemies only created new ones – as would soon become clear once the country went to war.

Why was the NEP abolished?

The revolutions from above, then, had decidedly mixed results. Why were they attempted in the first place? Some historians argue that the authoritarian turn at the end of the 1920s was unnecessary, un-Marxist, even counter-revolutionary.

A continuation of NEP was possible, indeed desirable. If properly managed, it would have yielded similar economic growth as Stalin's path, and with less destruction along the way. This argument has become known as the "Bukharin alternative," named after Nikolai Bukharin (1888–1938), a staunch defender of NEP and a one-time ally of Stalin in the fight against the anti-NEP "left opposition" headed by Trotsky.

In the English speaking world, this interpretation was gaining ground from the 1970s, particularly among Marxist historians of the "new left," who implicitly or explicitly tried to separate Leninism from Stalinism. Today the pendulum has swung the other way and it finds fewer supporters. Instead, an older argument has been revived, which stresses the incompatibility of NEP with the ideological commitment of the Bolsheviks to build a nonmarket society. It is indeed hard to see how the painful compromises of the NEP could have continued for very much longer without completely disillusioning the hard core of the Bolshevik Party, now made up of many proletarian cadres who had learned their politics in the civil war – not exactly a school of compromise and subtlety.

More recently, an economic interpretation has also been reinvigorated. The NEP depended on grain exports on the international market and on gaining access to loans from international lenders. Both the grain and the financial market were increasingly in crisis, well before the capitalist economy came crashing down on Black Friday in 1929. The strategies of the NEP, therefore, stopped working and clearly a different path had to be taken. Stalin expressed this economic necessity very clearly during a speech to the Central Committee of the Communist Party on July 9, 1928. "Our country doesn't have loans from abroad," he noted, "this path is closed to us." Hence, only "internal accumulation," or squeezing the peasants dry, could pay for the construction of industry.[1] Stalin knew that in 1926 the Germans had advanced 300 million marks in credit to the Soviets, but that by 1928 German capitalists had serious doubts about Soviet ability to repay, and hence were more reluctant. This was a disaster for the existing economic strategy, which thus far Stalin had supported. As late as December 1927 he had written to the Politburo that in order "to realize our program, we have to make use of foreign help," a hope now squashed by the worsening international economy.[2]

A variant of this argument focuses on the internal workings of the NEP, stressing that the leadership had been so distracted by the nasty mutual backstabbing they had engaged in ever since Lenin's demise, that they had had no time or energy to manage, recalibrate, and adjust the economy. Many of them, of course, also had no training or expertise in this kind of social democratic approach, and were more likely to reach for a gun rather than the economics textbook if things got tough. By 1928, the economy had so run out of kilter, that a radical solution became more and more attractive.

These three broad interpretations – political choice, ideological compulsion, and economic necessity – are not mutually exclusive. The Bolsheviks were, to adapt a metaphor once developed by an economic historian – in the situation of hungry vegans on a fixed budget. When buying their lunch, they need to decide if they go for a ham sandwich, which they cannot afford, a cheese sandwich, which they could just so afford, or a candy bar and a sugary drink for about the same price. Clearly, our vegans have to make a choice. If we see them reach for the candy bar, we can interpret this result as driven by economic necessity: they could not afford the ham sandwich, and they could only afford the cheese sandwich, but nothing to drink. Alternatively, we could understand the choice they made as ideological: their dietary preferences would have prevented them from choosing the cheese sandwich, to say nothing of the meat.

Team Stalin was in a similar situation by about 1928. Like our hungry vegans, political choice, ideological preference, and economic necessity interacted to push these men in the direction they took. First, they did have a choice: Stalin's team was in control, had eliminated the opposing factions, and could employ the significant powers of the coercive apparatus they now controlled to exert their will. One choice they could not afford: abolish the march to Communism, and return to capitalism and build a liberal polity. Such a course of action would have eliminated their own power, destroyed all they had fought for so long. It was the equivalent of choosing the ham sandwich. Continuing the NEP amounted to eating the cheese sandwich. It would not have the desired results and would still be an ideological compromise at best. Hence, the choice for the most radical solution to the problem (to eat a candy bar and soda despite the nutritional problems involved). To choose a coercive solution to the economic problems of the NEP made sense politically (within the Bolshevik party, many craved for more heroic times), economically (the situation on the world markets made internal accumulation a logical step), and ideologically (an elimination of the market could be seen as a step toward socialism).

A final consideration needs to be added: warfare. Neither economic necessity nor ideological purity would have forced the Bolshevik leadership to embark on an economic course that suppressed civilian consumption and focused nearly exclusively on heavy industry. While one could expect socialists to build an authoritarian welfare state out of conviction, Stalin's team in effect built the opposite: a warfare state. Here, the memory of war and civil war was essential – the historical experience recounted in Chapters 2 and 3, read through the lens of the apocalyptic Marxism of Lenin and his followers. The Soviet Union had to arm, and it had to arm quickly, as the next major conflict was just around the corner. The economy might have recovered to its prewar level, but further expansion of the nonconsumer goods sector was difficult under the NEP framework. Moreover, other societies had expanded their industry sector: The Soviet Union had fallen behind in comparative terms. Given that the competitor states could be expected to be hostile to the "first Socialist state," the very survival not only of the revolution, but of the partially reconstructed empire was at stake. Again, Stalin expressed this link very clearly. In a much-quoted speech to industrial executives in 1931 he memorably recounted the history of Russia, a legacy he wanted to escape:

> One feature of the history of old Russia was the continual beatings she suffered because of her backwardness. She was beaten by the Mongol khans. She was beaten by the Turkish beys. She was beaten by the Swedish feudal lords. She was beaten by the Polish and Lithuanian gentry. She was beaten by the British and French capitalists. She was beaten by the Japanese barons. All beat her—because of her backwardness, because of her military backwardness, cultural backwardness, political backwardness, industrial backwardness, agricultural backwardness. They beat her because it was profitable and could be done with impunity. ... Such is the law of the exploiters—to beat the backward and the weak. It is the jungle law of capitalism. You are backward, you are weak—therefore you are wrong; hence you can be beaten and enslaved. You are mighty—therefore you are right; hence we must be wary of you.[4]

The First Revolution from Above (1928–1932)

In order not to be beaten again, "backwardness" needed to be eliminated. A major seat of this "backwardness" – from the Bolshevik point of view – was the village. The revolution had liberated the peasantry from the landlords once and for all, and it had leveled them economically. Prosperous farmers were likely to be expropriated, while larger, sometimes more economically run estates were divided up among the toilers of the land. The result was a strengthening of peasant society, but also the locking in of unproductive, sometimes archaic production methods. The Bolsheviks had tolerated this development at first, because they needed the countryside to be neutralized while taking over power in the cities. Once the civil war was under way, however, the disdain of urbanites for the village asserted itself in often brutal grain requisitioning. This hostility towards the peasantry was reciprocated in the great peasant war at the end of the civil war. The rural rebels were brought to heel by massive force, but at the same time concessions were made: the compromise of the NEP.

Allowing peasants to market their produce led to a remarkable recovery of consumption levels throughout the 1920s, but also limited industrial expansion, as only the grain the peasants chose to sell could be sold on international markets to produce capital necessary to buy machines and know-how. Careful calibration of economic policy might have made a difference, but was not a real option for a leadership distracted by political infighting. The peasants had the Bolsheviks by the throat.

The solution seemed obvious: assert control over the village and extract as much grain as possible. After experiments with coercive methods, first in Ukraine, then in Siberia and the Urals during the winter of 1927/1928, the Stalinist leadership universalized this course of action. From 1929, peasants were forced into collective farms. They had to give up control over family plots, farm animals, and equipment. Not surprisingly, few were willing to do so. Hence, force needed to be applied, especially against the leaders of village society, dubbed "kulaks" ("fists"), for allegedly holding their own property as well as everybody else in their tight grip. Officially a class category, "kulak" soon became a label that could be affixed to anybody who resisted collectivization. And many did resist, either by slaughtering their cattle rather than handing it over, by hiding their grain, by fleeing to the cities, or by armed assaults on the collectivizers. Altogether, some 2.5 million peasants participated in a variety of disturbances, which reached their highest point in March 1930. The Bolsheviks retaliated with severity. In 1930 and 1931 over 1.7 million people were expropriated and deported to Siberia or other far-away regions, while other alleged kulaks were sent into exile in their own district. Over 30,000, who were seen as particularly dangerous enemies, were shot. This was a very large number, even for Soviet circumstances. In more "normal" years (not counting the extraordinary years 1937 and 1938), executions were in the hundreds or in the thousands, not in the tens of thousands.

With the resisters out of the way, the rest of the peasantry could be forced into the collectives, a "second serfdom" most resented deeply. To guard the recently stolen property of the new collectives from recovery by the peasants, a draconian law of August 1932 instituted the "highest measure of social protection—shooting and the confiscation of the entire property" for any theft of "harvest in the field, public reserves, cattle, cooperative warehouses and stores, etc." The death sentence could be reduced to 10 years imprisonment with confiscation of property if "mitigating circumstances" presented themselves. No amnesty was to be given to such "criminals."[5] Thus, a mother trying to feed her starving children with grain taken from the fields faced a prolonged prison term at best, should she be caught in the act. This law encapsulated the escalation of the coercive relationship between the Soviet state and the majority of the population.

Meanwhile, forced-paced industrialization was underway elsewhere. Established industrial centers grew by leaps and bounds. Others were created from scratch, such as the city of Magnitogorsk, behind the Urals. Here, newly minted proletarians and foreign guest workers displaced by the Great Depression lived in tents, dugouts, or over-crowded barracks. In other places, existing housing stock was stretched to the limits. Apartments were subdivided between several families to make "communal apartments." An innovation already from the days of revolution and civil war when proletarians took over the housing of the rich, these *kommunalki* now became central to the new urban habitat. They would survive until the end of the Soviet Union and beyond.

Flanking collectivization and forced industrialization was an assault on specialists of prerevolutionary vintage, suspected of disloyalty to the new regime. Doctors, engineers, professors, and teachers – all came under assault from young revolutionaries from the working classes intent on taking over. Crash courses trained these new cadres quickly and poorly to become the new, "red" ruling class. This cultural revolution also extended to the products of culture itself: "bourgeois culture" was to be discarded, replaced by "revolutionary culture," whatever that might mean in practice. In Ukraine, the assault on elites of prerevolutionary vintage victimized the native intelligentsia, whose embracement of the nativization campaign of the 1920 was now construed as "bourgeois nationalism" threatening the union.

Internal Colonization

In order to increase the state's control over the enormous and largely spontaneous flow of people from the countryside to the city, the state decreed the introduction of an internal passport system in late September 1932, and "passportization" of the cities began the following year. Passports were issued only to residents of cities and only passport holders whose personal identification document was registered with the police were legally entitled to reside in the cities. This system survived to the end of the Soviet Union. While in practice it was continually broken, it allowed heavy-handed policing of the cities by means of campaigns checking citizens' papers and expelling all illegals.

Collectivization and dekulakization amounted to a process of violent internal colonization of the countryside by the Bolshevik city. In non-Russian regions, the imperialist aspect was even closer to the surface. Ukraine became the first testing ground for the new, arbitrary and coercive grain requisitioning methods, before Stalin perfected them in the Urals and in Siberia. In Kazakhstan, collectivization disrupted the entire nomadic economy, with catastrophic results as we shall see. In many Muslim regions of the Caucasus and Trans-Caucasus as well as Central Asia, resistance to collectivization was organized, armed, and violent. It had to be put down with military force, including at times armored cars, artillery, and even aircraft. The rebels mobilized the language of Muslim resistance to the infidel colonizers:"Down with the collective and state farms, ... down with Soviet power, long live the Sharia!"[6]

The perception of the first revolution from above as an imperialist project was accurate. The control of Moscow over the non-Russian republics increased dramatically during these years. In Ukraine, the share of industry controlled by the government of the republic went from over 80% in the late 1920s to below 40% at the end of the First Five-Year Plan. This assertion of imperial control coincided with increasing national consciousness. The massive migration of rural dwellers to the cities not only transformed the latter into "peasant metropoleis" as it did elsewhere.[7] In addition, it led to their increasing Ukrainization. By the early 1930s, Ukrainians formed the majority of inhabitants of the previously Russian dominated cities in Ukraine. Stalin's revolution inadvertently instituted a "new and assertive Ukrainian national consciousness, which appeared national in form, socialist in content, and urban in residence."[8]

This nationalizing Ukraine faced unbelievably callous food requisitioning policies. In 1930 and 1931, 70% of the grain exported from the Soviet Union in order to raise capital for industrialization came from Ukraine, which until then had only provided about half of such exports. At the same time, Ukraine only received 18% of capital investments in 1933, falling further to below 14% by 1939. Seen from Moscow, this was a rational strategy: after all, the further away from the possible European frontline the new industries were located, the safer they were in time of war. For increasingly nationalized Ukrainians, however, the transfer of resources from Ukraine to the Urals and Siberia looked like colonial exploitation.

The Great Famine

The result of the massive disruption of village life as a result of collectivization, the destruction of draft animals, completely unrealistic grain collection targets stripping entire villages of all reserves, and some bad weather was catastrophic: a massive famine in 1932 and 1933, worse than its predecessor at the end of the civil war. Worst hit in absolute terms was Ukraine. The 1937 census showed 4.8 million fewer Ukrainians than its 1927 equivalent, a decrease of 15%. And this number already included children born in the "three good years" between the end of the famine and the start of the Great Terror. In relative terms, however, the Kazakhs did worse being a much smaller group, whose nomadic lifestyle had been disrupted by collectivization, by 1937 their number was down by a staggering 28%.[9] As one historian has pointed out, the unequal impact of the famine meant that the population of the Soviet Union overall "shifted radically" in favor of the Russians, who increased their share from 53% in 1926 to 58% in 1937.[10]

The famine triggered an acrimonious debate. At stake are the causes of the catastrophe. Most agree that this famine was manmade. In the final analysis, it was a result of the extreme grain requisitioning policies of the Soviet government. Greater disagreement exists with respect to the intentions of the Bolsheviks in general and Stalin in particular. Some assert that Stalin planned the famine in order to destroy resistance in the village. An extreme form of this position construes the famine as a genocidal attack on the Ukrainian nation. Given that Ukrainians, Jews, Poles, Russians, and others starved together, other historians see the target more in class than in national terms: it was the recalcitrant peasants who were meant to be brought to heel with the weapon of famine. Others assume that the catastrophe was an unintended consequence of callous policies: the Stalinists knew that the peasants were hiding grain and local authorities were likely to under-report available reserves. Thus, they increased the pressure until the peasants starved – at which point they knew that really nothing was left. Once famine developed, however, another choice had to be made: Would grain exports continue, or would the food be sent back to the starving villages? The leadership stayed the course of its ambitious industrialization program, leading some scholars to conclude that while the famine in 1932 was unintentional, its successor in 1933 was not. Facing the choice between continuing crash industrialization and saving peasant lives, Stalin chose "building socialism" over yet another "retreat." To the dictator, the peasants, Ukrainian or otherwise, were collateral damage in history's march towards Communism.

Different scholars find different interpretations more or less convincing, and their disagreements cannot be resolved by simple reference to "the facts." Each of the conclusions reached relies on interpretation of sources and on at least some conclusions relying on plausibility. Given that no clear evidence exists about the leader's state of mind, the most cautious position would be agnosticism. Given the unbelievable horror of the mass starvation of 1932 and 1933 and given that this debate is entangled not only in residual emotions from the Cold War (when historians would be routinely accused of being either red baiters or apologists for Stalin) but also in new Ukrainian and Russian nationalisms, such a stance is unlikely to find many followers.

Three Good Years

After the famine was over, consumption recovered somewhat. Rationing, which had been introduced in 1928 and 1929 and systematized in 1931, was discontinued in 1935. The cultural revolution ended, and "respectability" in dress, behavior, and lifestyle made a comeback. Life was still hard, the communal apartments were still stinking and crowded, pay was still low, and food still scarce. But the pressure was off for a while and some kind of normality returned. In retrospect, the years 1934 to 1936 became the "three good years" between two catastrophes. At the time, too, a sense of relief was widespread and officially encouraged. "Life has improved, comrades," cheerfully announced Stalin in 1935. "Life has become more joyous. And when life is joyous, work goes well."[11] A new dance craze was one of the outward signs of this recovery, as was the replacement of the leather coat with a suit for the aspiring Stalinist and a dress for his female counterpart.

Even during these years of relative relaxation, the clouds of war were always on the horizon, however. In 1933, the Nazis had taken over in Germany; in 1935, Fascist Italy invaded Abyssinia; in 1936, civil war erupted in Spain; and in

1937 war started between Japan and China. The Soviet Union was affected in a variety of ways by these wars: the German Nazis and the Italian Fascists saw Bolsheviks as among their deadliest foes; Soviet advisors were active in Spain as well as China, where Stalin also sent weapons.

These wars clearly worried the dictator. Not that Stalin feared war as such. As a Marxist-Leninist, he appreciated the destructive nature of war, its ability to pulverize the old and thus engender the new. It was war, after all, which had brought his Party to power. The long-term perspective was that capitalism would continue to lead to war, that war would breed civil war, and that – after "the final battle" – World Revolution would emerge victorious. In the short to medium term, however, Stalin needed peace. The Red Empire was still very vulnerable. Crash industrialization began to produce the machinery of destruction and the army began to expand. However, the enemies of the "first socialist state" were not asleep at the wheel either. The young Soviet republic was surrounded by heavily armed enemies and the Soviets had by no means caught up and surpassed them, despite all efforts.

Big Russian Brother

How could one mobilize the country for the coming war? The socialist slogans increasingly fell on deaf ears in a country where in reality food was scarce, housing crowded, public infrastructure poor, and social inequality steep. Hence, the leadership of this Marxist country, this multinational union of republics, began to wager on the nation – the *Russian* nation. In a cultural equivalent of the political and economic shift towards Moscow since the end of the 1920s as well as the demographic change in favor of the Russians in the wake of the great famine, Russian national heroes now became prominent offerings for identification. The history of the Soviet Union became an extension of the Russian Empire. By 1932, as we have seen above, Comrade Stalin had put the current industrialization drive in the context of the history of "Russia," which was beaten, beaten, and beaten by its enemies in the past. Now this line became ever clearer. What was needed, Stalin insisted in 1934, was a history of the USSR demonstrating that "the Russian people in the past gathered other peoples together and have begun that sort of gathering again now."[12]

The Second Revolution From Above (1937–1938)

As the previous quote shows the Russians were meant to lead the other peoples of the USSR in the way a big brother would his younger siblings. The problem was, however, that both the Russian and the non-Russian population seemed to teem with enemies of the current regime. For one, there were the remnants of the old order, those "former people" who had not been killed in the revolution and civil war or emigrated abroad. Second, there were the victims of the first revolution from above – peasants whose property had been confiscated and whose children had starved to death, "bourgeois specialists" whose careers had been destroyed, youth whose parents had been deported or shot. Even in the party itself, it appeared, there were hidden enemies everywhere. Could one really trust those who had once opposed Stalin's team and now claimed to toe the party line? Could one let all these fickle intellectuals run the party? Would they not destroy unity, so necessary for the coming war?

These nagging worries about internal and external enemies were dragged to the surface when one of Stalin's associates was murdered. Having learned from the Stalinists they study to think in conspiracies, historians have sometimes assumed that the shooting of Sergei Kirov, the boss of the Leningrad party organization, was a hit organized by Stalin himself. Newer research has discredited this view: the perpetrator was a lone and somewhat deranged gunman. Once Kirov was dead, however, Stalin used the execution as a starting point to first construct a conspiracy against his regime, then to arrest and execute those accused of this imaginary plot.

After a series of show trials starting in 1936 had pursued the most prominent victims – including the ill-fated Bukharin – a wider purge began to tear through the Communist Party, the intelligentsia, and the ruling elite in the first half of 1937. Given the dense networks of patrons and clients, friends and acquaintances that were necessary requirements for working and living in the economy of scarcity, "conspiracies" were quickly found by suspicious investigators. Every arrest yielded a whole group of people connected to the accused, and various forms of pressure and outright torture made sure that sinister motives were detected as well. The accumulated jealousies, resentments, and life pressures in this society of extreme scarcity encouraged denunciations of neighbors, colleagues, or superiors. What better way to get another room in a communal apartment, the promotion to the superior's job, or revenge on the collectivizers than to denounce "class enemies?"

The purge thus quickly extended its reach through the entire state and party apparatus.

A campaign for a new, more inclusive constitution (adapted in December 1936) was followed by a quickly suppressed census in January 1937 that showed how widespread discontent with the current regime was. This discontent spread outwards into wider and wider circles of society. First, in August, came the "operation" against "former kulaks" and other "anti-Soviet elements," who were tracked down, arrested, and shot. Diaspora nationalities with presumed ties to foreign governments – most prominently, Soviet Poles – came next. The officer corps of the Red Army, too, needed to be purified, and a massive blood-letting of elite soldiers suspected of disloyalty ensued in 1938.

Altogether, the "Great Purges" victimized about 1.3 million people during 1937 and 1938 alone. Nearly 0.7 million people were executed in these two years, the largest spike for the entire period between 1921 and 1953. Most of those shot fell victim to the "kulak" operation under order No. 00447 (57%), followed by victims of the "national operations" (36%). 0.6 million were sent to labor camps and prisons, some 18,000 were exiled.

The Violent Turn in Nationality Policy

As the national operations of the terror indicate, nationality policy turned from benevolent to nasty. The indigenization (*korenizatsiia*) policies of the 1920s, which had developed minority culture and minority cadres, transmogrified into arrests, deportations, and shooting operations in cases where the non-Russian ethnicity might either harbor secessionist aspirations (the Ukrainians) or could be suspected of loyalties to hostile foreign governments (the Poles, Germans, or Koreans). While affirmative action policies for minorities were never abolished, they were now subdued under increasing suspicion of the nationalism they helped to engender. This turn against minorities was the logical result of the rise of Russia and the Russians as the first among unequals, the ruling ethnicity of the Red Empire.

In Ukraine, the first revolution from above was accompanied by fears of a resurgence of nationalist separatism similar to the first epoch of violence. The Stalinists reacted to their own anxieties by arresting Ukrainian intellectuals and others accused of forming underground organizations. The Communist Party of Ukraine, too, was purged in 1933, and many of the now former communists were arrested soon thereafter. During the second revolution from above, things got worse. The now lethal party purge was so comprehensive that the Central Committee of the Communist Party of Ukraine "could not hold meetings because it lacked the required quorum."[13] The party lost most of its leaders in the purge. Of the membership 37% became victims of one form of repression or other in the year 1937 alone. And it was not only the communist party that was victimized disproportionally. Nearly 21% of those arrested in 1937 and 1938, and 32% of all those executed came from Ukraine, which at the time counted less than 18% of the total population of the USSR. In parallel with such extermination of people, Ukrainian-language instruction and Ukrainian-language publications were reduced, while the Russian language rose in prominence, in particular in the cities and as the major language of the state apparatus. Thus, while the cities of Ukraine were now more Ukrainian than ever, given the massive influx of Ukrainian peasants during the first revolution from above, Ukrainian culture and language were downgraded to second-best options. Anybody who wanted to make a career needed to speak the language of the empire: Russian.

For many diaspora nations living in Soviet Ukraine, the "three good years" of 1934 to 1936 were anything but. Germans, Poles, and other non-Slavs had been treated particularly harshly during collectivization, when in a fusion of ethnic and class hatred local Communists construed them all as "kulaks." In 1930, in the "first explicitly ethnic deportation" in Soviet history "kulak Polish counter-revolutionary elements" were deported "with maximum organization and without fanfare."[14] Now, while life normalized for some, over 10,000 Soviet Poles and Germans were arrested in 1934, tens of thousands were forcibly resettled from the western border regions to the more secure eastern Ukraine in 1935 and an even larger group of Poles, nearly 0.7 million strong, was deported to Kazakhstan in the same year.

For Soviet Poles, the first and second revolutions from above thus blurred into one. And things got worse as time went on. In the Polish operation of the Great Terror, nearly 56,000 people were arrested throughout the Union and the vast majority of them executed. At the other end of the empire, in the Far East in 1937, the Soviet Koreans had the privilege of being the first nationality to be deported in its entirety for nothing more than their potential links to Japanese imperialism.

Where neither a foreign sponsor nor aspirations to break apart the union could be intimated, the Stalinists left people more or less alone. The Roma (*Tsygane*) are a case in point: While repeated attempts to settle nomadic Roma were made and a very successful group of urban Roma activists developed a flowering cultural scene, the turn in nationality policy only affected Roma schools, which were closed in 1938 together with other national schools and national departments. Repression remained sporadic, focused on removing nomadic Roma from urban areas or persecuting settled Tsygane whose cooperatives seemed to be run as private businesses rather than socialist enterprises. Some of the nomads were swept up in the mass operations against "anti-Soviet elements" and social marginals, but there was no national operation against Tsygane: As they had no foreign government for which they could serve as a "fifth column" in times of war, no mass extermination was necessary.

Indeed, the lethal turn in nationality policy was neither complete, nor final. The majority of victims of repression remained Russians, who made up 63% of all Gulag camp inmates in January 1939, compared to 58% in the population as a whole. Meanwhile, affirmative action policies for national minorities continued. Despite the unbelievable brutality with which Ukrainian peasants were treated in collectivization and famine and despite the large-scale arrests among Ukrainian intellectuals and the purge of the Ukrainian Communist Party, Ukrainians remained essential parts of the imperial elite. They constituted the second largest national group after the Russians in the Communist Party of the Soviet Union. In 1941, they made up 16% of the membership, a share conforming to their percentage in the population in 1939 (before the annexations of eastern Poland). Within Ukraine, this central role of Ukrainians was even more pronounced. In 1930, Ukrainians constituted 54% of all communists in the Ukrainian branch of the Communist Party, in 1933 this had reached 60% to rise further to 63% in 1940. Thus, the nationalization of the Ukrainian republic continued despite, and in parallel with, the victimization of many Ukrainians.

Elsewhere, too, the indigenization program might have stalled, but was not undone. In Kyrgyzstan, Tadzhikistan, and Uzbekistan, the titular nations in the republican communist parties all remained at around half of the membership throughout the prewar years; white collar jobs, too, continued to be filled with natives. By 1939, writes the major authority on Soviet affirmative action, "titular nationals had on average achieved proportionate representation" in leadership positions and the cultural sector, if not always in technical jobs and engineering.[15] At the top of the political system, meanwhile, and despite the prominence of non-Russians like Stalin among the top leaders, the increasing assertion of Russian dominance was marked. The membership of the Central Committee went from 54% Russian before the second revolution from above, to 70% thereafter. The original under-representation of Russians in the Soviet Union's elite, thus, was replaced by a marked over-representation after the terror. However, there was a second national group that also moved from under-representation to over-representation in the Central Committee: Ukrainians!

Welfare

Affirmative action for minority nationalities was one aspect of the larger assertion of welfare the Soviet Union represented. As a socialist state, it claimed to be building a fairer society without national, class, or gender discrimination. This aspiration was popular. The desire to lead a "cultured" life marked by "a good suit, tasty food, and clean sheets" (or at least leather boots, iron bed frames, and mirrors) was widespread – from the village all the way to the Kremlin walls.[16]

There were advances in all spheres: Minority nations received preferential access to higher education, the Party, and good jobs. Poor peasants became proletarians, proletarians became managers, engineers, or professors, often catapulted upwards by the sudden mass of vacancies created by the terror. The new elite taking shape as a result of the two revolutions from above – maybe 4% of the overall population – was to a significant degree a new class of upwardly mobile former workers and peasants. The regime also opened new doors for women. Young enthusiasts from all nationalities aligned themselves with the Party-State, freed themselves from patriarchal oppression, and became Komsomol organizers, unveilers of other women, tractor drivers, scientists, or pilots.

But the Red Empire not only promised social mobility to its proletarians, it also declared itself responsible for their welfare. The 1936 constitution indeed instituted, on paper, a comprehensive socialist welfare state. Articles 118 to 121 "guaranteed" the rights to rest and leisure (including paid vacations and state-run rest-homes and sanatoria); to maintenance in case of old age, sickness, or inability to work (through "the extensive development of social insurance of workers and employees at state expense, free medical service for the working people and the provision of a wide network of health resorts for the use of the working people"); and to education ("ensured by universal, compulsory elementary education" and "by education, including higher education, being free of charge"). Article 122 promised "pre-maternity and maternity leave with full pay, and the provision of a wide network of maternity homes, nurseries and kindergartens." Discrimination on the basis of sex, nationality, or race was illegal (articles 122–123).[17]

The reality, of course, looked different and these claims could only be reconciled with reality if seen through the prism of socialist realism: Whatever difficulties occurred in the present were just temporary difficulties on the march towards Communism.

To be sure, some advances were made: By 1937, 50% of the population was literate (up from 28% at the turn of the century). Illiteracy was nearly eradicated among youth born after 1917, where the gap between women and men had also disappeared. The inability to read and write rose with age, and so did the gap between the sexes: men tended to be more literate than women.

In healthcare, the progress was more ambiguous. The first revolution from above enlisted health services in the industrialization effort. Preventative care – the backbone of Soviet successes in the 1920s – was abolished in favor of attempts to repair labor power in the individual. Clinics were attached directly to workplaces, with the result that, like housing, medical care became a benefit of employment, not a universalized right. A worker who left a job also lost the entitlements to housing and healthcare, such as they were. Medical services in the countryside were extremely basic, if they existed at all.

In 1938, the Third Five-Year Plan marked a transition from warfare spending to investment in welfare and consumption, but this transition was aborted by World War II. It was only after the war that welfare state building came on the agenda again, although here too it was inhibited by the demands of the Cold War.

It is no accident that the advances in medicine and education were directly relevant to defense: modern war needed fit and literate soldiers to fight and similarly functional workers to produce the means of destruction. The entire welfare sector, indeed, was instrumentalized for mobilization for the coming war. Welfare itself remained a soft-line concern for the Stalinist state, expressed in the fact that there was no Commissariat of Social Security at the Union level – this field was left to the republics instead. Old age pensions existed largely on paper and disability pensions were constructed in a way that ensured that if any labor power was left in the individual, he or she would continue to work.

This "workers' state" might have been run increasingly by former workers, then, but it was far from a welfare state for the proletariat. The years of Stalin's twin revolutions were by marred by miserable consumption levels, below those achieved during the NEP. Real wages, average living standards, and caloric intake plummeted after 1928 and would recover decisively only in the 1960s.

Support and Discontent

The support the Soviet system received under Stalin was thus not based on universal welfare, although the majority of citizens supported the principle. Instead, Stalin's popularity among a plurality, but almost certainly not a majority of the population was based on two pillars: social mobility and ideology. Both were stressed by an older cohort of scholars of "totalitarianism" in the 1950s and 1960s: sociologists, anthropologists, and political scientists, interested in "how the Soviet system works."[18] Social mobility then became a topic of interest for social historians of the 1970s and 1980s. These "revisionists" were sometimes accused of whitewashing Stalinism because they pointed to the undeniable fact that universalized primary education, affirmative action in technical training and higher education, and the extraordinary cadres exchange of the Great Terror led to incredibly steep careers for former proletarians turned functionaries. Most beneficiaries of the revolutions from above were grateful for their advancement and many of them believed in the words and jargon of official communications, the language they had learned to speak while moving up in the world.

The ideology of Marxism-Leninism also had its own attractions. It was hard to miss, as it pervaded the discourse distributed by the growing network of newspapers, radio, movie theaters, and grassroots agitators. And of course it did not simply come "from above" but had much deeper roots in revolutionary and prerevolutionary society. Youth in particular, as yet unencumbered by the numbing grind of caring for a family in the economy of scarcity, were often enough enthusiastic "builders of socialism," willing to see all crimes, poverty, and shortcomings as temporary ills of a transitional period. Many agonized terribly over the fact that their social background was "impure," and yearned to remake themselves into loyal Stalinists. Such impurities were widespread: Given the social, economic, and political upheaval since the turn of the century few could claim that they were of unambiguous poor peasant or proletarian background and had never associated with the many political enemies of Stalin's team. The phenomenon of self-identification with official ideology, both among Russians but also among the many minority populations of the empire, has recently interested cultural historians sometimes described as "post-revisionists." They tend to universalize the deep belief in Stalinism they find among their protagonists to the population at large. Other historians have exploited the wealth of newly available archival material to document the widespread discontent and opposition to Stalin's barracks socialism.

Warfare State

Wherever one stands in these scholarly debates, one fact is undisputed: By 1939, Stalin's position was more secure than ever. His own entourage – the team that had helped him win the factional struggles of the 1920s, the war against the peasantry, and the struggle for industrial growth – trembled in fear of "the boss's" whims. While discontent, disgruntlement, and silent opposition were rife throughout society, no effective resistance was possible. Should war come now, Stalin did not have to worry about a replay of the war-and-revolution complex, which had toppled the tsar. Stalin's state was politically much more in control than its Romanov predecessor.

Life in the Red Empire was considerably worse than under the final tsar. There was no freedom of speech, no ability to assemble on one's own initiative, and no political parties other than the Bolsheviks. Travel abroad was impossible even to those who could afford it and was only available to functionaries on official business. Libraries were purged of material from opposing political factions, and new literature, art, even music, was supposed to help in uplifting but also in entertaining the masses on the march to Communism.

This Socialist Realism did not show how life really was, but how it was to become. It was more than just a literary doctrine, enshrined in a canon of exemplary texts to be imitated by aspiring artists and writers. It was an approach to reality, a "dream world," where "caviar with champagne" became everyday staples.[19] In reality, by contrast, only elite stores stocked such items. Bread and watery soup, washed down with the increasingly available vodka, was the daily fare. Alcohol, indeed, was the only item in massive supply in this "economy of shortage," a deliberate tactic to raise money.[20] In order to equip "40 to 50" more divisions, wrote Stalin in 1930, "we need to get rid of a false sense of shame and directly and openly promote the greatest expansion of vodka production possible for the sake of a real and serious defense of our country."[21] The tactic worked: three years later, 20% of state revenue came from vodka sales.

Everyday life, then, was extremely hard, if not always sober. Most Soviets lived in dilapidated houses, overflowing with humans; in communal apartments awash in petty squabbles of strangers forced to share intimate spaces; in leaky tents and improvised dugouts; in barracks and crowded dormitories; in cities awash every spring in excrement, when the human waste that had been deposited in the backyards began to thaw; in villages stripped bare of draft animals and demoralized by the collective farm system. The most basic items of daily life – clothes, linen, kitchen implements – were expensive and hard to obtain. There were queues at bread shops and food rationing was in place until 1935.

Even after rationing had been abolished, access to housing, food, services, health, education, and consumer goods depended on one's position in the official hierarchy of distribution. People at the top, those who served the state as politicians, high-ranking soldiers, intellectuals, and managers were not only better paid, but also had special pathways to scarce goods and services distributed through the workplace and according to rank in the hierarchy. Those at the bottom – the slaves in the growing Gulag, the serfs in the collective farms, the large number of homeless and dispossessed – had to scrape together an existence as best as they could.

In this society of scarcity, access to goods was a major problem, more so than the access to money. The shops were frequently empty, first because the entire economy was geared towards heavy industry and defense and hence produced fewer consumer goods than necessary; second because whatever was produced often disappeared in warehouses; and third because all along the chain of production and distribution, workers, employees, and criminals siphoned off items for private use, distribution through networks of friends, and sale on the black market. Finally, much of what was produced was distributed through closed distribution systems attached to workplaces or accessible only with special privileges. "Connections" to people with access, whether legal or illegal, therefore, became crucial, particularly higher up in the hierarchy of consumption. They were called *blat* when others engaged in them and "friendship" when one did it oneself. These ties formed networks of friends and acquaintances, patrons and clients, which originated in the official structure, but spread their tentacles far beyond them. Anchoring the Stalinist state in the population at large, these informal networks were densest in the cities, where *blat* was "higher than Stalin," as the proverb had it, and they petered out the further one went into the countryside or the working-class districts.[22]

The economy, then, was an odd mixture of planning and irrationality, as similar mechanisms also applied in production. Given ever-changing planning figures, the managers of Soviet enterprises had every incentive to hoard goods of any description, should they become useful once the plan needed to be fulfilled and "over-fulfilled." Enormous stockpiles, which were not managed by the central allocation mechanisms, further increased scarcity but they could also be used to barter with other enterprises, in order to "obtain" the necessary resources to meet production norms. Hence, every major enterprise employed "pushers" (or "consultants" if we believe the accounting books), whose job it was to wheel and deal behind the scenes to make things work. In order to fulfill the plan, then, planning had to be circumvented. The planned economy relied on quasi-market mechanisms. In this "economy of favors," indeed, planning "disappeared in the plan."[23] Illegal transactions, constant trouble shooting, and working in mad bursts or "campaigns" were systemic features of this system. They therefore reappeared after each attempt to stamp them out.

Stalinist society relied on market mechanisms in a more overt form as well. For one, pay was not "according to need" (as should be the case in "Communism") but "according to effort" (which was said to be a feature of the society of "Socialism"). Wage differentials were enormous and geared towards rewarding certain activities – heavy industrial labor, but even more so managerial positions, and loyal service in the state, the Party, or the arts and sciences. Moreover, much of the food supply of the population came from a tiny but thriving private sector. Part of the pacification of the countryside during the great upheavals of collectivization had been a very limited retreat: peasant households were eligible to keep a small plot of land around the hut, where they could grow food for their own consumption. After hefty taxes, they were allowed to market any remaining surpluses on the "kolkhoz market" – a form of legal open-air bazaar. It was here, paying market prices, that much of the urban population got its food during the 1930s.

While small-scale peasant farming on the family plot thus prospered, the collective farms never produced the amounts of surplus grain the leadership had expected once "kulaks" and "speculators" were removed from the scene. Outside the agricultural sector, there were four things this economy was good at producing: first was a large quantity of increasingly standardized armaments; second was an immense amount of vodka to pay for them; third was a generalized scarcity of consumer goods; and fourth was conformism. No matter what individual citizens believed, if they wanted to have a roof over their head, if they desired to clothe and feed their families, they needed to conform to the system's demands. They needed to work long hours, stand even longer hours in line to obtain the necessities of life. They had to wheel and deal to the best of their abilities. Women, in particular, had to contend with the triple burden of working, tending the household, and hunting and gathering in the economy of scarcity.

The immense hierarchies, the state-centered distribution, the swollen state apparatus, the transfer of a large share of the public wealth to defense, and the resulting poverty of civilian consumption, the punitive laws, the severe repression, the long working hours and poor pay, the internal passport prohibiting the majority of the population to live where it pleased, the scarcity of consumer goods: they all resembled a society at war.

The Soviet Empire in the 1930s is thus best described as a warfare state. It had taken shape in the cauldron of war, revolution, and civil war explored in Chapter 2 and Chapter 3, it had been consolidated during the tactical retreat described in Chapter 4, but was jolted back into a new effort at coercion, discipline, and terror by the threat of war at the end of the 1920s and throughout the

1930s. Thanks to this single-minded focus, the Soviet Union became the world's largest weapons producer. By 1939, the Red Empire, as a result, was ready to join the aggressors in what became the start of World War II. If it would survive this new Armageddon was anybody's guess.

Notes

1   Lynne Viola and Viktor Petrovich Danilov, eds., *The War against the Peasantry. 1927–1930. The Tragedy of the Soviet Countryside* (New Haven, CT: Yale University Press, 2005), 98.

2   Oscar Sanchez-Sibony, "Depression Stalinism: The Great Break Reconsidered," *Kritika: Explorations in Russian and Eurasian History* 15, no. 1 (2014): 23–49; quotation: 37.

3   The original spoke of the rabbi who needs to choose between a ham and a cheese sandwich. Alex Nove, "The 'Logic' and Cost of Collectivization," *Problems of Communism* 25, No. 4 (1976): 55–59, here: 55.

4   Iosif Stalin, "The Tasks of Business Executives. Speech Delivered at the First All-Union Conference of Leading Personnel of Socialist Industry," (4 February 1931), available at:https://www.marxists.org/reference/archive/stalin/works/1931/02/04.htm, accessed December 29, 2017.

5   A translation of the law is available at: http://www.faminegenocide.com/kuryliw/corn_law.htm, accessed December 29, 2017.

6   Quotation from report from the North Caucasus (May 1930), *Tragediia sovetskoi derevni. Kollektivizatsiia i raskulachivanie. Dokumenty i materialy*, ed. V. Danilov, R. Manning, and L. Viola (Moscow: Rosspen, 2000), 5 vols, vol. 2: 430–2.

7   David L. Hoffman, *Peasant Metropolis. Social Identities in Moscow, 1929–1941* (Ithaca, NY and London: Cornell University Press, 1994).

8   George O. Liber, *Total Wars and the Making of Modern Ukraine, 1914–1954* (Toronto: University of Toronto Press, 2016), 129.

9   V. B. Zhiromskaia, I. N. Kiselev, and Iu. A. Poliakov, *Polveka pod grifom 'sekretno': Vsesoiuznaia perepis' naseleniia 1937 goda* (Moscow: Nauka, 1996), 88.

10   Liber, *Total Wars*, 160–1.

11   I. Stalin, "Speech at the First All-Union Conference of Stakhanovites," (17 November 1935), https://www.marxists.org/reference/archive/stalin/works/1935/11/17.htm, accessed December 29, 2017).

12   D. L. Brandenberger, and A. M. Dubrovsky, "'The People Need a Tsar': The Emergence of National Bolshevism as Stalinist Ideology, 1931–1941," *Europe-Asia Studies* 50, no. 5 (1998): 873–92, here: 875.

13   Liber, *Total Wars*, 188.

14   Terry Martin, "The Origins of Soviet Ethnic Cleansing," *The Journal of Modern History* 70, no. 4 (1998): 813–61, quotations: 839.

15   Terry Martin, *The Affirmative Action Empire. Nations and Nationalism in the Soviet Union, 1923–1939* (Ithaca, NY and London: Cornell University Press, 2001), 385.

16 Lewis Siegelbaum, "'Dear Comrade, You Ask What We Need': Socialist Paternalism and Soviet Rural 'Notables' in the Mid-1930s," *Slavic Review* 57, no. 1 (1998): 107–32; here: 121.

17 The 1936 constitution in its original redaction can be found here: http://constitution.garant.ru/history/ussr-rsfsr/1936/red_1936/3958676/; an English translation of the constitution in its amended form of 1944 can be found here: https://www.marxists.org/reference/archive/stalin/works/1936/12/05.htm. I quote here from the English translation after checking against the Russian original; both accessed December 29, 2017.

18 Raymond A. Bauer, Alex Inkeles, and Clyde Kluckhohn, *How the Soviet System Works. Cultural, Psychological, and Social Themes* (Cambridge, MA: Harvard University Press, 1956).

19 Jukka Gronow, *Caviar with Champagne. Common Luxury and the Ideals of the Good Life in Stalin's Russia* (Oxford, New York: Berg, 2003); Amy Randall, *The Soviet Dream World of Retail Trade and Consumption in the 1930s* (Basingstoke: Palgrave Macmillan, 2008).

20 Janos Kornai, *Economics of Shortage*, 2 vols. (Amsterdam: North-Holland Pub., Co, 1980).

21 Stalin to Molotov, September 1, 1930, reprinted in: Lars T. Lih, Oleg V. Naumov, and Oleg V. Khlevniuk, eds. *Stalin's Letters to Molotov 1925–1936* (New Haven, CT and London: Yale University Press, 1995), 208–9.

22 Sheila Fitzpatrick, "*Blat* in Stalin's Time," in: *Bribery and Blat in Russia. Negotiating Reciprocity from the Middle Ages to the 1990s*, ed. Stephen Lovell, Alena Ledeneva, and Andrei Rogachevskii (New York: St. Martin's Press, 2000), 166–82; here: 170.

23 Moshe Lewin, "The Disappearance of Planning in the Plan," *Slavic Review* 32, no. 2 (1973): 271–87; reprinted in Lewin's *The Making of the Soviet System. Essays in the Social History of Interwar Russia* (New York: New Press, 1994); Alena Ledeneva, *Russia's Economy of Favours. Blat, Networking and Informal Exchange* (Cambridge, New York, Melbourne: Cambridge University Press, 1998).

Bibliography

Alexopoulos, Golfo. *Illness and Inhumanity in Stalin's Gulag* (New Haven, CT: Yale University Press, 2017).

Applebaum, Anne. *Red Famine: Stalin's War on Ukraine* (London: Allen Lane, 2017).

Baberowski, Jörg. *Scorched Earth. Stalin's Reign of Terror* (New Haven, CT: Yale University Press, 2016).

Bernstein, Seth. *Raised under Stalin. Young Communists and the Defense of Socialism* (Ithaca, NY: Cornell University Press, 2017).

Bojko, Diana and Jerzy Bednarek, eds. *Holodomor. The Great Famine in Ukraine 1932–1933* (Warsaw and Kiev: Institute Pamieci Narodowej Komisja, 2009).

Brown, Kate. *A Biography of No Place. From Ethnic Borderland to Soviet Heartland* (Cambridge, MA: Harvard University Press, 2003).

Chatterjee, Choi, and Karen Petrone. "Models of Selfhood and Subjectivity: The Soviet Case in Historical Perspective." *Slavic Review* 67, no. 4 (2008): 967–86.

Conquest, Robert. *The Great Terror. A Reassessment* (New York and Oxford: Oxford University Press, 1990).

Davies, Sarah. *Popular Opinion in Stalin's Russia. Terror, Propaganda, and Dissent, 1934–1941* (Cambridge, New York, Melbourne: Cambridge University Press, 1997).

Davies, Sarah, and James Harris. *Stalin. A New History* (Cambridge: Cambridge University Press, 2005).

Davies, Sarah, and James Harris, *Stalin's World. Dictating the Soviet Order* (New Haven, CT: Yale University Press, 2014).

Edele, Mark. "Soviet Society, Social Structure, and Everyday Life. Major Frameworks Reconsidered," *Kritika: Explorations in Russian and Eurasian History* 8, no. 2 (2007): 349–73.

Edele, Mark. *Stalinist Society 1928–1953* (Oxford: Oxford University Press, 2011).

Edele, Mark. "Stalinism as a Totalitarian Society. Geoffrey Hosking's Socio-Cultural History," *Kritika: Explorations in Russian and Eurasian History* 13, no. 2 (2012): 441–52.

Edele, Mark. "The New Soviet Man as a 'Gypsy': Nomadism, War, and Marginality in Stalin's Time," *REGION: Regional Studies of Russia, Eastern Europe, and Central Asia* 3, no. 2 (2014): 285–307.

Filtzer, Donald. *Soviet Workers and Stalinist Industrialization. The Formation of Modern Soviet Production Relations, 1928–1941* (Armonk, NY: M. E. Sharpe, 1986).

Fitzpatrick, Sheila. *The Cultural Front. Power and Culture in Revolutionary Russia* (Ithaca, NY and London: Cornell University Press, 1992).

Fitzpatrick, Sheila. *Stalin's Peasants. Resistance and Survival in the Russian Village after Collectivization* (New York and Oxford: Oxford University Press, 1994).

Fitzpatrick, Sheila. "Intelligentsia and Power. Client-Patron Relations in Stalin's Russia," in: *Stalinismus vor dem Zweiten Weltkrieg. Neue Wege der Forschung*, ed. Manfred Hildermeier (Munich: R. Oldenbourg Verlag, 1998), 35–53.

Fitzpatrick, Sheila. *Everyday Stalinism. Ordinary Life in Extraordinary Times: Soviet Russia in the 1930s* (New York and Oxford: Oxford University Press, 1999).

Fitzpatrick, Sheila. "*Blat* in Stalin's Time." In *Bribery and Blat in Russia. Negotiating Reciprocity from the Middle Ages to the 1990s*, ed. Stephen Lovell, Alena Ledeneva and Andrei Rogachevskii (New York: St. Martin's Press, 2000), 166–82.

Fitzpatrick, Sheila, ed. *Stalinism. New Directions* (London and New York: Routledge, 2000).

Fitzpatrick, Sheila. *On Stalin's Team. The Years of Living Dangerously in Soviet Politics* (Melbourne: Melbourne University Press, 2015).

Getty, J. Arch, and Oleg V. Naumov. *The Road to Terror. Stalin and the Self-Destruction of the Bolsheviks, 1932–1939.* (New Haven, CT and London: Yale University Press, 1999).

Goldman, Wendy Z. *Terror and Democracy in the Age of Stalin. The Social Dynamics of Repression.* (Cambridge and New York: Cambridge University Press, 2007).

Graziosi, Andrea. *The Great Soviet Peasant War: Bolsheviks and Peasants, 1917–1933* (Cambridge: Ukrainian Research Institute, 1996).

Harris, James. *The Great Urals: Regionalism and the Evolution of the Soviet System* (Ithaca, NY: Cornell University Press, 1996).

Harris, James. ed. *Anatomy of Terror: Political Violence under Stalin* (Oxford: Oxford University Press, 2013).

Harris, James. *The Great Fear: Political Violence under Stalin* (Oxford: Oxford University Press, 2016).

Hellbeck, Jochen. *Revolution on My Mind. Writing a Diary under Stalin* (Cambridge, MA and London: Harvard University Press, 2006).

Hessler, Julie. *A Social History of Soviet Trade. Trade Policy, Retail Practices, and Consumption, 1917–1953* (Princeton, NJ and Oxford: Princeton University Press, 2004).

Hoffmann, David L. *Peasant Metropolis. Social Identities in Moscow, 1929–1941* (Ithaca, NY and London: Cornell University Press, 1994).

Hoffmann, David L. *Stalinist Values. The Cultural Norms of Soviet Modernity, 1917–1941* (Ithaca, NY and London: Cornell University Press, 2003).

Hoffmann, David L. *Cultivating the Masses. Modern State Practices and Soviet Socialism, 1914–1939* (Ithaca, NY and London: Cornell University Press, 2011).

Ivanova, Galina Mikhailovna. *Labor Camp Socialism. The Gulag in the Soviet Totalitarian System* (Armonk, NY, and London: M. E. Sharpe, 2000).

Khlevniuk, Oleg V. "The Objectives of the Great Terror, 1937–1938," in: *Soviet History, 1917–53. Essays in Honour of R. W. Davies*, ed. Julian Cooper, Maureen Perrie and E. A. Rees (New York: St. Martin's Press, 1995).

Khlevniuk, Oleg V. "The Reasons for the 'Great Terror': The Foreign-Political Aspect," in: *Russia in the Age of Wars*, ed. Silvio Pons and Andrea Romano (Milan: Fondazione Giangiacomo Feltrinelli, 2000), 159–69.

Khlevniuk, Oleg V. *The History of the Gulag. From Collectivization to the Great Terror.* (New Haven, CT and London: Yale University Press, 2004).

Khlevniuk, Oleg V. *Master of the House. Stalin and His Inner Circle* (New Haven, CT and London: Yale University Press, 2009).

Khlevniuk, Oleg V. *Stalin. New Biography of a Dictator* (New Haven, CT and London: Yale University Press, 2015).

Kotkin, Stephen. *Magnetic Mountain. Stalinism as a Civilization* (Berkeley, Los Angeles, London: University of California Press, 1995).

Kotkin, Stephen. "Modern Times: The Soviet Union and the Interwar Conjuncture," *Kritika: Explorations in Russian and Eurasian History* 2, no. 1 (2001): 111–64.

Lenoe, Matthew E. *The Kirov Murder and Soviet History* (New Haven, CT: Yale University Press, 2010).

Loring, Benjamin. "'Colonizers with Party Cards': Soviet Internal Colonialism in Central Asia, 1917–39," *Kritika: Explorations in Russian and Eurasian History* 15, no. 1 (2014): 77–102.

Martin, Terry. "The Origins of Soviet Ethnic Cleansing," *The Journal of Modern History* 70, no. 4 (1998): 813–61.

Martin, Terry. *The Affirmative Action Empire. Nations and Nationalism in the Soviet Union, 1923–1939* (Ithaca, NY and London: Cornell University Press, 2001).

McDermott, Kevin. *Stalin* (Basingstoke and New York: Palgrave Macmillan, 2006).

O'Keeffe, Brigid. *New Soviet Gypsies: Nationality, Performance, and Selfhood in the Early Soviet Union* (Toronto: University of Toronto Press, 2013).

Osokina, Elena. *Our Daily Bread. Socialist Distribution and the Art of Survival in Stalin's Russia, 1927–1941* (Armonk, NY, London: M. E. Sharpe, 2001).

Payne, Matthew. *Stalin's Railroad. Turksib and the Building of Socialism* (Pittsburgh, PA: University of Pittsburgh Press, 2001).

Petrone, Karen. *Life Has Become More Joyous, Comrades: Celebrations in the Time of Stalin* (Bloomington: Indiana University Press, 2000).

Randall, Amy, *The Soviet Dream World of Retail Trade and Consumption in the 1930s* (Basingstoke: Palgrave Macmillan, 2008)

Slezkine, Yuri. *The House of Government. A Saga of the Russian Revolution* (Princeton, NJ: Princeton University Press, 2017).

Stone, David R. *Hammer and Rifle. The Militarization of the Soviet Union, 1926–1933* (Lawrence: University Press of Kansas, 2000).

van Ree, Eric. *The Political Thought of Joseph Stalin. A Study in Twentieth-Century Revolutionary Patriotism* (London and New York: Routledge Curzon, 2002).

Viola, Lynne. *Peasant Rebels under Stalin. Collectivization and the Culture of Peasant Resistance* (New York and Oxford: Oxford University Press, 1996).

Viola, Lynne. *The Unknown Gulag. The Lost World of Stalin's Special Settlements* (Oxford and New York: Oxford University Press, 2007).

6

A Long Second World War (1937–1949)

On March 10, 1939, Stalin reported to the Eighteenth Congress of the Bolshevik Party on the work of the Central Committee. Startlingly, he announced that "a new imperialist war is already in its second year." "Imperialist war" was the Soviet term for what many in the West then called the "Great" or the "World War," and what we today know as World War I. According to Stalin, now another such "imperialist war" was underway. Where and when had World War II started? The General Secretary reviewed the major armed conflicts of the 1930s: Italy's attack on Abyssinia (1935–1936), the Spanish Civil War (raging since 1936 and in its final month as the dictator spoke), the German annexation of Austria (1938) and its occupation of Czechoslovakia (1938–1939). However, his remark that this war was in its second year suggested that its origin lay in Asia. Japan was a major culprit, who "having seized Manchuria, ... in 1937 invaded North and Central China, occupied Peking, Tientsin and Shanghai and began to oust her foreign competitors from the occupied zone."[1]

Stalin's analysis turned out to be right. In Asia, World War II had indeed already begun. This new global bloodletting was not one conflict but a conglomerate of several wars, whose merger into one interdependent whole by 1941 created the most destructive cataclysm of the twentieth century. First was a land war in Asia, fought between Japan and China in particular. It began with the battle of the Marco Polo Bridge near Beijing between July 7 and July 9, 1937. In 1945, with the defeat of Japan by the Allies, it transformed into the Chinese Civil War, which ended with victory by the Communists in 1949. Second was the European land war, the more common starting point for histories of World War II. It was considerably shorter than the Asian war,

The Soviet Union: A Short History, First Edition. Mark Edele.
© 2019 John Wiley & Sons, Inc. Published 2019 by John Wiley & Sons, Inc.

beginning with Germany's invasion of Poland on September 1, 1939 and ending with the defeat of the Nazis on May 8/9, 1945. Fighting continued in the western borderlands of the Soviet Union, pacified only in 1949, when the last of the big deportations from the western borderlands effectively ended the resistance. Even shorter was the war in the Pacific, which began with the Japanese bombing of Pearl Harbor on December 7, 1941 and ended with the defeat of Japan in 1945 after two atomic bombs were dropped in August and the Soviets had also entered the war. The shortest World War II was fought in North Africa, where fighting only lasted from 1940 to 1943.

The Soviet Union was involved in these four concurrent wars to different degrees. The land war in Asia was concerning, as it happened right on the eastern doorstep. Here, the Soviets focused on delivering military aid to Chinese proxies in order to bog down the Japanese. When forced to fight, the Soviet Union could do so victoriously, as the undeclared border war with Japan in 1938 and 1939 showed. Stalin, however, did not press his advantage but was careful to remain defensive in order to not be drawn into the quagmire of the Sino-Japanese war. As long as Japan was distracted, the Soviet eastern front was safe. This strategy succeeded and led to a neutrality pact with Japan in early 1941, which kept Stalin's back free for the war in Europe.

Here, we can distinguish three phases of Soviet involvement: in the first phase (1939–1941), the Soviet Union made common cause with Germany and continued the regathering of the empire in the west, a process that had remained incomplete at the start of the 1920s. Poland, Finland, the Baltic States, Bessarabia, and Bukovina all became objects of Soviet aggression. With the exception of Finland, which remained independent, they were all brought back into the empire during this period, Bukovina being the only acquisition that had not been Russian in 1914.

The second phase began with Germany's attack on the Soviet Union on June 22, 1941. Now the Soviet Union became a victim of aggression. It quickly lost all it had acquired since 1939 and much else besides. German troops marched deep into the Soviet heartland, occupying Ukraine, Belarus, the Baltics, and large sections of European Russia. The Red Army fought desperately, slowing the opponent down all the way, eventually reversing the direction of attack in the battle of Moscow in the winter of 1941. Germany went back on the offensive in 1942. The battles of Stalingrad in the winter of 1942/1943 and Kursk in the following summer, however, broke the German war machine. In the third phase of the Soviet war in Europe (1943–1945), the Red Army drove the Germans out of Soviet territory before marching through Eastern Europe all the way to Berlin.

With Germany subdued, the Red Army turned east again, this time going beyond the defensive stance of 1938 to 1939. The Manchurian campaign of August 1945 had been planned well in advance of the two US atomic bombs, which ultimately sealed the fate of the Japanese Empire. The attack brought the recovery of southern Sakhalin (lost by the Romanov Empire to Japan in the Treaty of Portsmouth in 1905) and the Kuriles (ceded even earlier, in the Treaty of St. Petersburg in 1875), and short-lived Soviet occupations of Manchuria and North Korea, but not of parts of Japan, as Stalin had hoped.

The Soviets thus played a crucial role in World War II. They were directly involved in all but two theaters (Africa and the Pacific), although what happened in these had repercussions on the Soviet war as well. The Stalinist contribution to the war against Hitler from 1941 was decisive, and the results of this war's destruction traumatic and of long-term consequence. The Soviet impact on the outcome of the war in Asia is a matter of historical debate. In 1937 and 1938, the Chinese would certainly have had an even harder time resisting Japan, were it not for Soviet assistance. For 1945, historians are divided over whether or not Japan would have fallen when it did even without the Soviet attack (after all, two atomic bombs had already done their destructive work when the Red Army was set in motion). Debate, sometime acrimonious, also continues over the evaluation of the overall Soviet war conduct, which is impossible to describe in black and white terms. The memories of Soviet liberations and occupations continue to arouse deep-seated national and residual Cold War emotions in various parts of the globe. This war was deeply ambiguous in moral and political terms, combining heroism and enormous sacrifice with criminality and imperial conquest. It came close to destroying the Soviet Union. It killed millions. It broke the Wehrmacht's back and saved the world from Nazism. And it transformed the Soviet Union from an embattled warfare state into a military superpower, an enlarged empire, secured now by a ring of satellites in the west, and friendly allies in the east.

The Eastern Front, 1937–1939

None of this future could be known on August 21, 1937, when the Soviet government reacted to the outbreak of war in China with a dual decision. One resolution ordered the deportation of the Soviet Koreans from the Far Eastern borderlands; on the same day, the Soviets signed the Mutual Nonaggression Treaty with China.

These two decisions were linked in a defensive strategy for the Soviet eastern front. The deportation of over 172,000 Koreans was the first forced removal of an entire ethnic group in Soviet history. As we saw in Chapter 5, there were precursors in the early 1930s, and the Great Terror, heating up in the background, also had its national operations. In each of these cases, however, only subgroups of the nationality in question were victimized, in particular those who were presumed to be particularly hostile to Soviet power. In the context of the hot war being fought in China, this practice was universalized: All Koreans were presumed to be potential spies or collaborators with the Japanese. Hence, they were herded into cattle trucks and after a long and arduous journey dumped in the steppes of Kazakhstan and Uzbekistan. Tens of thousands died as a result of the resettlement.

The deportation was one part of the fortification of the eastern front against a feared Japanese aggression. A military buildup in the Far East paralleled this measure. Soviet infantry divisions in the region went from 16 in 1936 to 20 in 1937, growing to 30 in 1939. Manpower increased from 300,000 to 570,000 and tanks from 1200 to 2200 in the same period. The Soviets prepared for an attack by Japan.

Meanwhile, the Nonaggression Treaty with China had the task of helping to fight the war instead of having to enter it. Tens of thousands of rifles, thousands of automatic weapons, hundreds of planes, tractors and other automobiles, scores of tanks, and well over 1000 artillery pieces were delivered to the Chinese in the following years. The goal was to bog down Japan and thus decrease the likelihood that it would turn north to attack the Soviet Union. Between 1937 and 1942, some 5000 pilots, military advisors, and support personnel aided the Chinese, including one Vasilii Chuikov, the later hero of the battle of Stalingrad. During the largely forgotten but incredibly bloody battle of Wuhan in 1938, Soviet combat pilots challenged Japanese air superiority, shooting down more than 90 enemy planes. By 1939, 195 Soviets had died in China or were missing in action.

In the long-term, the Soviet tactic was successful: Japan was denied victory in China. In the short run, the Soviets did not escape the fight. Border incidents had been steadily increasing throughout the 1930s, reaching over 200 in 1937. In 1938 and 1939, two major battles were fought as part of an undeclared border war between the Soviet Union and Japan. The first, the battle of Lake Khasan, also known as the Changkufeng Incident (July 29 to August 11, 1938), was triggered by one of the most spectacular defections of the 1930s: the flight of the commander of the NKVD troops in the Far East across the border, to escape his arrest in the Great Terror. The Soviets reacted with tightening the border, occupying in the process the Changkufeng hill, which commanded the surrounding countryside in the volatile region between Korea, Manchuria, and the USSR. Like many spots along this poorly mapped border, the hill was claimed by both sides. Japanese forces ejected the Soviets from the outpost, before being driven back by a massive and costly counter offensive. The Soviets first admitted only to 236 dead and 611 wounded, but archival reports put the total losses at 960 dead and 3279 wounded. For every Japanese soldier lost nearly two Soviet soldiers died in this battle, largely because commanders insisted on frontal attacks against entrenched positions – a sign of things to come later in the war.

The second major battle of the Soviet–Japanese border war was fought at Khalkhin Gol (or Nomonhan, in the Japanese version of events; May 11 to September 16, 1939). This "most important World War II battle that most people have never heard of,"[2] was technically fought not on Soviet, but Mongolian territory, showing that de facto the Soviets treated its satellite as home territory. This battle was much larger than its predecessor. It took four months and tens of thousands were killed and wounded on both sides. Again, Soviet casualties exceeded Japanese losses, but again the Soviets won.

If the battle of Khalkhin Gol is remembered at all, it is largely for General Georgii Konstantinovich Zhukov's (1896–1974) brilliant use of massed armor, an anticipation of later operations against the Germans. Also anticipating the later war, however, this "modern" Red Army – the result of the Stalinist industrialization push since the late 1920s – was embedded in a nineteenth-century army relying on horses, trains, and forced marches for its mobility. This mixture of old and new would also remain a constant throughout the Soviet's World War II, when motorized spearheads of maybe 20% of the forces were embedded in a horse-drawn army of foot-sloggers. As late as 1945, requisitioned peasant carts allowed the regular infantry to more or less keep pace with the advancing elite units. Later that same year 16,507 more horses than machines were transferred to the Far East to help fight Japan in the Manchurian campaign. Luckily, the major adversary – the German Wehrmacht – did not do much better in terms of mechanization of transport. Here, too, the horse and the boot prevailed.

The victorious border war against Japan in 1938/1939 had serious implications for the further history of World War II. Soviet victories pushed Tokyo away from schemes to attack the Soviets and nudged Japan's government towards a Soviet–Japanese treaty of neutrality in April 1941, which would keep Stalin's back free to face the Germans. Bogged down in China and facing a Red Army that clearly could fight, the Japanese moved south instead, eventually challenging the United States in the Pacific. Arguably, this successful avoidance of a two-front war against Germany and Japan was one of Stalin's greatest military-diplomatic triumphs.

Offensive War in Europe, 1939–1941

While the battle of Khalkhin Gol was raging in the east, a shocking development took place in the west: on August 23, 1939, Germany and the Soviet Union signed a nonaggression treaty. Known as the Molotov-Ribbentrop pact after the two foreign ministers, or Hitler–Stalin pact after the dictators they represented, this document continues to haunt Eastern Europe. In a secret protocol to the pact, the two dictators carved up Central and Eastern Europe into a German and a Soviet sphere of influence. Historians and politicians continue to debate whether this pact with the devil was forced upon Stalin because of the reluctance of the western powers to unite with the Soviets in a framework of collective security against Hitler, or if Stalin willingly helped unleash war in Europe because he hoped the capitalist powers would wear themselves out and the

Soviet Union could reap the benefits. A second debate circles around the question as to whether Stalin had a grand plan for these borderlands. Archival documents suggest instead that Soviet actions in the years 1939 to 1941 were improvisations, often hasty ones.

The end result of the pact with Nazi Germany and of subsequent decisions was that the Soviet Union entered the war as an aggressor on the side of the Nazis. The German attack on Poland on September 1 triggered declarations of war against Germany from France and Britain. World War II in Europe had begun. Stalin bided his time while the Germans made short work of Poland's army. Despite repeated pleas by its fascist ally to start the second front, the Red Army only entered the fray on September 17, the day after a cease fire had ended the battle of Khalkhin Gol. Under the pretext that the Polish state had ceased to exist (a claim disputed by Polish historians), the Soviet Union took over the eastern half of the country, as had been agreed to in the Hitler–Stalin Pact. Poland was carved up between the two victorious powers and its Soviet half annexed to the Belarusian and Ukrainian republics.

The Polish campaign was the thus far largest Soviet military operation in this war, involving close to half-a-million troops. Nearly twice as many, 0.8 million, would be necessary to fight the next war, against Finland at the year's end. This conflict became a major embarrassment for the Red Army, after direct meddling by Stalin, who rejected the plan worked out by military specialists and sent in too few troops in a poorly prepared attack. The Finns, led by the old tsarist General, somewhat reluctant Finnish nationalist and violent anticommunist of civil war days, Carl Gustaf Mannerheim (1867–1951), fought bravely. Only once Stalin began listening to his generals after the initial disaster and adjusted his tactics did the attrition by an overwhelming enemy eventually wear the defenders down. The Reds could have marched on Helsinki, but settled for negotiations, as the Finns were ready to accept very harsh terms. That Britain and France had made moves to stand with the Finns also helped in moving from war to peace. Historians remain divided over the question of whether the dictator had originally planned to take over all of Finland – another of the old Tsarist domains, after all, which like Poland had escaped reincorporation into the Red Empire. That a puppet government of Finnish communists stood at the ready suggests that Stalin at least kept his options open. In the end, the Finns escaped annexation, but had to give up parts of Karelia, Salla, and the Rybachi peninsula and demilitarize the arctic coastline. The border was pushed away from vulnerable Leningrad (as Petrograd had been called since 1924) and the Murmansk railroad – central for access to the port – was safer as well.

In June 1940, it was the turn of the three Baltic republics, like Finland old Tsarist domains, who had escaped reincorporation during the first epoch of violence. Estonia, Latvia, and Lithuania had already been bullied into accepting Soviet military bases in 1939. Now ultimatums were issued. The three republics chose not to start a war they could not win. The Soviets took over, installed "people's governments," held rigged elections which delivered communist majorities who demanded admission of their now "Soviet republics" into the great Soviet Union. Their requests were granted. The Baltic States became three new union republics, a status they suffered until 1991.

Sovietization of the newly acquired western borderlands was extremely violent: a shift of the focus of repression from the Soviet heartland to its borders in the west, which can be described as a "revolution from abroad."[3] By the summer of 1941, a total of 383,000 people had been deported to remote regions of the Soviet Union, because Stalin's police believed that they were "class enemies" and "counter-revolutionaries." They included Poles, Jews, Latvians, Lithuanians, Estonians, and others, often women and children, who were sent to "special settlements" – a form of forced labor without a concentration camp. In addition, the security forces arrested and imprisoned many other political and class enemies. Arrests and deportations only ceased with the German attack on June 22, 1941. Altogether as much as 3% of the population of the new territories was either arrested or deported, a scale of repression superseded in the Soviet heartland only by collectivization at the start of the 1930s.

At the extreme end of the spectrum of "Sovietization" efforts, executions were meant to eliminate possible opposition. The most appalling of these was the mass extermination of 21,857 Polish officers, policemen, military settlers, and other representatives of the old regime. They were shot on direct orders from the Kremlin in the forest of Katyn and several other execution sites in 1940. Reminiscent of the "mass operations" of the Great Terror, this shooting spree had the same goal: to "cleanse" the home-front from possible enemies in anticipation of war. These massacres, however, turned into a major public relations debacle for the Soviets once the Germans uncovered the remains of some of the victims in 1943 and exploited them for their propaganda. In a major coup for the Nazis, these revelations led to a break in diplomatic relations between the Polish exile government in London and the Soviets during a critical phase of the war against Germany. The Soviet government only admitted responsibility in 1990.

The Greater Soviet Empire, 1941

At first sight, Stalin had played his cards well in the first period of the war in Europe. The annexations of 1939 and 1940 expanded the Soviet Union from 11 to 16 union republics, while its population grew from 167 to 190 million, living on a total of now 8.5 million square miles. The borders were pushed outwards in the west and north, providing a greater sense of security against possible German and Finnish aggression. Much of the regathering of the Russian Empire, which had stalled at the end of the civil war, now seemed to be completed, even if parts of Poland as well as Finland remained beyond the reach of the Red Empire. Indeed, Stalin's state had expanded even beyond the territories the Romanovs had ruled over: northern Bukovina, annexed together with Bessarabia from Romania in 1940, had never been part of the Russian Empire.

On closer inspection, however, the expansion of the empire came with serious costs. The resources of the Stalinist state were spread thinner. Police capability did not grow in step with the expansion of territory and population, leading to a decrease in control at a time when millions of new subjects entered the Soviet realm. The military benefits of the change in borders were also dubious. Established defensive lines had to be dismantled and new ones needed to be built further west, increasing military vulnerability along a western borderline. The gains in territory from Finland were nullified by the impression that the poor performance of the Red Army in the Winter War had made on German military men who were convinced now more than ever that they could beat this stumbling colossus. And the Soviets now faced the German juggernaut directly, no longer shielded by a series of, however unfriendly, buffer states along the western frontier.

All along this new border, the loyalties of much of the population were at best suspect. Whether or not the Great Terror actually achieved its goal of eliminating enemies to Stalin's regime, there can be no doubt that whatever "positive" effect this bloodletting might have had was undone by the incorporation of millions of new citizens. They had been socialized under fundamentally different regimes and often felt that their nation had been subjected to an imperialist takeover. Nobody thought that recruits from the former Polish territories or the Baltics could be trusted and this suspicion sometimes turned out to be correct once the Germans attacked. Even more extreme, the expansion to the west had effectively imported militant nationalists, most prominently the Organization of Ukrainian Nationalists (OUN), who would play a major anti-Soviet role later in the war.

Less than 4% of the new population was Russian. Their predominance within the Soviet Union, then – which had grown first as a result of the amputation of so many non-Russian regions in the first epoch of violence and then by the disproportional victimization of non-Russians in the revolutions from above – was now weakened. In early 1939, 58% of the Soviet population were Russians, at the eve of the war with Germany in 1941 this share had decreased to below 52%. The growth of minorities came at exactly the time when military mobilization relied heavily on Russian nationalism.

The Catastrophe of 1941

The Soviet expansions in 1939 to 1940, then, were detrimental to the security of the Red Empire. Stalin had miscalculated. The German war effort was much more successful in the west than the experience of World War I could have possibly suggested. Hitler was also much less cautious than the Soviet dictator. While Stalin moved only in the west after his eastern flank was secure, Hitler was willing to risk a two front war and attack the Soviet Union before Britain was subdued. Despite repeated warnings from a variety of sources, Stalin refused to believe that his German counterpart could be so stupid. The German attack on June 22, 1941 thus came unexpectedly. The Soviet Union was not prepared.

The results were catastrophic. Nearly 2% of the 1941 population became military casualties in the first six months of this war. The entire standing army was wiped out in the summer and fall of this terrible year. Soviet soldiers and civilians displayed an extreme variety of behaviors. Some fought doggedly, making the German army pay for every inch of Soviet soil; others defected to the enemy to fight against Stalin on the side of the invaders; many more simply gave up when cut off by German encirclement, disoriented by lack of leadership, and frightened by the apparent superiority of the Germans. The populations in the west often greeted the Wehrmacht as liberators, but even among Russians in the Soviet heartland defeatism was widespread. Many saw their own interests as separate both from the Soviet and the German regimes. Meanwhile, many others volunteered for the army in order to help defend the Socialist homeland, or indeed "Mother Russia."

The fighting was terrible and German successes crushing. By the end of the year, the Wehrmacht had occupied Ukraine, Belarus, and the Baltics as well as a large chunk of European Russia. In the south-west, Romania had invaded together with Germany on June 22, recovering Bessarabia and Bukovina and eventually occupying the rest of the Moldavian ASSR, Odessa, and parts of the Vynnitsa region. In the north, after botched Soviet airstrikes on June 25, which targeted Finnish airfields used by the Luftwaffe, Finland attacked the Soviet Union in what came to be known as the "Continuation War," quickly taking back all that had been lost in the Winter War. Mannerheim's troops stopped 30 kilometers from Leningrad, though, not pressing their advantage beyond what they saw as Finnish lands. They dug in, occupying the territory until 1944, when Finland exited the war in a separate peace with the Soviets.

By the end of 1941, the frontline ran from encircled Leningrad in the north to Moscow in the east, and south to Rostov. The lost regions included some of the most fertile and most industrialized regions of the empire. Before the war, nearly 45% of the population had lived in the now occupied lands, and despite flight and evacuation, between 65 and 68 million Soviets, or around a third of the prewar population, remained behind.

In the end, the Germans were unable to win the quick and decisive war they had hoped for. The enormous territory they had occupied amounted only to 9% of the prewar Soviet Empire: there was plenty of space for the Soviets to retreat into without having to concede defeat. And the Soviet Union did not give up. The imperial apocalypse of 1914 to 1917 did not repeat itself. Although the defeats of 1941 were much more crushing than even the great retreat of 1915, the empire did not fall apart under the strains imposed by wartime. In Stalin's empire, there was no revolutionary movement, not even a loyal opposition, which could have fomented rebellion. Local unrest in October, such as the looting and beating of departing officials during the Moscow panic as well as strikes in Ivanovo, were small-scale, localized, and easily suppressed. While poorly led and unprepared troops often gave up quickly, and while a sizable minority actively went over to the Germans, many others slowed the Wehrmacht down in a fighting retreat. The Red Army implemented a most aggressive tactic of relentless counter attack, which cost it many casualties, but also bled the Wehrmacht dry. Rather than a war that would be "over by Christmas," the Germans had engaged in a war of attrition with an empire, which had been preparing for exactly this eventuality for the past decade. The Soviet dictatorship thus kept the population in its grip and mobilized the extensive resources of this vast country for the most terrible war of the twentieth century.

Defensive War on Soviet Soil, 1941–1943

From the very start, the Soviets had more men, tanks, aircraft, guns, and artillery than the Germans, and more were churned out once industry shifted to a war footing. Germany could not keep pace, and it was just a matter of time until the Soviets learned to use their resources more efficiently. Having failed to win a quick victory in 1941 – which had always been an enormous gamble – the Germans had lost the war.

This material superiority was a result of the forced-paced industrialization that had been overseen by Stalin since 1928. It puts the failures of 1941 in even sharper relief – failures which, like Soviet strengths, were also due to the actions of the dictator. Stalin's prewar policies had left the country poorly prepared for the actual war when it did break out. The military was still shaken from the Great Purge. The humiliation of the Finnish war taught the wrong lessons, and it took a while to unlearn them. Commanders were in short supply and often poorly trained. The army was unprepared for the attack and in the middle of an enormous reorganization. Redeployment to the western frontier and fortification of this new borderline had not been completed, equipment was often poorly maintained, and in many cases already technologically obsolete. Much was wiped out in the first month of the war, including the air force at the western front, which was destroyed on the ground.

Stalin indeed knew that he had "fucked up," to use his own colorful language. But he did not give up, and was ready to do whatever was necessary to defend Lenin's "inheritance."[4] The political system was recalibrated to deal with the emergency of wartime. On the one hand was further centralization: a "State

Defence Committee" (GKO) was formed, with Stalin at its head. It brought together the tentacles of state and the Party in a supreme dictatorial executive running the entire war effort. On the other hand was quite radical decentralization of anything not directly connected to the war. Civilian consumption and the provision of welfare to civilians, for example, devolved to the localities, often the enterprises. Even the work of the GKO was in practice relying on decentralized decision makers: plenipotentiaries sent to the fronts or the hinterland to fix problems and enforce resolutions. If before the war, as a result of the terror, Stalin's team had disintegrated, it now quickly reconstituted itself. The war effort was a team effort.

Beyond the immediate political system, too, society began to reconverge around defense and a sense of patriotism. Conscription of nearly all adult males to fight meant that the majority of the population had either a family member in the army, or had lost one in the war. Wartime mobilization entangled the fates of families, nations, and the empire in new ways. The focus of the propaganda on Russian patriotism and German atrocities, on the defense of home, hearth, women, and children, helped in a "crystallization" of Russian national consciousness.[5] Nearly half the population, of course, was not Russian, but special propaganda was developed for non-Slavic servicemen in particular, and the themes of violated mothers, executed infants, and burning homes had a universal resonance.

For the first time since the Revolution, official pronouncements simply told the truth: German behavior was atrocious. Propaganda exploited in particular the destruction of entire villages on German-held territory in the context of anti-Partisan operations, the execution of civilians, and the terrible plight of Soviet POWs in German detention, where millions died of hunger, exposure, and disease. Soviet media were more muted about the destruction of the Jews, because the leadership worried that the many anti-Semites in the population would not find much to object to in the physical annihilation of all Soviet Jews. "Good, the war's begun," said Moscow workers the day after the invasion began, "they'll kill the Jews."[6]

When it turned out that the Germans killed not only Jews and Communists, but also Russians, Ukrainians, Belarusians, and their children, larger and larger sectors of the population saw their own interests better served by rallying behind the regime. Military successes and their implications – that the Soviets were there to stay, or would return to the occupied regions – further added to this groundswell. Earlier battles in 1941, especially at Smolensk and Kyiv, had decidedly weakened the attackers. Now, the first clear victory of the Soviets came at the end of the year: the Battle of Moscow. For the first time, the supposedly invincible Wehrmacht was beaten and forced to retreat. Although German advances resumed in 1942, this time in the south, trying to reach the Baku oilfields, the war had now effectively turned in the Soviet favor. The German economy was not big enough to withstand a war of attrition against the much larger Soviet economy, let alone an international alliance including the Soviets, the United States, and the British Empire.

Offensive in Europe and Asia, 1944–1945

It was part of this alliance that the Soviet Union now fought. The second half of 1941, in this respect, was a pivotal year in World War II. First it brought the Soviets from the side of the Germans over to the side of the anti-Hitler coalition; then it brought the United States fully into the conflict, when war spread to the Pacific.

Nevertheless, the defensive war in the Soviet Union did not come easily. Only after the battle of Stalingrad at the end of 1942 and the start of 1943 did the tables turn decisively. By late 1944, most of the Soviet territory was liberated from Nazism. Finland had sued for peace and was let off the hook with a punishing peace treaty, but without a Soviet occupation.

From late 1944, then, Soviet troops began to fight well beyond territories that had been part of the empire. By May 1945, the Red Army had swept through Eastern Europe and into Germany and Austria. After the German defeat in May, the Red Army regrouped to return to the war on the eastern front, which had been relatively quiet, thanks to the April 1941 treaty of neutrality, which both sides observed despite some local irritations and a continuing trickle of border incidents.

The offensive against Japan began on August 9, exactly three months after Germany's defeat, as Stalin had promised at the Yalta Conference in February 1945. It was also the same day as the second atomic bomb was dropped on Japan, which surrendered on August 15. The Soviet advance continued as did sporadic resistance from the Japanese army.

Civil Wars

Fighting also continued in what now again became the western borderlands: the former Baltic, Polish, and Romanian territories incorporated from 1939. Here, the world war had transformed into a civil war. It was fought between various nationalists and the Soviet conquerors. In contrast to the civil wars in the first epoch of violence, however, one participant had a clear advantage in the mobilization of the means of violence from the outset: the Soviet Union.

The civil wars following liberation of the western borderlands by the Red Army had their roots in the years of German (or Romanian) occupation. Several forces were in conflict. On the one hand were local nationalist groups. Sometimes these fought each other as much as the Germans, as was the case with the Ukrainian OUN/UPA and the Polish Home Army (AK). They faced German counter-insurgency troops, collaborator units formed from former Soviet citizens (until the latter were transferred to the western front in 1943), and local armed militias in charge of defending their own villages. They further confronted several types of Soviet "partisans": spontaneously founded resistance groups of Party and NKVD functionaries; surrounded Red Army units who did not give up but continued to fight behind the lines; Red Army commandos sent into the rear, largely to gather information about the enemy; and NKVD troops in charge of terrorizing and exterminating collaborators. Armed Jewish survival and resistance groups completed the mix. Most of these units had to behave like "bandits" at one time or other: they needed to requisition food, fodder, clothes, and other supplies. But there were also bandits pure and simple: armed gangs without a political goal, who lived off the land.

The civilian population stood between these armed groups, having to suffer requisitions, reprisals, and forced mobilization to fight or to work for the Germans. Jews faced the exterminationist policies of the Nazis, often supported by local nationalists and collaborators. But other groups were targeted, too. In Volhynia in 1943, UPA killed Poles by the tens of thousands, and Poles retaliated by forming self-defense groups, by joining the German police or the Soviet partisans. Thus armed and organized, they began shooting Ukrainians in response to the ethnic cleansing they had experienced at the hand of their Ukrainian neighbors.

The German-occupied areas, then, were the site of an at times low-level, and at others hot and often multisided civil war within and under the conventional war and occupation regime. At the beginning, the non- and anti-Soviet groups were the most influential. As time went on and the Soviet fortunes increased, the partisans grew in influence. The Soviet leadership now opened the movement up to all comers, and German reprisals against civilians, the general brutality of the occupation regime, and eventually the rising recognition that the Soviets would come back strengthened the movement. Defections from collaborator units became frequent and eventually entire regions were liberated from German control and run as "partisan districts."

When the Red Army arrived, the Soviet partisan units were either transformed into regular army units or disbanded, and their personnel drafted into the armed forces. In either case, they marched west, leaving collaborators and anti-Soviet nationalists behind, soon to be joined by farmers resisting collectivization. The Soviet counter-insurgency strategy combined the carrot and the stick. Collaborators were arrested and nationalist resisters tracked down and if necessary destroyed militarily. Given the overwhelming firepower of the Red Army and the security services, this task was achieved relatively easily. The anti-Soviet resistance then turned from military opposition to terrorism, killing representatives of Soviet power and their local allies. The Soviets reacted with a mixture of police investigation and counter-terror. Families of nationalist terrorists were deported. At the same time, offers of amnesty were extended to the insurgents and their kin, should they give up and turn against their former comrades. This tactic was successful; the borderlands were pacified and collectivized. The revolution from abroad was finally complete.

Why the Soviet Union Won the War in Europe

Once the counter-insurgency was over with the final deportations in 1949, the Soviet Union had won the war in Europe. The contribution of the Red Empire to the fall of Nazi Germany cannot be over-estimated. The Soviets consistently faced the largest share of Hitler's armies. 75% of German weaponry was destroyed on the Soviet front, and 78% of the German divisions and those of Germany's European allies were taken prisoner or were destroyed by the Red Army. Both Soviet historians and their Russian successors rightfully stress this basic fact, often ignored in the western world, obsessed as it is with the Normandy invasion and the Pacific theater.

Why did the Soviet Union win? We can distinguish between political, geographic, and military-economic factors. We have already mentioned the politics of this war: the German war of extermination gave little room for maneuver and forced many enemies of Stalinism to take the Soviet side as the lesser evil. To many historians, this fact is the most important circumstance: it rallied the population behind the regime, uniting leaders and led in a way that they had never been before. Dictatorship was a second reason, as it prevented the successful organization of any kind of effective resistance to the regime. Those who did not want to fight would be forced to do so.

Geography is another candidate in many explanations. The idea that the German army was only defeated by "General Frost" and "General Winter" was a favorite of German generals, who had to explain why they lost this war so comprehensively against an allegedly inferior enemy. The fact of the matter was that the Germans encountered heavy resistance by the Red Army long before the weather turned. As one German general wrote to his wife on August 1, 1941: "We have all underestimated the Russian. It was always said that his leaders are pathetic. Well, they have proved their leadership skills with the result that our operations have come to a halt."[7] That the Soviet Union was big, that the roads were poor, that the railroads had a different gauge than in the west, and that the Eurasian plains descend into mud in fall and are terribly cold in winter were also not military secrets somehow springing on unsuspecting German soldiers. They were facts one glance at an encyclopedia could have revealed. That Hitler's soldiers were not prepared for these conditions is not the conditions' fault. Finally, what one historian has called the "Eurasian funnel" – the phenomenon that the frontline lengthened the farther east the Wehrmacht marched – could also have been understood through a simple look at a map.[8] Geography, of course, was real; but it was also democratic: the Red Army dealt with the same conditions as the Germans. And military strategy, of course, has to take such basic facts as weather, road conditions, and distances into account.

The most important reasons for the Soviet victory, then, were neither geographic, nor political, but military and economic. The Soviet economy was much larger than its German counterpart, and the Soviets consistently out-produced the Germans in war materiel. In many ways, war was the natural habitat of the Soviet state, which had emerged from the first epoch of violence and had prepared for the next one with a determined single-mindedness, which turned the entire empire into an armed camp, indeed "one single forced labor camp," as one historian has written.[9] Civilian consumption could be suppressed without too much trouble, given the terrorist regime. The Soviets never worried as much as Hitler did about how much and what civilians ate. As long as they ate enough to be able to go to work, that was sufficient. Production was geared towards defense before the war, society was already mobilized and partially militarized. In contrast to the wide variety of war machines in action on the German side, Soviet production was standardized, which made maintenance and the delivery of spare parts much easier.

The economic superiority of the Soviet Union was further enhanced by the fact that it was in alliance with the largest economy of the globe, the United States. Much has been made of the impact of allied material assistance to the Soviet Union. By the end of December 1941, 25% of all medium and heavy tanks were of British origin, which had been delivered via the hazardous "northern route" to Archangel and Murmansk. In the Battle of Moscow, up to 40% of tanks were British. These deliveries plugged important holes. As the war went on, British deliveries were increasingly replaced by US ones. The preferred route now shifted to the south. Most deliveries now came through the Pacific, via Japanese waters, a path made possible by the neutrality of the Soviets in the Pacific War, the result of the April 1941 treaty with Japan. A second southern route came through the Caucasus, from Iran, occupied since 1941 by the Soviets in the north and the British in the south. Tanks were now replaced by food, machines, tools, and trucks, which allowed the Soviets to focus their industry on the production of tanks, artillery, and aircraft. The motorized spearheads of the Red Army relied on US Studebaker trucks.

The wider allied war effort also helped with Soviet victory. Remember the central role of China in helping to keep the Soviet back free from Japanese attack. Developments in other theatres of war also had an impact. In 1941, Italy was threatened by British successes, prompting the transfer of German aircraft from the Soviet front to the Mediterranean. British fighting thus lessened German air superiority in the east at a critical junction. The Allied airstrikes against German cities from 1942 drew more German fighter planes away from the Soviet front and thus helped the red air force establish air superiority over the Germans. The bombing campaign also had a significant impact on war production from early in 1943, further pushing Soviet superiority upwards. The Pacific theater played a role as well. US victory in the battle of Midway convinced the Soviets that Japan would be too occupied to break the neutrality pact. Thus, more Soviet divisions could be transferred from the Far East to join the fight against the Wehrmacht. In early September 1943 the Allies landed in Italy and on June 6, 1944 in Northern France. To the Soviets, this opening of the second front in Europe came far too late: the war had already turned in the Red Army's favor. Nevertheless, from now on the Germans did have to devote part of their forces to fight British, US, and French troops, no longer only Soviets. The Soviet advance in Europe picked up speed as a result.

How the Soviet Union Won the War

None of this diminishes the centrality of the Soviet war effort for the defeat of National Socialism. The Soviets beat the Germans largely on Soviet soil, spilling the blood of Soviet citizens armed with Soviet-produced tanks, planes, artillery, automatic weapons, and rifles.

That Soviet victory in Europe helped save the world from a dark fascist future, is an ongoing source of pride in Russia and Belarus today. In other parts of Eastern Europe, the legacy of this war is much more complex, partially because of the political situation in these countries, but partially also because this war was fought with often harsh methods and at times criminal conduct. It is these aspects of the war that dominate non-Russian East European memory. They are as historically real as the fact of Soviet victory over Nazism.

We can distinguish three types of Soviet violence: troop violence, revolutionary violence, and economic violence. Economic violence could take the form of marauding by groups of soldiers or individuals. A variant was more systematic, state-led confiscations and removal of equipment and even entire factories. Both types were prompted by the extreme poverty of Soviet society and the relative plenty the Soviets encountered in the outside world. These could be understood as reparations for war damage, as in Germany, but they also happened in all other territories the Red Army marched into, even where potential allies were the victims.

Troop violence beyond what was necessary to subdue the enemy was technically illegal and could be prosecuted, although the powers that be sometimes looked the other way. Only in rare cases, for example, were direct orders given to execute prisoners of war; more often, the military leadership tried to stop its troops from such deeds. Civilians, too, became victims of unauthorized excesses, from theft to murder and rape. These were most ubiquitous in Germany, but also took place on all other territories, including the liberated Soviet heartland. They were the results of poor discipline and driven by small-group dynamics, which created and reproduced a culture of violence in the Red Army. Revenge played a major role in Germany. Changing signals from above helped unleash or restrain such violence, but they did not cause it in the first place.

Revolutionary violence was different. It was planned by the state and instituted from above. Its goal was the transformation of society and the elimination of resistance to Sovietization. At times, as in the Caucasus or Crimea, it was punitive, revenge for perceived treason and collaboration with the Germans. Mass deportations were the most prominent means of this violence.

Deportations were ubiquitous in the war years. Between 1937 and 1945, some 2.8 million Soviet subjects were forcibly removed from their places of residence. By 1949, this number had increased to 3.2 million, an average of nearly 250,000 per annum for these 13 violent years. The selection of victims continued a trend away from class and towards nationality. This shift was already evident in the 1930s, in parallel with the re-evaluation of Russia and the Russians as central pillars of the empire, but now both trends became more acute. The deportation of the Koreans in 1937 set the pattern for what was to come: peoples identified as "enemy nations" because of presumed or real links to the wartime opponent, were subject to forced relocation to the "safety" of the hinterland. To list only the most prominent of these operations: Soviet Germans were deported in 1941, Italians, Greeks, and Romanians in 1942, Kalmyks and Karachai in 1943, and, Chechens, Ingush, and Crimean Tatars in 1944.

This shift from class to nationality was, however, neither complete nor escalating. While the deportations from "old" Soviet territory were overwhelmingly national, their equivalent in the newly acquired western borderlands both in the period 1939 to 1941 and from 1944 combined class, politics, and ethnicity: during the "revolution from abroad" the victims were identified as "class enemies," "former people," or "bourgeois nationalists" and the resumption of these operations after "liberation" from the Germans followed the same pattern. Now, Lithuanian and Ukrainian nationalist resisters and their families and "kulaks" found themselves in the deportation trains.

Soviet war-making was thus extremely violent and often criminal. Counter to what common sense might suggest, however, Soviet policies were not brutalized by the war. Mass executions on the model of the "mass operations" of the Great Terror took place in Poland in 1940, and again among prisoners during the chaotic summer of 1941. Such mass killings, however, did not return in 1945, not even in Germany, where one could have expected such a course of action. Instead, the somewhat milder form of "cleansing" by deportation became widespread in Eastern Europe. The difference to the Nazi pattern of relentless radicalization is striking. Even troop violence did not escalate in one continuous cycle of violence. Rather, brutalization came and went through several waves of radicalization and de-radicalization, which historians are only beginning to understand.

Notes

1 Report on the Work of the Central Committee to the Eighteenth Congress of the C.P.S.U.(B.), https://www.marxists.org/reference/archive/stalin/works/1939/03/10. htm, accessed December 29, 2017.

2 Stuart D. Goldman, *Nomonhan, 1939. The Red Army's Victory That Shaped World War II* (Annapolis: Naval Institute Press, 2012), 5.

3 Jan T. Gross, *Revolution from Abroad. The Soviet Conquest of Poland's Western Ukraine and Western Belarus*, expanded edition (Princeton, NJ and Oxford: Princeton University Press, 2002).

4 "Lenin left us a great inheritance and we fucked it up." Alternatively translatable as "Lenin left us a great inheritance and we shat on it." Reported by A. I. Mikoian in his memoirs, published in: *Govoriat stalinskie narkomy*, ed. G. Kumanov (Smolensk: Rusich, 2005), 55–80 here: 62.

5 Geoffrey Hosking, "The Second World War and Russian National Consciousness," *Past and Present* 175 (2002): 162–86.

6 John Barber, "Popular Reactions in Moscow to the German Invasion of June 22, 1941," *Soviet Union/Union Soviétique* 18, no. 1–3 (1991): 5–18; here: 14.

7 Johannes Hürter, *A German General on the Eastern Front. The Letters and Diaries of Gotthard Heinrici, 1941–1942*, translated by Christine Brocks (Barnsley: Pen & Sword, 2014), 73.

8 Chris Bellamy, *Absolute War. Soviet Russia in the Second World War* (New York: Alfred A. Knopf, 2007), 167.

9 Karel C. Berkhoff, *Motherland in Danger: Soviet Propaganda during World War II* (Cambridge, MA: Harvard University Press, 2012), chapter 3.

Bibliography

Alexievich, Svetlana. *The Unwomanly Face of War* (London: Penguin Books, 2017).

Arad, Yitzhak. *The Holocaust in the Soviet Union* (Jerusalem: Yad Vashem, 2009).

Barber, John. "Popular Reactions in Moscow to the German Invasion of June 22, 1941," *Soviet Union/Union Soviétique* 18, no. 1–3 (1991): 5–18.

Barber, John, and Mark Harrison. *The Soviet Home Front, 1941–1945: A Social and Economic History of the USSR in World War II* (London and New York: Longman, 1991).

Berkhoff, Karel C. *Harvest of Despair. Life and Death in Ukraine under Nazi Rule* (Cambridge and London: The Belknap Press of Harvard University Press, 2004).

Berkhoff, Karel C. *Motherland in Danger. Soviet Propaganda during World War II* (Cambridge, MA: Harvard University Press, 2012).

Bischl, Kerstin. "Presenting Oneself: Red Army Soldiers and Violence in the Great Patriotic War," *History* 101 (2016): 464–79.

Brandenberger, David. *National Bolshevism: Stalinist Mass Culture and the Formation of Modern Russian National Identity, 1931–1956* (Cambridge and London: Harvard University Press, 2002).

Budnitskii, Oleg. "The Intelligentsia Meets the Enemy. Educated Soviet Officers in Defeated Germany, 1945," *Kritika: Explorations in Russian and Eurasian History* 10, no. 3 (2009): 629–82.

Budnitskii, Oleg. "The Great Patriotic War and Soviet Society: Defeatism, 1941–42," *Kritika: Explorations in Russian and Eurasian History* 15, no. 4 (2014): 767–97.

Coox, Alvin D. *Nomonhan. Japan against Russia, 1939* (Stanford: Stanford University Press, 1985).

deGraffenried, Julie. *Sacrificing Childhood. Children and the Soviet State in the Great Patriotic War* (Lawrence: University Press of Kansas, 2014).

Edele, Mark. "Militaries Compared: Wehrmacht and Red Army, 1941–1945," in: *A Companion to World War II*, ed. Thomas W. Zeiler and Daniel M. DuBois (Oxford: Wiley-Blackwell, 2013), 169–85.

Edele, Mark. "'What Are We Fighting For?' Loyalty in the Soviet War Effort, 1941–1945," *International Labor and Working-Class History* 84, no. Fall (2013): 248–68.

Edele, Mark. "The New Soviet Man as a 'Gypsy': Nomadism, War, and Marginality in Stalin's Time," *REGION: Regional Studies of Russia, Eastern Europe, and Central Asia* 3, no. 2 (2014): 285–307.

Edele, Mark. "Toward a Sociocultural History of the Soviet Second World War," *Kritika: Explorations in Russian and Eurasian History* 15, no. 4 (2014): 829–35.

Edele, Mark. "Soviet Liberations and Occupations, 1939–1949," in: *The Cambridge History of the Second World War*, ed. Richard Bosworth and Joe Maiolo (Cambridge: Cambridge University Press, 2015), 487–506.

Edele, Mark. "The Second World War as a History of Displacement. The Soviet Case," *History Australia* 12, no. 2 (2015): 17–40.

Edele, Mark. "Take (No) Prisoners! The Red Army and German Pows, 1941–1943," *The Journal of Modern History* 88 (2016): 342–79.

Edele, Mark. *Stalin's Defectors. How Stalin's Soldiers Became Hitler's Collaborators* (Oxford: Oxford University Press, 2017).

Edele, Mark. "Fighting Russia's History Wars. Vladimir Putin and the Codification of World War II in Russia," *History and Memory*, 29, No. 2 (2017): 90–124.

Edele, Mark, and Filip Slaveski. "Violence from Below: Explaining Crimes against Civilians across Soviet Space, 1943–1947," *Europe-Asia Studies* 68, no. 6 (2016): 1020–35.

Exeler, Franziska. "The Ambivalent State: Determining Guilt in the Post-World War II Soviet Union," 75, no. 3 (2016): 606–9.

Fitzpatrick, Sheila. "War and Society in Soviet Context: Soviet Labor before, during, and after World War II," *International Labor and Working-Class History* 35, no. Spring (1989): 37–52.

Gellately, Robert. *Stalin's Curse. Battling for Communism in War and Cold War* (Oxford: Oxford University Press, 2013).

Goldman, Stuart D. *Nomonhan, 1939. The Red Army's Victory that Shaped World War II* (Annapolis: Naval Institute Press, 2012).

Goldman, Wendy Z. and Donald A. Filtzer, eds. *Hunger and War. Food Provisioning in the Soviet Union During World War II* (Bloomington and Indianapolis: Indiana University Press, 2015).

Harrison, Mark, ed. *"The Economics of World War II": Six Great Powers in International Comparison* (Cambridge: Cambridge University Press, 1998).

Harrison, Mark. "World War II," in *Encyclopedia of Russian History*, ed. James R. Millar (New York: Macmillan, 2004), 1683–92.

Harrison, Mark. "The USSR and Total War. Why Didn't the Soviet Economy Collapse in 1942?"in: *A World at Total War. Global Conflict and the Politics of Destruction, 1937–1945*, ed. Roger Chickering, Stig Förster, and Bernd Greiner (Cambridge: Cambridge University Press, 2005), 137–56.

Hasegawa, Tsuyoshi. "The Soviet Factor in Ending the Pacific War. From the Neutrality Pact to Soviet Entry into the War in August 1945," in *The End of the Pacific War. Reappraisals*, ed. Tsuyoshi Hasegawa (Stanford, CA: Stanford University Press, 2007), 189–227.

Haslam, Jonathan. *The Soviet Union and the Threat from the East, 1933–1941: Moscow, Tokyo, and the Prelude to the Pacific War* (Pittsburgh, PA: University of Pittsburgh Press, 1992).

Hellbeck, Jochen. *Stalingrad: The City that Defeated the Third Reich* (New York: Public Affairs, 2015).

Hill, Alexander. "British 'Lend-Lease' Tanks and the Battle for Moscow, November–December 1941 – A Research Note." *Journal of Slavic Military Studies* 19, no. 2 (2006): 289–94.

Hill, Alexander. "The Allocation of Allied 'Lend-Lease' Aid to the Soviet Union Arriving with Convoy Pq-12, March 1942 – a State Defense Committee Decree," *Journal of Slavic Military Studies* 19, no. 4 (2006): 727–38.

Hill, Alexander. "British Lend-Lease Aid and the Soviet War Effort, June 1941–June 1942," *The Journal of Military History* 71 (2007): 773–808.

Hill, Alexander. *The Great Patriotic War of the Soviet Union, 1941–45. A Documentary Reader* (London: Routledge, 2009).

Ironside, Kristy. "Stalin's Doctrine of Price Reductions during the Second World War and Postwar Reconstruction," *Slavic Review* 75, No. 3 (2016): 655–77.

Krylova, Anna. *Soviet Women in Combat. A History of Violence on the Eastern Front* (Cambridge and New York: Cambridge University Press, 2010).

Kucherenko, Olga. *Little Soldiers: How Soviet Children Went to War 1941–1945* (New York: Oxford University Press, 2011).

Kudryashov, Sergey, and Vanessa Voisin. "The Early Stages of 'Legal Purges' in Soviet Russia (1941–1945)," *Cahiers du Monde russe* 49, no. 2/3 (2008): 263–95.

Majstorović, Vojin. "The Red Army in Yugoslavia, 1944–1945," *Slavic Review* 75, no. 2 (2016): 396–421.

Manley, Rebecca. *To the Tashkent Station. Evacuation and Survival in the Soviet Union at War* (Ithaca, NY and London: Cornell University Press, 2009).

Markwick, Roger D., and Euridice Cardona. *Soviet Women on the Frontline in the Second World War* (Basingstoke: Palgrave Macmillan, 2012).

Mawdsley, Evan. *World War II. A New History* (Cambridge: Cambridge University Press, 2009).

Mawdsley, Evan. *December 1941. Twelve Days That Began a World War* (New Haven, CT and London: Yale University Press, 2012).

Mawdsley, Evan. *Thunder in the East. The Nazi-Soviet War 1941–1945*, 2nd revised edition (London: Bloomsbury, 2016).

Merridale, Catherine. *Ivan's War. Life and Death in the Red Army, 1939–1945* (New York: Metropolitan Books, 2006).

Moskoff, William. *The Bread of Affliction; the Food Supply in the USSR during World War II* (Cambridge: Cambridge University Press, 1990).

Naimark, Norman. *The Russians in Germany. A History of the Soviet Zone of Occupation, 1945–1949* (Cambridge, MA: Harvard University Press, 1995).

Overy, Richard, *Why the Allies Won* (New York: W. W. Norton, 1997).

Pleshakov, Constantine. *Stalin's Folly. The Tragic First Ten Days of World War II on the Eastern Front* (Boston, MA and New York: Houghton Mifflin Co., 2005).

Pohl, J. Otto. *Ethnic Cleansing in the USSR, 1937–1949* (Westport, CT: Greenwood Press, 1999).

Reese, Roger. *Why Stalin's Soldiers Fought. The Red Army's Military Effectiveness in World War II* (Lawrence: University Press of Kansas, 2011).

Rieber, Alfred J. "Civil Wars in the Soviet Union," *Kritika: Explorations in Russian and Eurasian History* 4, no. 1 (2003): 129–62.

Roberts, Geoffrey. *Stalin's Wars. From World War to Cold War, 1939–1953* (New Haven, CT and London: Yale University Press, 2006).

Schechter, Brandon. "'The People's Instructions': Indigenizing the Great Patriotic War among 'Non-Russians,'" *Ab Imperio* 2012, no. 3 (2012): 109–33.

Slaveski, Filip. *The Soviet Occupation of Germany. Hunger, Mass Violence, and the Struggle for Peace, 1945–1947* (Cambridge: Cambridge University Press, 2013).

Slepyan, Kenneth. *Stalin's Guerrillas. Soviet Partisans in World War II* (Lawrence: University Press of Kansas, 2006).

Snyder, Timothy. "The Causes of Ukrainian-Polish Ethnic Cleansing 1943," *Past and Present* 179 (2003): 197–234.

Stahel, David. *Operation Barbarossa and Germany's Defeat in the East* (Cambridge: Cambridge University Press, 2009).

Stahel, David. *Kiev 1941. Hitler's Battle for Supremacy in the East* (Cambridge: Cambridge University Press, 2012).

Statiev, Alexander. *The Soviet Counterinsurgency in the Western Borderlands* (Cambridge and New York: Cambridge University Press, 2010).

Stone, David R., ed. *The Soviet Union at War, 1941–1945* (Barnsley: Pen & Sword, 2010).

Voisin, Vanessa. "Retribute or Reintegrate? The Ambiguity of Soviet Policies towards Repatriates: The Case of Kalinin Province, 1943–1950," *Jahrbücher für Geschichte Osteuropas* 55, no. 1 (2007): 34–55.

Part IV

From Warfare to Welfare

7

Normalization (1944–1957)

The Effects of World War II

As the Red Army liberated German occupied territories and then swept through Eastern Europe and Northeast Asia, the Soviet regime began to face a new set of challenges. First was expansion itself: By early September 1945, the Red Empire had reached its maximum size. The Red Army had regained all the territories lost to Germany, Romania, and Finland. Next, it had occupied much of Eastern Europe – Poland, Czechoslovakia, Hungary, Romania, Bulgaria, parts of Austria, and parts of Germany. Its furthest outpost in the northwest was the Danish Island of Bornholm; in the north, the eastern Finnmark in the far north of Norway was occupied by Soviet troops and in the Far East, Manchuria and the north of Korea were in Soviet hands, as was southern Sakhalin and the Kuril Islands. In the south, the Soviets continued to occupy northern Iran and had annexed Tuva in 1944, a hitherto nominally independent satellite next to Mongolia. Could Stalin's war-battered state really rule this enormous territory?

Second was the destruction this war had brought. Between 25 and 27 million people had died in excess to what could have been expected under normal conditions. These losses of between 14% and 15% of the population were staggering in international comparison. Only Poland suffered greater death levels, and of course Europe's Jews, who had had the most lethal war of all, having been singled out for extermination by the German genocidal machine. The Roma, another group targeted by the Nazis for extermination, lost probably about the same share as the Soviets. Germany lost considerably less, as did all other combatants. Even in China, locked in a long and terribly costly war, and

The Soviet Union: A Short History, First Edition. Mark Edele.
© 2019 John Wiley & Sons, Inc. Published 2019 by John Wiley & Sons, Inc.

in Japan, hit by two atomic bombs and more conventional carpet bombing, a smaller share of the population perished in the war. Most of the Soviet dead were civilians, but military losses were such that every fifth married woman turned a widow during this war.

Destruction and population loss were worst in the western parts of the Union, in particular in Belarus and Ukraine. It was here that the fighting, the scorched earth retreats by both sides, the guerilla wars of pro-and anti-Soviet irregulars, German genocide and counterinsurgency had combined in a perfect destructive storm. Altogether 1,710 cities and towns, above 70,000 villages, more than six million buildings, 32,000 industrial enterprises and 98,000 collective farms had been shelled, bombed, burned, or otherwise destroyed by 1945. Millions lived in dugouts. Belarus lost a quarter of its population, followed by Ukraine with 16%. The Baltic States, under a somewhat milder form of German occupation, lost between 8% (Estonia) and 14% (Latvia). Outside the fighting zones, too, wartime neglect, over-crowding, lack of sanitation, and improvised accommodation of the many wartime displaced meant that housing stock was in terrible condition. Living quarters were cramped, overcrowded, and unsanitary. As the largest Union Republic, Russia had the greatest absolute losses in population, both in terms of civilians and among soldiers, but because of its sheer size and the fact that much of it was not occupied, it lost "only" 13% of its prewar population.

The destruction was paralleled by social dislocation. Millions of war veterans returned physically impaired and emotionally damaged. Vagrants and beggars, some of them war invalids, others homeless children and youth, were ubiquitous in the cities and along the train lines they used to move from place to place. Their number increased further by the famine, which struck the country in 1946 and 1947, killing well over a million people.

Again, the borderlands were the most prominent sites of displacement. Hundreds of thousands of ethnic Germans, Finns, Poles, and Jews left the Soviet Union permanently during the war and immediately after its end. Millions of captured Red Army soldiers, civilian slave laborers, military collaborators, and civilian evacuees left temporarily; 37% of the population fell under German occupation. Over 80% of these people were recovered as the war went on, including over four million "displaced persons" (DP) and 55 million who had survived the German occupation. Other Soviet citizens were displaced within the borders of their own state, including several million deportees (about 2% of the population), evacuees and refugees to the Soviet hinterland (as many as 10% of the population). At least 18% became "military migrants" mobilized to fight in the armed forces.[1]

This was unsettlement on unprecedented scale. The Red Empire had a history of upheaval and displacement, but the second age of violence superseded both the first violent epoch of 1904–1921 and the first revolution from above of 1928–1932 in nearly every respect. We have already mentioned the escalation of deportations, but other types of displacement also exceeded precedent. During World War I, the millions mobilized to fight or into defense work made up less than 11% of the population. In 1941 to 1945, military mobilization alone touched 18%. The number of deportees grew by leaps and bounds, as did the tally of refugees. By the summer of 1917, there were approximately 7.4 million refugees and evacuees in the Russian Empire. In 1941 and 1942 alone, more than twice as many suffered a similar fate.

Only emigration was smaller in World War II than it had been in the wake of war, revolution, and civil war since 1914. During the first epoch of violence, some 1.5 to 2.5 million people had left to live abroad while the new, "second wave" of émigrés in the period 1939 to 1945 was only 0.6 million strong. This smaller number was due to the concerted efforts of the Soviet government to repatriate each and every citizen – a striking shift in attitude to potential "enemies." With the support of the western allies and at times against the resistance of those subject to the policy, the Soviets repatriated 5.4 million citizens, which included 1.8 million prisoners of war by 1946.

The massive dislocation of wartime had long-term consequences. To an extent unseen before, the war brought people of different backgrounds, education, nationality, social class, and politics into contact with each other. Easy convictions were shattered. Young urban communists were confronted with old peasants, who thought that Stalin was a hoofed demon. Anti-Bolshevik Cossack women learned that evacuated city folk also had husbands and sons fighting and dying at the front. They might be communists, but they were also mothers, daughters, sons, and siblings – human beings like any other. Kyrgyz learned that they were Soviets in encounters with both the conscription office and deported "traitor nations" dumped on their territory. Millions saw life outside the Soviet Union and could not but see that many claims about the Soviet paradise were incorrect. Ideas about alternative economic and political organization circulated with greater vigor, but hatred of the outside world also increased through these entanglements. Ethnic tensions rose, including but not limited to anti-Semitism, but the melting pot of war also fostered a new sense of connectedness between the many peoples that made up the empire.

The war engendered among the population hopes and aspirations not easily reconciled with Stalin's system – another challenge the regime had to face. The peasants longed for land and the dismantling of the collective farm system. In some regions they had decollectivized spontaneously, either in the interim between Soviet retreat and German occupation, or with German support. Even nominally "Soviet" partisans sometimes divided the land in regions they had liberated behind the lines of the Wehrmacht. Everywhere, peasants had encroached on the public lands by increasing the size of the private plot the household controlled directly. Would they be allowed to keep these additions? Would the wartime sacrifice be rewarded with dissolution of the hated collectives? In the cities, too, hopes ran high. The intelligentsia dreamed of liberalization and more freedom of expression; veterans expected a special status in return for wartime service; black marketeers hoped for a continuation of their business; and nationalists of all stripes – from Russians to Kyrgyz, from Ukrainians to Jews – strove for the advancement of their co-nationals, either within the victorious Soviet Union, or without.

Stalin rose to these challenges through a triple strategy: consolidation of the empire abroad; reconstruction of both the physical assets and the dictatorship at home; and a barely concealed campaign against the Jews as the universal, "rootless" and "cosmopolitan" enemy all other nationalities could project their resentments onto.

Consolidating the Empire

The Soviet position in September 1946 was not sustainable, given the state of exhaustion the empire was in. Thus, Stalin consolidated. Historians are divided over how to interpret this period of Soviet foreign policy: Did Stalin have a clear plan? Did he intend to expand the Soviet Union? Was the fate of Eastern Europe sealed by the time the Red Army marched in? Was the Cold War caused by the Soviets, the West, or the dynamic between the two sides?

The confrontation that became the Cold War was over-determined. The Soviets had always seen the capitalist world as a threat; and the capitalists reciprocated with fear of the specter of communism. The wartime alliance between the first communist state and the leading capitalist nations had always been an odd one, dictated by the overwhelming threat of Nazi Germany and militaristic Japan. There is considerable evidence, though, that Stalin originally intended to continue the wartime alliance. While he clearly wanted security for the Soviet Union, he had no blueprint for how this goal was to be achieved, and that he acted according to trial and error. He made tactical decisions as he went along. Stalin did not "plan" the Cold War, but he desired security for his empire. The resulting confrontation with the West was "an unwelcome but acceptable price to pay" for a secure western flank.[2]

By 1949, the result of the tactical decisions Stalin had taken in the realm of international politics was a consolidation of the prewar Soviet Empire as it had emerged by 1941, secured in the West by a ring of satellites and in the east by friendly, communist regimes in China and North Korea. The Red Army soon began to shorten its over-extended frontline, retreating from Norway in September 1945, Bornholm, Manchuria and Iran in 1946, and Korea in 1948. Stalin did not press on with the reincorporation of formerly Tsarist domains, which had not been "regathered" by the time of the German attack. (The exception was southern Sakhalin, which had been Japanese since the Treaty of

Portsmouth in 1905 but now became Soviet and the Kurile Islands, which remain a bone of contention between Russia and Japan today.) The rest of Poland was not reincorporated, but instead became a formally independent satellite. Its borders were pushed west and a population exchange brought Poles to their new nation state, while Ukrainians and Belarusians were transported east, to become citizens of the now ethnically more consolidated Belarusian and Ukrainian SSRs. Finland had to give up some additional territories, but was not forced under Soviet suzerainty. It was even spared the status of a satellite, but instead became a neutral country carefully avoiding alienating its powerful neighbor, but nevertheless building one of the most successful liberal democracies of the postwar years. In principle, this model of "Finlandization" might have been available to others in Eastern Europe, who eventually became satellites instead. Austria is a case in point: the Soviet occupation here ended in 1955 after promises of neutrality and a prohibition to unite with Germany.

The rest of Eastern Europe was less fortunate and was transformed into only nominally independent satellite states. In 1949, communist Poland, Czechoslovakia, Hungary, Romania, Bulgaria, and Albania united with the Soviet Union in the Council for Mutual Economic Assistance (Comecon), an extension of the Soviet economic empire beyond its borders. After the establishment of two German states in the same year, the Soviet-dominated German Democratic Republic (GDR) joined in 1950. In 1955, the satellites also united with their Soviet sponsor in a formal defense alliance (the Warsaw Pact) to counter the formation of the North Atlantic Treaty Organization (NATO) in 1949.

Behind the security screen these new satellites provided, the Red Empire covered approximately the same area as it had at the start of 1941. In addition, in the west, the formerly Prussian region of Königsberg became Kaliningrad region, a 6000 square mile exclave of the RSFSR; Transcarpathian Ukraine was taken from Czechoslovakia; in the north, Finland lost the Petsamo region. In the east, Southern Sakhalin and the Kurile Islands were annexed from Japan, adding 35 square miles. Overall, the Soviet territory now covered 8.6 million square miles, just slightly more than it had in June 1941. By 1959, when the first postwar census was held, the overall population had recovered to 208.8 million, up from 190 million on the eve of the German invasion. Russians made up nearly 55% of the Union's population, which was a larger share than they had had in June 1941 (below 52%), but still a much smaller percentage than before the westward expansion from 1939 (58%). The shares of Ukrainians (17.8%) and Belarusians (3.8%) were slightly up as well, despite the devastating population losses in Ukraine and Belarus during the war. This strengthening of the three large Slavic nationalities was likely due to Jews killed in the Holocaust, emigration from the Baltic republics, and the Polish–Ukrainian population exchanges, which led to ethnically much more homogenous regions in Ukraine, Belarus, and Poland.

Stalinist Reconstruction

If the consolidation of the empire abroad combined retreat with entrenchment, at home reconstruction meant a return to prewar structures, if at all possible. Stalin reasserted his personal dictatorship, which had weakened during the war due to the necessity of teamwork among the leaders. But first, the regime had to deal with those who had aided and abetted the enemy during the war. From the earliest liberations onwards, hundreds of thousands of collaborators were arrested, tried, and convicted to anything from deportation to Siberia to execution or, during the period when the death sentence was suspended (1947–1950), to 25 years labor camp with confiscation of all personal property. This was a surprisingly differentiated treatment of traitors by a state that had equated simple captivity by the enemy with treason during the war. Many liberated POWs and former forced laborers of the Germans were thus rightfully apprehensive when confronted with forced repatriation. But they, too, were treated with comparative discrimination: the majority was either re-enlisted into the army, into labor battalions, or sent home. Only a minority was arrested during the screening process in special "filtration camps." The information available during these screenings was so poor that many former military collaborators slipped through the net and returned home. Only some of them were later picked up by more regular, and increasingly professional, police investigations.

Treason was not the only result of the war that required the attention of the state in the 1940s. Breaches in the kolkhoz order had to be reversed and the black market needed to be brought under control. The intelligentsia was brought to heel through a campaign against anybody who "kowtowed before the west." Even war veterans were put back in their place. By 1948, most of the special privileges they had enjoyed at least on paper had been abolished and repeated attempts to organize frustrated. In the villages, where most of these former peasants returned to once released from the army, they found that rumors about the dissolution of the kolkhoz were unfounded and that the regime was intent on reconstructing the prewar agrarian order, or on introducing it, where it did not yet exist, such as in the Baltics or much of Western Ukraine. Soon, then, the veterans fled the villages in search of a better life in the cities – a return to prewar patterns of migration and urbanization.

Stalinist demobilization, thus, meant a return to much of the prewar status quo in the "old" Soviet Union. What did not return, however, were mass killings as in the Great Terror. There were executions both of traitors and of certain members of the elite (such as in the Leningrad affair in 1949 to 1950), but there was no relapse into the frenzy of the Great Terror. Instead, new property laws of 1947 resulted in an incredible number of arrests, swelling the Gulag population to an unprecedented 5.5 million by the time Stalin died, nearly half of them citizens who had stolen as little as a loaf of bread.

In the newly reacquired "western borderlands" (the Baltics, Western Belarus and Western Ukraine), the "revolution from abroad" returned. But even here, it was deportations, not mass executions, that were the order of the day. In 1949 and 1950 these newly Soviet areas, which had escaped collectivization (as in the Baltics) or had not seen it through (as elsewhere) had the collective farm system established and "kulaks" and their families removed. Deportations also played a major role in the pacification of these regions, as they also targeted the families of nationalist guerillas.

Beyond the reconstruction of the Soviet regime in the old territories and its imposition in the new ones, the state also faced the effects of the physical destruction the war had wrought. It needed to rebuild the country and replace the dead. The former was accomplished by a combination of state programs focusing on industry and the encouragement of private initiative to build housing. From May 1944 state loans were made available to private citizens who wanted to build their own home (often a hut or a shack). The number of personally owned dwellings thus increased by 69%, while those in control of local Soviets only rose by 23% by 1950. The concerted attempts of private citizens to look after their own needs, however, could not overcome the immense wartime destruction of already scarce housing stock. By the time of Stalin's death, the Soviet Union still faced a housing crisis of massive proportions, and the leadership knew it.

Replacing the dead was an even more complex task, which required the cooperation of rank-and-file citizen in the most intimate aspect of human life. How were the few men who had survived the war to father children to the many more women? This sexual problem became a real political worry for the leadership. The Soviets, once champions of easy divorce and legal abortion, had already turned in a pro-natalist direction in the 1930s. Pregnancy termination had been outlawed in 1936. The war's human cost pushed the government further down the same path. A tax on "bachelors, single and childless citizens of the USSR" was introduced in late 1941 and remained in force until 1958. It punished all those who did not participate in the repopulation of the country. In 1944, subsidies for single mothers and those with many children added positive incentives to the mix. Men were now liberated from responsibility for children they had fathered outside marriage in the hope that this new freedom would encourage promiscuity. These measures, together with the shortage of men, had long-term effects on the relationships between the sexes in the Soviet Union. Male irresponsibility became accepted. Women became the real centers of families and households.

Seeds of Change

As an older literature has rightly asserted, then, postwar "normalization" meant a return to the Stalinism of the prewar years, even if in a somewhat less bloodthirsty form. As historians look closer at the society that emerged from the war, however, they find a lot of dynamism under the surface of the "high Stalinism." Among educated youth oppositional Marxisms gestated, only to be quickly suppressed once such dissident leftists came to the attention of the authorities. Less overtly critical forms of youth protest, such as the "stiliagi" (a form of home-grown Soviet hipsters, who made their appearance among the privileged classes of urban society in the late 1940s) or working-class dandies who developed their own distinct style, were left more or less in peace. The same was true for religious believers, at least of Orthodox Christianity, who could practice their faith relatively unmolested, as long as they did not try to enter the communist party. More far reaching was the intellectual freedom given to physicists working on the Soviet atomic bomb project, which would produce some of the most prominent critics of later years, such as Andrei Sakharov. Stalin was well aware of the dangers this leniency might cause, but also that he needed these intellectuals to get the superweapon. "Leave them in peace," he told one of his enforcers, "we can always shoot them later."[3]

Another social formation that began to crystallize after the war was war veterans. The state did not allow them to organize and from 1948 no longer reciprocated their entitlement claims – *we fought for you, you now owe us* – with actual privileges. Nevertheless, the desires to organize and to obtain a special status in Soviet society never went away and would come into its own decades later, forming one of the pillars of late Soviet society. Until 1951, Ukraine was an exception from the general ban on veteran associations. Here, Nikita Khrushchev, party boss until 1949, allowed an organization in Kyiv to grow into a republic-level affair – something of a model for the Soviet Committee of War Veterans he would permit on an all-Union level from 1956.

The state itself was not stagnant, either. The war and its aftermath saw an incredible surge of professionalization of many aspects of statecraft. Policing became more regularized and less dependent on blunt terror; investigations into war crimes were more forensic and less reliant on producing evidence by framing, beating, or otherwise coercing the suspects; the bureaucracy became more worthy of that name, developing routine procedures and professional personnel. Thus, a modern state finally emerged, but the dictator remained unconstrained and could interfere at will – a system that has been dubbed "neo-patrimonialism."[4] Within this state, a range of reform programs were worked out, but had to be shelved because the dictator would have none of them. Some enlightened bureaucrats envisioned a comprehensive welfare state, greater social inclusivity, and a decrease in repression; architects, engineers, and town planners developed the tools and visions necessary eventually to tackle the housing crisis; others even contemplated the legalization of the black market, which could then be taxed rather than suppressed.

Some of these plans remained pipe dreams; others would form the basis of reform under Khrushchev. Meanwhile, a fundamental transformation of the urban economy did take shape, nearly unnoticed, while Stalin was still alive. The wartime decentralization of food provision to the civilian population had enforced the spread of a semi-private gardening movement. Enterprises and institutions grew their own food, but also parceled out land to their employees so they could feed their families. This encouragement of the self-sufficient family would flower into a fully blown society of weekend home owners – the "dacha," a central social and economic institution in the final decades of the Soviet Union.

Anti-Semitism

Less positive were other subterranean developments the state first tolerated and then exploited. The most important of them was the rise of anti-Semitism not just as a popular sentiment but as part of state discourse. Historians are divided over the origins of this somewhat surprising turn of events in a state where anti-anti-Semitism had been a central pillar of the official ideology ever since the revolution. Some argue that the German anti-Jewish propaganda during the war seeped across the trenches and infected the Soviet armed forces and from here society at large. Others point to anti-Semitic instances early in the war, which would be hard to explain in this manner. Instead, the war might have simply seen deeply held popular resentments bubbling to the surface. A third explanation focuses on the massive influx of Jews into the expanded Soviet Union in the wake of the Hitler-Stalin pact. A large share of this new Jewish population was then distributed across the Soviet Union by deportation, flight, and evacuation. In the context of the extreme poverty and the heated competition over housing in particular, hostility to these newcomers expressed itself in time-honored anti-Jewish outbursts.

A related question is why the state did not resist such popular moods, as it had in the past, but instead exploited, even encouraged them. From the middle of 1946 a central campaign tried to rid Soviet culture from "groveling before the West." A major cause for such "kowtowing" was said to be "rootless cosmopolitanists," a fairly transparent euphemism for Jews, who began to lose their jobs all over the Union. In 1948, the director of the Moscow State Jewish Theater, Solomon Mikhoels, was assassinated by Stalin's secret police. The theater, established in 1919, was closed. The members of the Jewish Anti-Fascist Committee (JAC), created during the war to mobilize public opinion overseas for the Soviet fight against Nazism, were arrested as "bourgeois nationalists." The publication of the *Black Book of Soviet Jewry*, a documentation of the Holocaust on Soviet territory, was shelved. In 1949, Polina Zhemchuzhina, foreign minister Viacheslav Molotov's wife, was arrested after she had been too friendly to Golda Meir, the first envoy of the newly created state of Israel. Charged with Zionism, she was sent to internal exile in Kazakhstan. From now on, things began to escalate. In August 1952, the JAC members arrested in 1948 were executed as counter-revolutionaries. In September began arrests of Jewish doctors accused of a plot to kill the Soviet leaders they had been treating. These allegations were disseminated in a vicious article in the newspaper *Pravda* in January 1953, beginning a campaign further stoking anti-Semitic passions by claiming the conspirators were Zionist terrorists in the pay of US intelligence. Further escalation ended abruptly with Stalin's death. His lieutenants had never supported this unpleasant anti-Semitism and immediately abandoned the campaign and released the doctors – to the protest of many rank-and-file Soviets.

Historians are still unsure why Stalin took this anti-Semitic turn after the war. One theory has it that he had always hated Jews, and that this trait simply affirmed itself in older age. A second explanation focuses on the foundation of the state of Israel in 1948, which transformed Jews from a minority nationality without ties to foreign countries into a diaspora group potentially loyal to another state. The self-affirmation of a Jewish sense of identity when confronted with the Holocaust only made matters worse. A third explanation sees Stalin essentially as a tactician, exploiting popular anti-Semitism to gear up for another purge of the elite. Whether or not Stalin prepared a major purge in the period 1952 to 1953, he clearly liked to keep his underlings on their toes and mobilizing popular anti-Semitism might well have been a means to do so.

A final possibility should be considered. As a Marxist, Stalin commanded a fairly sophisticated analysis of anti-Semitism as a tool of the ruling class to distract the oppressed from their real source of oppression. According to this theory, anti-Semitism was directing the resentments of the exploited against a minority instead of the source of their suffering: the system and its beneficiaries. There is no reason to believe that Stalin did not understand this theory; and there is equally no reason to believe that he was not cynical enough to turn it to his own advantage. That Jews were prominent in the Soviet elite was an asset in this context. What better way to distract from the fact that the fruits of victory tasted rotten for the large majority of the population? What better way to paper over the fact that, after demobilization was over, resources were again pumped into the military sector in preparation for war with the United States, which in the context of the proxy war in Korea seemed very much on the cards? Why not blame the Jews for the continuing misery of daily life in Stalin's warfare state? After all, it seemed to work.

Warfare and Welfare in Late Stalinism

The return of war-like mobilization in peacetime was not preordained. It was a reaction to the worsening international environment: the beginning of the Cold War. After 1945, the Soviet leadership had tried to wind back the warfare state and increase the welfare of the exhausted population. The immediate postwar years saw a radical demobilization of the army. Well over 8.5 million troops were released into civilian life between 1945 and 1948, just as the wartime alliance began to crumble into the new confrontation of the Cold War. Always cautious, Stalin kept his options open by largely demobilizing other ranks while keeping the officers in place. Should a continuation of the wartime alliance prove impossible, his army was thus prepared for escalation: the top heavy skeleton of a cadre army with a bloated officer corps could be quickly filled with the flesh of remobilized men, as indeed it was.

The demobilized men were given basic entitlements to ease their reintegration, and this welfare legislation overlapped with cover for war invalids, repatriated citizens, and recipients of major war decorations. Unlike elsewhere, however, veteran welfare did not act as a spearhead for a wider benefits system. First, much of it remained undelivered, only increasing the resentment many felt when returning to civvies. Second, by the end of 1947, most of this legislation had been dismantled and only war disabled received some assistance. Third, veterans competed for scarce resources with other nominally privileged groups, such as war widows, war orphans, wartime evacuees returning to their places of origin, the families of active servicemen, and members of the civilian service class.

Meanwhile, welfare-state building focused on the provision of medical care to the population, a field most directly connected to both the efforts at repopulation and for maintaining readiness for labor and defense. Between 1945 and 1953, the number of doctors nearly doubled and concerted efforts were made to ensure these specialists were properly qualified. Maternal mortality decreased as a result, as did death after surgery. A more universalized healthcare system began to supplement the production-based provisions of the 1930s, which had tied medical care to the place of employment. The public health outcomes of this change were impressive.

Life expectancy began to rise partially because the crisis years of the Soviet experience were over after the last Soviet famine of 1946 to 1947. Prewar production levels in wool, cotton, sugar, and shoes began to surpass prewar indicators from 1948. As operations became more routinized, the Soviet economy began to deliver respectable growth rates. In retrospect, we can see that the 1950s were the decade of the "triumph of the Soviet economy," before its eventual demise.[5] While the command system continued to produce scarcity to the end of its existence, it now produced scarcity of consumer goods rather than a catastrophic lack of everything not directly related to war making. Life did, finally, become better, if slowly.

For the time being, however, the defense sector continued to cripple civilian consumption. Under Stalin the relationship between the two fields of state action continued to be conceptualized as a zero-sum-game: if money needed to be spent on guns, less would be available to pay for butter. Defense spending constituted between 20% and 24% of the state budget in the final years of Stalinism. The atomic bomb program, central to superpower status in the new bipolar world, sucked up enormous resources, and the leadership knew it. When the Minister for Health complained about shortage of resources in healthcare, Stalin remarked dryly that the comrade "knows about the development of atomic weapons," and should therefore "understand where our resources are deployed."[6] The Soviets succeeded in building their own A-bomb in 1949, but this triumph of science and spy-craft did not end the growth of the warfare state. Instead, the Korean War (1950–1953) accelerated the trend to transfer of resources from welfare to warfare. Consumption levels dropped, consumer goods and agricultural production suffered, taxes increased, and the army grew again to a size larger than it had been on the eve of the German attack, let alone after demobilization was over in 1948.

Stalin's Death and the Succession Struggle

On March 5, 1953, Stalin died in his dacha in Kuntsevo, outside Moscow. The 74-year-old dictator had suffered a severe stroke in the night of March 1/2, and medical attention was delayed, first because nobody dared to enter his room when he did not appear in the morning, then because the country's best (Jewish) medicos were being tortured in the dungeons of the secret police in order to beat out of them confessions about their alleged plot to kill the leadership.

Reactions to the leader's death ranged from elation ("One swine fewer"[7]) to grief, even hysteria. Large crowds visited the display of the dead body, many dying in a resulting stampede. Stalin was laid next to Lenin in the mausoleum on Red Square, the faithful student united with his mentor.

Meanwhile, the affairs of state were in the hand of his immediate entourage, who pledged to rule as a collective: Georgii Malenkov, Lavrentii Beriia, Viacheslav Molotov, Klim Voroshilov, Nikita Khrushchev, Nikolai Bulganin, Lazar Kaganovich, and Anastas Mikoian. The most likely contender to destroy such collective leadership was Beriia, in charge of the security services. Afraid of the rise of a new dictator, his colleagues arrested him with the aid of the army on June 26 and sentenced him to death as an alleged spy and traitor in late December. He was shot in the head, a rag in his mouth to stifle his sobs.

Normalization and its Discontents

This execution was the last murder of a political opponent in the Stalinist tradition. From now on, losers in factional struggles would be allowed to live. This normalization of politics expressed a consensus of the ruling elite that the excesses of the 1930s were not normal politics.

Normalization also extended to wider domestic affairs. Almost immediately after the dictator's death the many reform ideas that had been brewing below the surface in the postwar years were implemented. The Gulag was dismantled, prisoners released. The anticosmopolitanism campaign came to an abrupt end, and the doctors were released. Censorship was eased, making the publication of Ilia Erenburg's landmark novel *The Thaw* possible in 1954, which would give Khrushchev's years in power their popular name. The draconian theft laws of 1947 were replaced with much more lenient legislation in 1955. Housing construction received more attention. Taxes on the collective farmers' household plots were eased, leading to a massive growth of food production. The proxy-war in Korea, which had driven the remilitarization of the Soviet Union, was ended, and the number of Soviet troops was reduced in 1953, 1955, and 1956. The counter-productive abortion ban was abolished in 1955, with positive public health results. The ban, intended to increase the birth rate, instead had only led to a growth of illegal terminations and the inevitable injury or even death of women undergoing them.

Internationally, however, the political thaw did not translate into a liberalization of rule over the perimeter of satellites surrounding the empire. If anything, the opposite happened. When workers struck in East Berlin on June 16 and June 17, 1953, demanding lower working norms and the resignation of the communist government, a massive military response by the Soviet Union quashed the uprising. The pictures of civilians hurdling stones against tanks became icons of the Cold War.

Domestically, too, liberalization did not mean decommunization. There were some radical campaigns, driven by ideological zeal and revolutionary enthusiasm. The best known of these was the "Virgin Lands Campaign." Conceived in 1953 and begun in 1954, it attempted to bring hitherto untilled land in Siberia, Kazakhstan, the Caucasus, and the Volga under the plow. Komsomol youth were mobilized in the honored tradition of Soviet propaganda, which promised adventure and self-fulfillment while also building communism and thus contributing to the public good. As an attempt to overcome food shortages without giving up the Stalinist antimarket fundamentalism, it was a failure in more than one regard. The results for agricultural output were meager at best, and the social problems created in tent cities swarming with uprooted young men were impressive. Riots became a common phenomenon in the "virgin lands" and the campaign was one example of the silly schemes dreamt up by Khrushchev.

Secret Speech

Meanwhile, the First Secretary planned his boldest move yet. The context was the ongoing struggle for supremacy within the leadership team, which had taken control of the empire after Stalin's death. Like many a man with a vision,

Khrushchev found it hard to work within a collegial framework. Sooner or later, the collective leadership thus had to come to an end. Khrushchev took his chance to position himself ahead of his colleagues in 1956, with what was maybe the most famous speech of the entire Soviet experience.

"On the Cult of Personality and Its Consequences" was delivered to a closed session of the Twentieth Party Congress in February 1956. It amounted to a carefully calibrated denunciation of Stalin while defending much of the policies of Stalinism, which Khrushchev of course had helped to implement. After citing Marxist classics about the inadmissibility of personality cults in a communist party, Khrushchev cited Lenin's late recognition of Stalin's rudeness and the conflict between the late leader of the Party and the General Secretary over boorish remarks towards Krupskaya, Lenin's wife. This set the tone for much of the speech, which contrasted Lenin's stern but fair leadership with Stalin's egocentric brutality. Curiously, however, most of Stalin's policies turned out to be correct: the fight against the various oppositions, dekulakization and collectivization, and the building of the hyper-centralized warfare state in the prewar years were all fine in Khrushchev's opinion. It was only the extermination of "honest communists" in the Great Terror that Khrushchev abhorred, not the general direction of Stalinism. Citing Lenin, he approved of terror if it was "necessitated by the resistance of the exploiting classes" in an "era when the exploiting classes existed and were powerful." This situation no longer existed in 1937 and 1938 and the victims of Stalin's terror were "honest workers of the Party and of the Soviet state." No mention was made of the simple fact that nonparty people made up the largest number of victims of Stalin's repressions. They did not matter to Khrushchev.

In a momentous juncture in the construction of the Soviet memory of the Great Patriotic War, Khrushchev also pinned all setbacks in the war on Stalin. Stalin knew from a variety of sources that the Germans would attack; Stalin chose to ignore these warnings; Stalin thus was to blame for the catastrophe of 1941. The situation was made worse by poor preparation and equipment of the army (Stalin's fault), Stalin's elimination of many military cadres in the Great Terror, and Stalin's alleged retreat from the leadership once the catastrophe of the German invasion became clear. "Therefore, the threatening danger which hung over our Fatherland in the initial period of the war was largely due to Stalin's very own faulty methods of directing the nation and the Party." Everything else that went wrong in this war, too, was the result of Stalin's "nervousness and hysteria;" the leader was constantly "interfering with actual military operations" and "planned operations on a globe." Khrushchev, who had served on the frontline and was proud of it, was particularly bitter about Stalin's postwar appropriation of all military honors for himself. "In various ways he tried to inculcate the notion that the victories gained by the Soviet nation during the Great Patriotic War were all due to the courage, daring, and genius of Stalin and of no one else." This focus on Stalin was wrong: "Not Stalin, but the Party as a whole, the Soviet Government, our heroic Army, its talented leaders and brave soldiers, the whole Soviet nation – these are the ones who assured victory in the Great Patriotic War."

Khrushchev also raised the case of the mass deportations of national minorities during the war, "together with all Communists and Komsomols without any exception," as another of Stalin's crimes. This section of the speech ended with the remarkable claim that "Ukrainians avoided meeting this fate only because there were too many of them and there was no place to which to deport them." This was the closest Khrushchev came to acknowledging the victimization of ordinary citizens, rather than communists. Moving to the postwar years he again shifted to the victimization of the elite in the Leningrad (1949–1950) and Mingrelian Affairs (1951–1952) as well as the Doctors' Plot (1953). His own participation in the murder of Beriia after Stalin's death seems to have weighed on Khrushchev's consciousness, as he spent a large section of the speech on this renegade's crimes against the party, concluding that "he assisted Stalin in everything and acted with his support." Leaving such dangerous territory, the First Secretary then recalled with bitterness and in great detail Stalin's own involvement in the creation of his personality cult before moving to an extensive discussion about how the dictator had been able to take control of the party. The speech ended in a call "to restore completely the Leninist principles of Soviet socialist democracy, expressed in the Constitution of the Soviet Union, to fight willfulness of individuals abusing their power."[8]

The Secret Speech was a bombshell. It caused a crisis in the international Communist movement. In the west, many intellectuals left the Party, because they were unable to confront the fact that they had willingly accepted lies about Soviet crimes for decades. Others refused to reform, founding Stalinist splinter parties, which, incredibly, are still alive today in places as distant as Australia. In the Soviet Union itself, the speech ushered in a period of excited discussion among the educated all over the empire. Reactions went well beyond the permissible, demanding more far-reaching democratization of the system. Others were critical of the demotion of Stalin from a genius to a political criminal. In Georgia, days of, at times violent, demonstrations followed the realization that the nation's greatest son had fallen out of favor. The politics of these protests were varied and indeed confused. Calls for secession were heard alongside calls to preserve Stalin's legacy. What united the demonstrators was their dismay at Khrushchev. The republic had to be brought to heel by a military crackdown.

Dangerous Liberalization

Decisions to liberalize certain aspects of the postwar order, taken in the wake of the Twentieth Party Congress, quickly moved beyond the control of the center. The ban on forming a veterans' organization was finally lifted in 1956, but only as a propaganda measure. The Soviet Union wanted to join the World Veterans' Federation in order to counter anti-Soviet views espoused by the American Legion in this international umbrella organization. In order to do so, the Soviet Union needed its own veterans' union, which the leadership duly tried to create as a front organization with no real domestic role. Khrushchev's experience with a staunchly loyal union of old soldiers in postwar Ukraine helped to facilitate the shift. To allow the veterans of Stalin's war to organize was hardly a revolutionary endeavor. However, it proved hard to control.

The war veterans who were drafted to fill the positions in this *Potemkin* organization, consistently misunderstood the goal of the Soviet Committee of War Veterans (SKVV). They saw it as a lobbying group for the needs and desires of veterans and began to organize their own, unauthorized and technically illegal groups in a range of localities once they had returned from the founding congress in Moscow. This spontaneous self-organization within the context of a misunderstood Soviet institution would set the pattern for the relationship between the Soviet veterans' movement and the state for the decades to come.

The organized veterans misunderstood the central party line, but they did not challenge the overall political system. Other reactions to liberalization were more serious. One was the rehabilitation of some of the "punished peoples" of World War II, in particular the Chechen and Ingush, whose status as "special settlers" was revoked and whose autonomous republic was recreated in January 1957. What followed was uncontrolled and unauthorized migration from Kazakhstan back to the Caucasus. The authorities tried to stem the tide with ad-hoc detentions and roadblocks, but ultimately were unsuccessful. The returning mountaineers began to clash with the migrants from elsewhere in the Soviet Union, who had taken their homes and lands after the war. Interethnic tensions, and violence, thus increased as a result of liberalization.

The most serious reactions to the secret speech came from Eastern Europe. In late-October 1956, student demonstrations in Budapest sparked an anticommunist rebellion all over Hungary, leading to the downfall of the communist regime and the installation of a new government intent on leaving the Warsaw Pact to become a neutral country like Austria. After some hesitation, Khrushchev decided to crush the rebellion with military force. By November 10, the Hungarian revolution was history, making it clear that the Soviet Empire would not allow a breach in its defensive perimeter of satellites in the west.

Leadership Challenge

Eventually, the unrest caused by liberalization caught up with the Soviet leader. In the debates about how to react to Hungary, Khrushchev faced opposition from hardliners within the Party, who, not unreasonably, blamed the Secret

Speech for the uprising. Soon, they moved to depose the First Secretary, who had further aggravated them by trying to decentralize the state bureaucracy, in particular the economic management of the country. This attempt to weaken central power appears to have been the final straw. Molotov, Malenkov, and Kaganovich moved to sack Khrushchev in June 1957. The conspirators had a majority in the Presidium of the Communist Party (as the Politburo was now called), the central decision making body. However, formally only the Central Committee itself could replace a First Secretary, a provision Khrushchev, who had built strong networks of clients all through the Party apparatus, managed to exploit. With the backing of Minister of Defense and World War II hero Zhukov, whom Khrushchev had praised in the Secret Speech and who mobilized military planes to fly in delegates from all over the Union, Khrushchev managed to turn the tables on his former comrades. The Central Committee re-elected Khrushchev.

His opponents were dubbed the "Anti-Party Group" and were removed from the leadership. In a major innovation in Soviet politics, however, they were not executed. Instead, Molotov was sent to Mongolia, to become the ambassador in the Soviet satellite, while Kaganovich and Malenkov were appointed directors of enterprises in the Soviet provinces. For the first time since the 1930s, then, the losers of a factional struggle kept their lives. The years of "living dangerously in Soviet politics" were over.[9]

Notes

1   The term belongs to Joshua A. Sanborn, "Unsettling the Empire: Violent Migrations and Social Disaster in Russia during World War I," *Journal of Modern History* 77, no. 2 (2005): 290–324.

2   Mark Kramer, "Stalin, Soviet Policy, and the Establishment of a Communist Bloc in Eastern Europe, 1941–1948," in: *Stalin and Europe. Imitation and Domination, 1928–1953*, ed. Timothy Snyder and Ray Brandon (Oxford: Oxford University Press, 2014), 264–94, here: 265.

3   David Holloway, *Stalin and the Bomb. The Soviet Union and Atomic Energy 1939–1956* (New Haven, CT and London: Yale University Press, 1994), 211.

4   Yoram Gorlizki, "Ordinary Stalinism: The Council of Ministers and the Soviet Neopatrimonal State, 1946–1953," *The Journal of Modern History*, vol. 74, no. 4 (2002): 699–736.

5   G. I. Khanin, "The 1950s – the Triumph of the Soviet Economy," *Europe-Asia Studies* 55, no. 8 (2003): 1187–212.

6   A. A. Danilov and A. V. Pyzhikov, *Rozhdenie sverkhderzhavy. SSSR v pervye poslevoennye gody* (Moscow: Rosspen, 2001), 114.

7   O. V. Edel'man et al. (ed.), *58–10 nadzornye proizvodstva prokuratury SSSR po delam ob antisovetskoi agitatsii i propagande. Annotirovannyi katalog mart 1953–1991* (Moscow: Demokratiia, 1999), 13.

8   Quotations in this and the previous paragraph are taken from *Speech to 20th Congress of the C.P.S.U.* https://www.marxists.org/archive/khrushchev/1956/02/24.htm (last accessed January 2, 2018).

9   Sheila Fitzpatrick, *On Stalin's Team. The Years of Living Dangerously in Soviet Politics* (Melbourne: Melbourne University Press, 2015).

Bibliography

Blackwell, Martin J. *Kyiv as Regime City: The Return of Soviet Power after Nazi Occupation* (Rochester, NY: University of Rochester Press, 2016).

Brent, Jonathan, and Vladimir P. Naumov. *Stalin's Last Crime. The Plot against the Jewish Doctors, 1948–1953* (New York: Perennial, 2003).

Burton, Christopher. "Minzdrav, Soviet Doctors, and the Policing of Reproduction in the Late Stalinist Years," *Russian History/Histoire Russe* 27, no. 2 (2000): 197–221.

Burton, Christopher. "Soviet Medical Attestation and the Problem of Professionalisation under Late Stalinism, 1945–1953," *Europe-Asia Studies* 57, no. 8 (2005): 1211–29.

Dale, Robert. *Demobilized Veterans in Late Stalinist Leningrad. Soldiers to Civilians* (London: Bloomsbury Academic, 2015).

Dobson, Miriam. *Khrushchev's Cold Summer. Gulag Returnees, Crime, and the Fate of Reform after Stalin* (Ithaca, NY and London: Cornell University Press, 2009).

Duskin, Eric. *Stalinist Reconstruction and the Confirmation of a New Elite, 1945–1953* (New York: Palgrave, 2001).

Edele, Mark. "Strange Young Men in Stalin's Moscow: The Birth and Life of the Stiliagi, 1945–1953," *Jahrbücher für Geschichte Osteuropas* 50, no. 1 (2002): 37–61.

Edele, Mark. *Soviet Veterans of the Second World War. A Popular Movement in an Authoritarian Society, 1941–1991* (Oxford: Oxford University Press, 2008).

Edele, Mark. "Veterans and the Village: The Impact of Red Army Demobilization on Soviet Urbanization, 1945–1955," *Russian History* 36, no. 2 (2009): 159–82.

Edele, Mark. *Stalinist Society 1928–1953* (Oxford: Oxford University Press, 2011).

Edele, Mark. "Veterans and the Welfare State: World War II in the Soviet Context," *Comparativ. Zeitschrift für Globalgeschichte und vergleichende Gesellschaftsforschung* 20, no. 5 (2011): 18–33.

Edele, Mark. "The Impact of War and the Costs of Superpower Status," *The Oxford Handbook of Modern Russian History* (online), ed. Simon Dixon, November 2015. At: http://www.oxfordhandbooks.com/view/10.1093/oxfordhb/9780199236701.001.0001/oxfordhb-9780199236701-e-028, accessed January 6, 2018.

Edele, Mark. "Soviet Liberations and Occupations, 1939–1949," in: *The Cambridge History of the Second World War*, ed. Richard Bosworth and Joe Maiolo (Cambridge: Cambridge University Press, 2015), 487–506.

Edele, Mark. "The Second World War as a History of Displacement. The Soviet Case," *History Australia* 12, No. 2 (2015): 17–40.

Edele, Mark, Sheila Fitzpatrick, and Atina Grossmann, eds. *Shelter from the Holocaust: Rethinking Jewish Survival in the Soviet Union* (Detroit: Wayne State University Press, 2017).

Fieseler, Beate. "The Bitter Legacy of the 'Great Patriotic War.' Red Army Disabled Soldiers under Late Stalinism," in: *Late Stalinist Russia. Society between Reconstruction and Reinvention*, ed. Juliane Fürst (London and New York: Routledge, 2006), 46–61.

Fieseler, Beate. "The Soviet Union's 'Great Patriotic War' Invalids: The Poverty of a New Status Group," *Comparativ. Zeitschrift für Globalgeschichte und vergleichende Gesellschaftsforschung* 20, no. 5 (2010): 34–49.

Filtzer, Donald. *Soviet Workers and Late Stalinism. Labour and the Restoration of the Stalinist System after World War II* (Cambridge and New York: Cambridge University Press, 2002).

Filtzer, Donald A. *The Hazards of Urban Life in Late Stalinist Russia. Health, Hygiene, and Living Standards, 1943–1953* (Cambridge and New York: Cambridge University Press, 2010).

Fitzpatrick, Sheila. "War and Society in Soviet Context: Soviet Labor before, during, and after World War II," *International Labor and Working-Class History* 35, no. Spring (1989): 37–52.

Fitzpatrick, Sheila. "The World of Ostap Bender: Soviet Confidence Men in the Stalin Period," *Slavic Review* 61, no. 3 (2002): 535–57.

Fitzpatrick, Sheila. "Social Parasites. How Tramps, Idle Youth, and Busy Entrepreneurs Impeded the Soviet March to Communism," *Cahier du Monde russe* 47, no. 1–2 (2006): 377–408.

Fitzpatrick, Sheila. *On Stalin's Team. The Years of Living Dangerously in Soviet Politics* (Melbourne: Melbourne University Press, 2015).

Florin, Moritz. "Becoming Soviet through War: The Kyrgyz and the Great Fatherland War," *Kritika: Explorations in Russian and Eurasian History* 17, no. 3 (2016): 495–516.

Fürst, Juliane, ed. *Late Stalinist Russia. Society between Reconstruction and Reinvention* (London and New York: Routledge, 2006).

Fürst, Juliane. *Stalin's Last Generation. Soviet Post-War Youth and the Emergence of Mature Socialism* (Oxford: Oxford University Press, 2010).

Gellately, Robert. *Stalin's Curse. Battling for Communism in War and Cold War* (Oxford: Oxford University Press, 2013).

Gorlizki, Yoram, and Oleg Khlevniuk. *Cold Peace. Stalin and the Soviet Ruling Circle, 1945–1953* (Oxford and New York: Oxford University Press, 2004).

Hachten, Charles. "Separate Yet Governed: The Representation of Soviet Property Relations in Civil Law and Public Discourse," in: *Borders of Socialism. Private Spheres of Soviet Russia*, ed. Lewis Siegelbaum (New York and Basingstoke: Palgrave Macmillan, 2006), 65–82.

Heinzen, James. *The Art of the Bribe. Corruption under Stalin, 1943–1953* (New Haven, CT and London: 2016).

Hessler, Julie. "A Postwar Perestroika? Toward a History of Private Trade Enterprise in the USSR," *Slavic Review* 57, no. 3 (1998): 516–42.

Holloway, David. *Stalin and the Bomb. The Soviet Union and Atomic Energy 1939–1956* (New Haven, CT and London: Yale University Press, 1994).

Jones, Jeffrey W. *Everyday Life and the "Reconstruction" of Soviet Russia during and after the Great Patriotic War, 1943–1948* (Bloomington, IN: Slavica Publishers, 2008).

Kostyrchenko, Gennadii. *Out of the Red Shadows: Anti-Semitism in Stalin's Russia* (Amherst, MA: Prometheus Books, 1995).

Kozlov, Vladimir A. *Mass Uprisings in the USSR. Protest and Rebellion in the Post-Stalin Years* (Armonk, NY: M. E. Sharpe, 2002).

Lovell, Stephen. *Summerfolk. A History of the Dacha, 1719–2000* (Ithaca and London: Cornell University Press, 2003).

Lovell, Stephen. *The Shadow of War. Russia and the USSR 1941 to the Present* (Oxford: Wiley-Blackwell, 2010).

McBride, Jared. "Peasants into Perpetrators: The OUN-UPA and the Ethnic Cleansing of Volhynia, 1943–1944," *Slavic Review* 75, no. 3 (2016): 630–54.

McCallum, Claire E. "The Return: Postwar Masculinity and the Domestic Space in Stalinist Visual Culture, 1945–53," *Russian Review* 74, no. 1 (2015): 117–43.

McCallum, Claire E. "Scorched by the Fire of War: Masculinity, War Wounds and Disability in Soviet Visual Culture, 1941–65," *The Slavonic and East European Review* 93, no. 2 (2015): 251–85.

Nakachi, Mie. "N. S. Khrushchev and the 1944 Soviet Family Law: Politics, Reproduction, and Language," *East European Politics and Societies* 20, no. 1 (2006): 40–68.

Nakachi, Mie. "Population, Politics and Reproduction: Late Stalinism and its Legacy," in: *Late Stalinist Russia. Society between Reconstruction and Reinvention*, ed. Juliane Fürst (London and New York: Routledge, 2006), 167–91.

Qualls, Karl. *From Ruins to Reconstruction. Urban Identity in Soviet Sevastopol after World War II* (Ithaca, NY and London: Cornell University Press, 2009).

Rieber, Alfred J. *Stalin and the Struggle for Supremacy in Eurasia* (Cambridge: Cambridge University Press, 2015).

Rubenstein, Joshua, and Al'tman, Il'ia, eds. *The Unknown Black Book: the Holocaust in the German-Occupied Soviet Territories* (Bloomington: Indiana University Press, 2008).

Shearer, David R. *Policing Stalin's Socialism. Repression and Social Order in the Soviet Union, 1924–1953* (New Haven, CT and London: Yale University Press, 2009).

Slezkine, Yuri. *The Jewish Century* (Princeton, NJ: Princeton University Press, 2004).

Smith, Mark B. "Individual Forms of Ownership in the Urban Housing Fund of the USSR, 1944–64," *Slavonic and East European Review* 86, no. 2 (2008): 283–305.

Smith, Mark B. *Property of Communists: The Urban Housing Program from Stalin to Khrushchev* (DeKalb: Northern Illinois University Press, 2010).

Taubman, William. *Khrushchev. The Man and His Era* (New York and London: W. W. Norton & Co., 2003).

Veidlinger, Jeffrey. *The Moscow State Yiddish Theater. Jewish Culture on the Soviet Stage* (Bloomington and Indianapolis: Indiana University Press, 2000).

Weiner, Amir. *Making Sense of War. The Second World War and the Fate of the Bolshevik Revolution* (Princeton, NJ and Oxford: Princeton University Press, 2001).

Zubkova, Elena. *Russia after the War. Hopes, Illusions, and Disappointments, 1945–1957*, translated by Hugh Ragsdale (Armonk, NY and London: M. E. Sharpe, 1998).

Zubkova, Elena. "The Soviet Regime and Soviet Society in the Postwar Years: Innovations and Conservatism, 1945–1953," *Journal of Modern European History* 2, no. 1 (2004): 144–45.

8

Mature Socialism (1956–1985)

Housing Revolution

Approximately one month after his victory over the "Anti-Party Group" in 1957 Khrushchev launched what one historian has called "the greatest housing program in the world."[1] The July 31 decree "On the Development of Housing Construction within the USSR" began unprecedented building activity. Within the next half a decade millions of prefabricated houses were built at incredible speed. The construction was often shabby and incomplete. These five-story housing blocks did not age well. Nevertheless, the "Khrushchev houses" (*khrushchevki*) were a major improvement over the barracks, communal apartments, dugouts, or self-constructed shacks much of the population had called home before. With individual apartments for families they provided at last some basic privacy; equipped with a toilet and a small bathroom they were a major advance in public health; and with a small kitchen in each unit, they freed women from the perennial fights in communal cooking facilities. At long last, they provided a space where family and friends could sit, drink, eat, sing, and talk. Shabby and depressing as they look to a twenty-first century observer, the "Khrushchev slums" (*khrushcheby*) showed that the state had finally begun to care about the basic needs of the long-suffering population.

Khrushchev's housing program, then, was a double rift in Soviet history. First, it shifted the initiative for housing construction for the vast majority of the population from individuals and their families to the state. The major policy of the Stalin period as far as reconstruction of residential buildings was concerned, was the May 1944 decree making state loans available to citizens desiring to

The Soviet Union: A Short History, First Edition. Mark Edele.
© 2019 John Wiley & Sons, Inc. Published 2019 by John Wiley & Sons, Inc.

build their own home (usually a wooden construction, often not more than a hut or a shack). Personally owned houses in the cities, therefore, increased by 69% in 1950, while housing controlled by local government (Soviets) only rose by 23%. Private initiative, not the state, was the most important source for the reconstruction of residential space in the late Stalin years. From 1957, the state stepped in to a degree hitherto unseen.

It did so at an opportune time. The Russian Empire had been an overwhelmingly rural place, with a few cities housing a minority. The Soviet Union, by contrast, had become a more and more urban country ever since the massive migration to the cities in the first Five-Year Plan. The trend continued, and by 1959 48% of Soviet citizens were urbanites. Ongoing urbanization made dealing with the housing crisis more difficult. Together with overall population growth (the 1959 census counted nearly 209 million people in the empire), the shift to living in the city prevented the state from ever satisfying demand for new homes. Nevertheless, the command economy proved able to ease significantly the pressure for millions – a real urban revolution (which came, as usual, "from above.")

The new focus on the housing of the population was part of a more general move of government attention from warfare to welfare. This shift had begun with Stalin's death, as discussed in Chapter 7: it had included the ending of the Korean War, the reduction of troop numbers, the dismantling of the Gulag, and increased attention to housing construction. Under Khrushchev, this change of focus truly came into its own.

Pension Reform

One landmark policy preceded Khrushchev's final victory in the succession struggle: the Law on State Pensions of July 14, 1956. It simplified, unified, and extended the pension system to larger sectors of the urban population. Nearly to the day eight years later, a new law of July 15, 1964 applied these benefits to collective farmers, who had been considered second-class citizens since collectivization. Together, these legal acts and their implementation "amounted to one of the most significant reforms of the Khrushchev era."[2] Social insurance budgets exploded as a result, rising from 18 billion rubles in 1950 to 72 billion ten years later to reach 171 billion in 1970. The number of pensioners rose from 4 million in 1940, to nearly 19 million in 1960 and above 40 million 10 years later.

Despite such numbers, historians still debate if the Soviet Union can be described as a welfare state. Some embrace the label, and date its advent back to the 1930s or the late-Stalinist years. Others point out, correctly in my view, that during those decades, welfare existed only in the realm of political rhetoric, or was part of the mobilizational regime, thus, in the final instance an aspect of the warfare state. Still others dispute that the Khrushchevian Soviet Union can be labeled a "welfare state," because provisions were so all-encompassing that they outstripped anything categorized under this term in capitalist societies. This argument relies on a fairly technical definition of what a welfare state is, which seems too narrow for our purposes here. Seen in the longer trajectory of Soviet history, the central point is that a transition was made, which displaced warfare from the center of the Soviet project and put welfare in its place.

Motivations for Socialist Welfare

Why this shift? Part of the explanation is ideological. The Bolshevik revolutionaries had never intended to build a barracks state where people lived in poverty and could barely feed their families, while heavy industry churned out tank after tank, and people disappeared into labor camps or mass graves. Instead, the revolution had promised "communism": from each according to ability, to each according to need. No state, no money, no police, no religion, no exploitation, but freedom and self-actualization for all. That this utopia had never arrived might not surprise people living in more sobering times, but the extent of the squalor in which most Soviets were forced to live in provided an extreme contrast to official aspirations. And contemporaries knew it, raging about the vast canyon between the communism they had been promised and the "hungerism" and "expensivism" they saw all around themselves.[3] Khrushchev was determined to eliminate this gap. Once the Soviet state seemed fairly secure, defended by a ring of satellites and a shield of atomic weapons, it was time to make good on the promises to build a good life for working people. Stalin had already announced that "socialism" had been achieved in 1936, a major disappointment in a country, where living standards had not recovered to the 1928 standard. Now the higher stage of "communism" was on the horizon, as the new program of the Communist Party of 1961 announced optimistically.

According to this vision, by 1970, the United States would be surpassed in per capita production. "The people's standard of living and their cultural and technical standards" would "improve substantially" and "everyone will live in easy circumstances." "Hard physical work" would "disappear" and Soviet citizens would enjoy "the shortest working day." Only with regards to real estate a more cautious formulation was chosen: "the demand of Soviet people for well-appointed housing will, in the main, be satisfied."

But then, this was just the beginning. In the following 10 years, things would become even more satisfying:

> The material and technical basis of communism will be built up by the end of the second decade (1971–80), ensuring an abundance of material and cultural values for the whole population; Soviet society will come close to a stage where it can

introduce the principle of distribution according to needs, and there will be a gradual transition to one form of ownership – public ownership. Thus, a communist society will in the main be built in the USSR. The construction of communist society will be fully completed in the subsequent period.[4]

These were not the words of a "retiring revolution." This was Marxist utopianism at its best, animating a leadership intent on actually building what, 45 years earlier, the revolution had been made for.[5]

Marxist utopianism, then, fueled the building of the Soviet welfare state. The war, too, played its role. It had driven home to the leaders how dependent they were on the sacrifice of rank-and-file citizens. Many, including Khrushchev, came out of the war with a sense that they owed the people. Even Stalin expressed such thoughts after the war, when he spoke of the trust the Russian people had shown in the government during the war, or when he toasted the "screws" making up the machine of the state.[6] He, of course, did not act on such grudging feelings of gratitude but Khrushchev did.

Competition with the West was another component of the shift towards the welfare state. As developed capitalist countries reacted to the double challenge of fascism and Soviet socialism, they developed welfare systems shielding their citizens from the worst risks of market economies. In the long term, the Soviets could not ignore that living conditions were higher in "the West." Through its ring of satellites, the Red Empire now extended far into central Europe; it bordered on one of the most dynamic postwar countries – West Germany – and living standards there could not be kept a secret. Capitalist prosperity thus served as a constant taunt to rulers who claimed to have built the first socialist state in the world. Proletarians surely were meant to live better under socialism than under the rule of capital. One could, of course, seal the borders and build a wall, as the Soviets did in Berlin in 1961, but this only highlighted that "Socialism" could not keep its citizens with anything but coercive means.

The new focus on the living conditions of ordinary Soviets was popular. During the Stalin years, even critics of the regime often embraced the officially promoted vision of a society where education, healthcare, and housing were free and where everyday people lived on a diet of "caviar with champagne."[7] Under conditions of decreased coercion, moreover, citizens had new ways of expressing their dismay. When in 1961 to 1962 the regime tried to get on top of economic imbalances through the combination of currency reform, increase of work norms, and price rises for food, protests, strikes, and disturbances erupted throughout Russia and Ukraine. The most famous uprising occurred in Novocherkassk in 1962, which was put down by troops sent in by the central leadership. These disturbances drove home the message that, absent mass repression on a Stalinist scale, only increased or at least sustained welfare would guarantee social peace. Rather than resorting to further repression, the regime began importing grain in 1963 in order to keep prices low and the population content. Remarkably, then, the social contract between the regime and the population in the "first socialist country," supposedly well on its way to "communism," became dependent on the capitalist world market.

The Thermonuclear Welfare State

The shift to welfare did not mean to neglect warfare. Khrushchev was not a wide-eyed idealist who thought that an army was not necessary in a world of armed superpower rivalry. Indeed, military strength in the international arena was seen as a precondition of transforming the Soviet Union from a warfare into a welfare state. Grasping the perverse potential of nuclear weapons to frighten the enemy into avoiding aggression, he gambled on their peace-making potential. By late 1955, both the United States and the Soviet Union had the bombs and planes necessary for this tactic of deterrence. Soon, they would add intercontinental missiles to the mix, a field the Soviets took a lead in. They successfully tested long-range rockets in 1957, before demonstrating their ability by shooting the first satellite into space later in the same year. The "Sputnik shock" ("beep, beep") was followed by an even greater coup: the first human being to rocket beyond the earth's atmosphere – Iurii Gagarin in 1961. Clearly, the command economy was able to deliver. Such achievements obliged the West to follow suit, as it did with copies of the Soviet way of doing things: The United States' National Aeronautics and Space Administration (NASA) or the Australian Institute of Sport (AIS) even copied the Soviet love for acronyms. More substantially, they replaced the spontaneity of the market with state planning and centralized allocation of resources. The success of such imitation was resounding. Forgetting about the niceties of liberal economics allowed the United States to put the first man on the moon; Australia, a comparatively small nation, became a great sporting power punching well above its weight in international competitions.

Investing heavily in the military-industrial and international sporting arenas, the Soviet Union also continued to build housing at home, grow its pension fund, and spend prolifically on other welfare measures. How could that be done? Did one not have to decide between guns and butter? Was there no trade-off between international prestige and domestic development? Khrushchev thought the two could be combined. His tactic was to build nuclear and rocket forces, which could act as a shield against attack, and then demobilize the now irrelevant land forces. The released manpower and resources could then be put to use to increase the standard of living of the population, to provide better and more consumer goods, build more apartments, introduce a pension system – in one word: focus on welfare rather than warfare. This plan, however, came with both domestic and international risks. At home, it alienated the military and its supporters in the military-industrial complex; abroad, it brought the world to the brink of nuclear war when Khrushchev tried to make the threat to the United States real by stationing nuclear ballistic missiles in Cuba in 1962.

Despite the enormous amount of resources thus committed to nuclear arms and the space race the civilian economy improved steadily under Khrushchev. The shift from a crisis economy to a more normal economy of scarcity had been accomplished already by the early 1950s. Adjustments to agricultural policy eased the plight of the collective farms and increased productivity. By 1960, 15 years after the end of World War II, finally, food consumption levels approximating 1928 were reached again in the "old" Soviet Union. The destruction wrought by Stalin's revolutions from above and World War II had finally been overcome. Elsewhere, it took longer: many citizens in the Baltics, which had started from a higher baseline, still consumed fewer eggs and less meat or dairy products than they had before the Soviet annexation. Moreover, the agricultural recovery was short lived. By the early 1960s, problems returned – leading to the unrest described above.

"The Thaw"

For the majority of the population, the material recovery, the housing construction boom, the better nutrition, and the increased social security were the most tangible results of the Khrushchev years. For intellectuals and the educated public, however, another aspect loomed at least as large: cultural and political liberalization. Indeed, Khrushchev's years in power have gone down in history as "the Thaw," named after a 1954 novel of the same name. And indeed, the cultural deep freeze of the Stalin years melted away. The Secret Speech of 1956, discussed in Chapter 7, marked the beginning of a far-reaching de-Stalinization. Censorship was relaxed, foreign, noncommunist literature was published in translation, and formerly banned Soviet authors re-emerged from their internal exile. In July 1957, tens of thousands of youth from all over the world attended the Festival of Youth and Students, held in Moscow. It became the site of unprecedented contact between young Soviets and their coevals from elsewhere. A mini baby boom with international parentage followed nine months later, worrying the authorities, as did the increasingly popular scene of song and poetry of the so-called "bards." Bulat Okudzhava, Vladimir Vysotskii, and Aleksandr Galich were the heroes of a new subculture for the young, the educated, and the urban. Despite some ups and downs, the Thaw continued as long as Khrushchev was in power. Its most spectacular moment came in 1962 with the publication of Alexander Solzhenitsyn's Gulag novella *One Day in the Life of Ivan Denisovich*.

The cultural liberalization and the end of terror allowed the emergence of an illegal opposition – the dissidents. This was a small group of intellectuals, led by scientists (Sakharov) and writers (Solzhenitsyn), who had no mass following in society and no effective organization beyond personal networks. Their habitat was the kitchens of the new *khrushchevki*, where one could talk to friends without too much fear of being overheard and reported (informers, of course, remained a problem and there was a consistent fear of having phones or lamps bugged by the authorities). Their forms of exchange were heated arguments around the kitchen table on the one hand and illegal publications, on the other. Dissident literature came in two forms: *tamizdat* and *samizdat*. The former – "over there publications" – were books that had been published abroad, after the manuscripts had been smuggled out of the country in sometimes hair-raising operations. Brought back into the Soviet Union illegally, they were typed up with multiple carbon copies and then distributed to friends. The same method was used for *samizdat* – "self-publishing," which relied on typescripts in the first place.

Dissidents came in several ideological stripes, and factionalism and mutual dislike were as rampant as they had been in the radical intelligentsia of the nineteenth century. There were four main factions: "Pure Leninists," such as the historian Roy Medvedev (born 1925), who prefigured ideas that would drive the reforms of the 1980s discussed in Chapter 9. His critique of Stalinism stood squarely in the Marxist tradition. Critics in this school usually escaped arrest, although they would be harassed by the security services under Khrushchev's successor from 1964, Leonid Il'ich Brezhnev (1906–1982). More radical were the other factions, whose ideas would become part of the heady ideological mix, which would help blow the Soviet Union apart in 1991. Liberals like Sakharov and Alexander Esenin-Volpin (1924–2016) would try to take Soviet laws literally, and attempted to force the state to live up to its own claims. Esenin-Volpin took particular delight in quoting the constitution or the criminal code to the prosecutors sent after him and his friends. The authorities repeatedly declared him insane. He was locked up in psychiatric hospitals under Stalin (1949), Khrushchev (1959), and Brezhnev (1968). The third branch of dissidents revived the long tradition of nationalist challenges to Bolshevik rule that extended back to 1917. They existed in Russian (Solzhenitsyn), Ukrainian, Crimean Tatar, Soviet German, Lithuanian, Estonian, Georgian, or Armenian versions. Russian Orthodox, Catholic, and Protestant dissenters attempted to fight against the repression of religious worship. Religious dissenters alone had relatively effective underground organizations, although they, too, were deeply penetrated by the security services.

Intrusion and Surveillance

While the cultural thaw of the Khrushchev years and the dissident movement it spawned has strongly colored the image of post-Stalin socialism, more recently historians have pointed to darker aspects of the same period. For one, the cultural defreezing came in fits and starts, dependent on the volatile mood of the First Secretary, his perceptions of internal and external threats, and his fairly unsophisticated tastes. Khrushchev did not like modernist paintings, which looked to him "as though some child had done his business on the canvas," as he noted while visiting a scandalous art exhibition in December 1962, only weeks after he had approved the publication of *Ivan Denisovich*. Formalist painters were not "normal people" but "pederasts" who created "art for donkeys." Their work was "simply anti-Soviet" and "amoral;" looking at it gave the First Art Critic "constipation." He also did not like jazz, which made him feel as if he had "gas on the stomach." Such music, he opined, "comes from the Negroes." "Indecent" dances like the foxtrot, which had already scandalized Soviet moralizers in the 1920s, also riled this socialist prude: "You wiggle a certain section of the anatomy, if you'll pardon the expression." Concluding his rant he promised the artists: "Gentlemen, we are declaring war on you."[8] No wonder that Khrushchev did not have many fans among the intelligentsia – until after his fall, when things got worse.

Second, the regime became "less repressive, but more intrusive" than under Stalin.[9] First within the communist party, then increasingly in society as a whole "communist morality" became a watchword. Drinking, wife-beating, infidelity all became subject to more and more extensive surveillance, often by peers rather than state agents. Busy-bodies and petty moralizers were thus mobilized to sober up and civilize their "uncultured" comrades. A sign of the time was that the fashionable Cocktail Hall on one of Moscow's major streets was turned into an ice-cream parlor. Once a hangout of the stiliagi in Stalin's final years (and source for "vile concoctions … dispensed under the name of 'koktails'," as a foreign sophisticate reported), it became the scene for much tamer urban pleasures.[10] The Soviet hipsters themselves, no longer just members of the Stalinist upper classes but more democratic in their social origin, became subject to Komsomol patrols who cut their ties, clipped their hair, and shamed them as "parasites." A variety of antisocial behavior became labelled "hooliganism" and subject to comrade courts. Nomadic Roma, who hitherto had been victimized by sporadic expulsions from cities, were now targeted in a major campaign of late 1956 and 1957. They were to become sedentary members of Soviet society, once and for all. Religious belief, once left more or less alone in Stalin's final years, as long as it was orthodox and hence "Russian," now became subject to a renewed atheist onslaught in 1957. In the Protestant and Catholic regions of the Baltics this campaign merged with the antinationalism drive described below. In March 1959 a citizens' auxiliary police force of Soviet vigilantes, the *druzhinniki*, was established to enforce socialist morality in their neighborhoods.

The Gulag also continued to exist in Khrushchev's time. It is true that it contracted radically after Stalin's death, but the archipelago never entirely disappeared. Between 1953 and early 1956, amnesties and mass releases had reduced the camp and prison population to under a million, a third of its late-Stalinist size. It would remain at or below that level over the next decade, with periodic ups and downs depending on the balance between new arrests and releases. The Gulag, rather than withering away, transformed "from an economic empire of its own into a supply company of a mobile workforce capable of filling gaps and clearing backlogs," as one historian has written. From 1966, the number of inmates began to rise again, reflecting the more repressive atmosphere under Brezhnev. By now, what once had been "a gigantic and omnipresent repressive machine" had transformed into "a more regular imprisonment system" with the task "to inhibit public disorder and political opposition."[11]

The Empire

Incomplete as it was, the liberalization after Stalin's death still had important repercussions for the Soviet Empire. The communist leadership in the Baltic republics attempted to assert more independence from Moscow and worked hard at indigenizing the local leadership, a tactic most successful in Lithuania, less so in Estonia, and least in Latvia. The Secret Speech further helped in this self-affirmation, as the denunciation of illegality could be extended towards the constitutional principle of the alleged autonomy of the Union Republics. The regular police was separated from state security and the prosecutor's office became a republican rather than a union affair. Republic-level police and prosecutors now enforced republic-level criminal codes – a strengthening of federalism within the Soviet Union. The cultural corollary was a more open expression of local nationalisms, including demands to replace Russian cadres with indigenous ones. The Thaw in culture also had its Baltic variant. Exiled writers and poets returned and prewar literature was republished.

The affirmation of local identity blended over into separatism, such as during student protests in support of the Hungarian uprising in 1956. These did lead to denunciations of "national communism," to a hardening of the cultural line from 1957, and some dismissals of cultural and academic functionaries, but not to an end of Baltic autonomy. Rather the reverse: Khrushchev's 1957 introduction of regional economic councils (*sovnarkhozy*) added economic decentralization to the ongoing cultural revival. Soon, each republic served as its own planning unit and local elites thus had a larger role to play in running their republic, albeit within a Union-wide framework. The population of the Baltics also became more homogenous as nonindigenous cadres and forced laborers left the republics and the survivors of the postwar deportations returned. This process was completed by 1959, the year the reaction from Moscow set in. Latvia was the first victim when a purge ripped through the republic's Communist Party. Many of the leading cadres were replaced by Russians or by Latvians who had spent significant time in Soviet exile and had returned as agents of Moscow.

Things seemed to get worse from a Baltic standpoint after 1959. In 1960, Moscow called for a Soviet identity to supersede local nationalisms, however "socialist in substance." In practice, this meant a campaign to learn Russian, the lingua franca of the empire, and to rewrite history to show the long and benevolent role of Russia in the Baltic states. In 1961, the new Party Program forecast the disappearance of borders between Union republics. A first step towards this goal was the creation of regional economic councils not based on Union republics in 1962.

With growing industrialization of the region, the influx of Russians also grew again, making the population more diverse. By 1965, a million Russians lived in the Baltics, and in both Latvia and Estonia immigration continued to outstrip natural population increase over the next decade and a half. This migration was not a conscious Russification policy, but was often perceived as such by the locals, who saw much of the new housing stock go to the newcomers. The republics were also tied into ever tighter economic networks with the rest of the Union. Within the empire-wide division of labor, the Baltics produced various types of specialist equipment, light-bulbs, radios, motorcycles, and refrigerators, while importing coal, cotton, iron, and cars.

In Ukraine, too, Russian immigration, pressures towards linguistic russification, and economic integration into the empire – Ukraine became a major producer of planes, missiles, and computers – competed with continued national self-affirmation. With the death of Stalin, the republic's titular nationality became a junior partner of the Russian big brother. Under Khrushchev, Ukraine became a favored republic, the First Secretary's power base. In 1954, the erratic leader transferred Crimea from the Russian Republic to Ukraine to show his appreciation and to aid in regional economic integration, a decision still haunting us today. Ukrainization of the state and party apparatus had gained steam after Stalin's death and continued throughout the Khrushchev years. Like in the Baltics, the control of industry by the republic's political elite increased dramatically as a result of Khrushchev's decentralization policy. Many Ukrainians made careers in Moscow as clients of the First Secretary, repaying their debt with loyal support in the 1957 leadership challenge. On the other end of the political spectrum, tens of thousands of postwar deportees – former nationalist guerrillas and their families – were allowed to return to the republic from their places of exile from 1956.

While policies towards the non-Russian republics oscillated between granting some measure of autonomy on the one hand and centralization on the other, the Red Empire also ran into trouble in its immediate perimeter. In 1960, irritations between Mao and Khrushchev, simmering ever since the Secret Speech, finally escalated to the breaking point. The Sino-Soviet split deprived the Soviet Union of security on its eastern front and changed the Cold War from a bipolar to a multipolar game. The western front did not remain quiet either after the uprisings in Germany in 1953 and Hungary in 1956. Eastern Germany remained a headache. The continued economic lag of the "socialist" part of the country vis-a-vis its "capitalist" and "miraculous" cousin next door led to a continued trickle of skilled workers and professionals westward. This brain drain helped push Khrushchev into the Berlin crisis (1958–1961) with its ultimate "resolution" of building the "anti-fascist defense rampart" in 1961: the Berlin Wall, a major symbol of the Cold War. The construction of that monstrosity only showed to the world that when push came to shove the Soviets could do no better than transform an entire country into an open air prison.

Khrushchev's Ouster, 1964

International upheaval was the least of Khrushchev's problems. More consequential than Hungary, Berlin, or even the Cuban Missile crisis became the enemies he made at home. The First Secretary had done much to alienate the political elite of his country. His attempt to demobilize the conventional forces had raised the army's hackles; his political reforms had disturbed the politicians; his zigzag course on culture had irritated the intelligentsia. Moreover, he was not really successful either. His economic policies did not work, once the boom of the 1950s ran out. His obsession with corn, to be planted everywhere because it seemed to make US farmers rich, was a joke; his international adventures got the world to the brink of nuclear war. Given that Khrushchev, unlike Stalin, did not rule by terror and did not personally control the levers of the Soviet police state, it was only a matter of time until opposition within the apparatus would lead to a coup. It came in 1964 and was led by the then chairman of the Presidium of the Supreme Soviet, the empire's nominal parliament: Leonid Il'ich Brezhnev. Khrushchev was sacked by the conspirators and sent into retirement – the second time a major leadership spill did not lead to bloodshed. Khrushchev, then, became a beneficiary of his own political innovation: that losers in factional struggles were not murdered, but put out to graze, and, in the case of Khrushchev, to write their memoirs – a major source for the political history of the Soviet Union.

Leadership change mattered in the centralized, undemocratic, dictatorial Soviet Union more than elsewhere. While historians have recently shown how the policies of one period often had their roots in the previous one, their work has also consistently demonstrated that the rhythm of political history was decisive. The change from Khrushchev to Brezhnev was not as deep a rupture as the death of Stalin, but it was a rift nonetheless. The new First Secretary, called General Secretary again from 1966, was less volatile, less passionate, but also less dictatorial than his predecessor had been. He was more prone to rule by committee, to ensure continuity, to guarantee the ruling elite of his generation

177

security of tenure. These were men, and a few women, who had risen through the ranks as a result of Stalin's revolutions, and who now wanted some peace and quiet to enjoy the fruits of their labors. The destabilizing experiments in politics and culture were ended. The cultural Thaw was over. Dissidents were intimidated, put under house arrest, arrested, or locked up in insane asylums. Regional economic management in the *sovnakhozy* was ended and replaced by vertical integration in production branches – an economic recentralization, which did nothing to stop the continued economic slowdown after the reconstruction boom of the 1950s was over.

Prague Spring

Hopes for a quiet retirement were premature, however. Soon, new unrest broke loose in the empire's western perimeter. In 1968, the Czechoslovakian government attempted to get control over its slowing economy. What happened next in some way prefigured what would happen in the Soviet Union in the 1980s: The magnitude of the economic problems called for radical change not only in economics but also in politics. Once the floodgates of public debate were opened, the communist regime was threatened with being washed away. Czechoslovakia was too important for the Soviets to let this happen. On August 20–21, 1968, Warsaw Pact troops invaded the country and quashed the Prague Spring. The West condemned this bloody intervention, but could do little than stand by in distress, given Soviet nuclear power.

The Prague Spring had fewer than expected repercussions in the empire itself. No crackdown on local culture occurred in the Baltics. Instead, the dual and contradictory developments of the previous decades continued: immigration and Russification as well as continuing economic integration into the Soviet orbit on the one hand, development of local national culture and orientation towards the western cultural sphere on the other. Plans to demolish the federal structure, fake and limited as it was, were shelved. Union republics remained union republics, autonomous in form but not content. A new Russification campaign started in the late 1970s; predictably, it led to a grass-roots assertion of local nationalisms instead of the intended assimilation to the empire's leading nation. The grievances caused by such politics would smolder under the surface, to break loose in the second half of the 1980s (Chapter 9).

Jewish Emigration

If Eastern Europe began to resemble a prison house of nations, many others were trapped in the Soviet Union proper. Besides intellectuals, ethnic minorities were feeling less and less at home in an empire that had taken an ethnic Russian turn in the 1930s, a mobilization strategy locked in by its success in World War II. Most prominent among the victims of this shift were Jews, once a favored minority within the Soviet system. The late Stalinist anti-Semitic campaign had disturbed many of Stalin's closest companions, who remained committed to the Bolshevik tradition of anti-anti-Semitism; but the projection of all resentments onto the traditional scapegoats proved popular among a large sector of the population, including many officials. The anti-Semitic turn in Soviet politics became a lasting legacy of late Stalinism: Jews would never again be as welcome in this state as they once had. Discrimination further increased in an anti-Zionist campaign in the wake of the Six-Day-War and the resulting suspension of diplomatic relations with Israel in 1967.

An increasing number of Soviet Jews now began to apply for exit visas to leave the Soviet Union and move to Israel. Many were denied, growing the group of so-called "refuseniks." After an attempt by a group of them to hijack a small plane in order to leave the country in 1970, the Soviet government relented and eased emigration. In the next decade, hundreds of thousands left, growing the Soviet-Jewish diaspora in Israel, New York, and Melbourne. The enormous brain drain represented by heightened emigration of a group better educated than the Soviet average explains why the Soviet policies continued to fluctuate between anti-Semitic discrimination and imposing restrictions on Jews leaving for a life abroad.

Recalibration of Warfare and Welfare

In other policy areas, too, balancing contradictory demands remained problematic. Both within the "old" Soviet Union and in its new western borderlands, social peace continued to be manufactured by increasing material well-being rather than repression. Fueled by oil exports, the expanding welfare state and the growth of Soviet consumerism allowed citizens to retreat into private life, to go on holidays (to the resorts in Crimea, the "western" Baltics, or, since 1955, to the eastern bloc countries of the Soviet perimeter), and to chase possessions (refrigerators and TV sets, shoes and clothes, including the ever-popular blue jeans). For the more culturally discerning, there were encyclopedias and book collections to acquire, record sets and sheet music, short-wave radios to listen to the Voice of America and the BBC, tape recorders to capture the jazz and the new rock music played on these stations. Never in adequate supply, always subject to scarcities and lines, both physical and metaphorical, these objects of desire were now accessible to the ordinary Soviet. Obtaining and maintaining them could fill one's days. Buying a car, which became more and more widespread among the better off, was a major endeavor; owning it became a time-consuming activity. The "car lover" needed to learn to repair the machine, obtain spare parts on the black or gray market, and find like-minded friends to help with both. Busy with such endeavors, he (and it was mainly men who pursued the car as a status symbol and lifestyle choice) would find less time for reading samizdat. Busy discussing where to obtain parts, he was less likely to stray into politics.

The political leadership knew that material well-being led to social and political peace, while their absence spelled potential unrest. Thus the challenge became how to provide welfare and consumption, while also maintaining the warfare state, which had secured the empire and was clearly necessary to enforce and defend it. How to balance warfare and welfare thus became a central political problem. Both Stalin and Khrushchev had conceptualized the relationship between these two aspects of statecraft as a zero-sum game: if resources were devoted to guns, they could not be spent on butter, and vice versa. The difference was that Stalin never felt safe enough internationally to concentrate on consumption, while Khrushchev, behind the shield of nuclear warheads, saw that the time for housing construction and material benefits had come. He thus tried to demobilize the conventional armed forces to allow for the transfer of resources to where they were needed most.

Brezhnev departed from his predecessors' view that a choice had to be made. He continued to expand the welfare state, while also expanding the armed forces, achieving nuclear parity with the West in the late 1970s. This dual growth of state activity and expenditure was seen as possible, because the leadership assumed that increased welfare would also grow productivity and hence partially pay for itself. At the same time, detente in international relations (1969–1980) made aggressive export of raw materials, in particular oil, to the capitalist world possible. It was the latter that truly paid for the expansion of welfare and warfare at the same time.

Brezhnev was wrong. The hopes for increased productivity and economic growth turned out to be misplaced. The domestic economy continued to stagnate after the boom years of the 1950s. Once the Soviets made the disastrous decision to invade Afghanistan in 1979, detente also came to an end. Under President Ronald Reagan (1981–1989), the United States again embroiled the first socialist state in an aggressive arms race. The new confrontation between the superpowers might have brought the world yet another time to the brink of nuclear war in 1983, when the Soviets mistakenly shot down a Korean airliner over Soviet air space and then mistook a NATO exercise for actual war preparation. The crisis passed, but the confrontation continued. For the Soviets, this military competition was even more costly, because since the Sino-Soviet split, the empire needed to match not only capitalist NATO but also communist China. In the long run, the Soviet Union could only win in this contest if it again suppressed civilian consumption and repressed the resulting conflicts – a return to Stalinism few were willing to contemplate.

Brezhnev's refusal to decide between warfare and welfare, then, failed as a political strategy. Under conditions of declining economic growth, a clear choice would have to be made: either stop the expansion of the warfare state and concede defeat in the arms race with the United States, or rein in welfare spending and risk mass unrest, which would require increased repression. Instead, the regime continued to commit to both. In the ensuing struggle for resources the more powerful military-industrial complex won out.

Neither Brezhnev nor anybody else in the regime had the stomach to return to the Stalin model – brutal suppression of civilian consumption. Hence, the leadership settled on a tacit pact with the population: the state would be allowed to focus on warfare, while the population would look after itself. Gardening and the acquisition of a weekend home outside the city – the much-loved *dacha* – became mass preoccupations. Such self-provisioning had helped to win World War II, but had been scorned during the ideologically charged years of Khrushchev as a "petty bourgeois" practice. Now, it was enshrined in law. Once food shortages returned in the 1970s the regime turned "from reluctant acceptance of private plots to their enthusiastic support," reaffirming not only the right of citizens to farm for their own consumption, but also decreeing, in the words of the 1977 constitution, that the state would "assist citizens in keeping their private plots."[12]

The final, constitutional acceptance of the dacha economy was part of a new realism that allowed citizens to "pretend we work" while the authorities "pretend they pay."[13] This state of affairs has been described as "acquisitive socialism," a social formation where the aspirations for material advancement were at the very least tolerated.[14] The workplace began to function less as a unit for the production or distribution of goods and services but as a mechanism for discipline and welfare. Combining surveillance of its members with the provision of healthcare, subsidized meals, access to housing, closed shops, holiday resorts, and other perks, the workplace was central in the lives of Soviet citizens. In the words of one dissident, it had evolved into an institution, in which "several hundred people can live …, kill their time …, expend … their best feelings and talents, and be allotted living space, holiday entitlement, and other such benefits."[15] This type of dysfunctional welfare society had emerged under Khrushchev, but now came into its own as the government no longer tried to interfere with the established equilibrium.

Overall, the strategy to let people find their own niche in an economy of predictable scarcity worked to preserve social peace without the need of too frequent repression: uprisings and disturbances continued at a rate of about one major incident every other year, but that was a major decrease in comparison to the Khrushchev period. Moreover, violence was used less often now to suppress such protests: while under Khrushchev 264 people had been killed or wounded during crackdowns, under Brezhnev only 71 citizens suffered the same fate. To many who lived through the 1970s, the Brezhnev years became, in retrospect, a golden time of security, harmony, and relative well-being. They are nostalgic for a period when, in reality, Soviet citizens spent much of their lives standing in line for scarce consumer goods of dubious quality. Nevertheless, even at the time it seemed to many observers both within the Soviet Union and abroad, that Soviet society had found some kind of steady state after decades of upheaval and suffering.

The Brezhnev equilibrium implied widespread everyday criminality in the cities in particular, where the everyday pilfering by ordinary citizens shaded over into a thriving black market dominated by hardened criminals on the one hand, and corrupt officials stealing at a larger rate than ordinary citizens on the other. And it fueled the desperation of a growing urban underclass with lots of resentments but no hope for social advancement. Young men vented their frustration in acts of hooliganism and senseless violence, while many others drowned their lack of opportunity in the bottle. In 1978, the police temporarily detained above nine million citizens for public drunkenness – above 3% of the entire population of men, women, and children!

Subterranean Developments

In a negative version of the golden past, then, the period between Khrushchev's ouster in 1964 and Mikhail Gorbachev's appointment to General Secretary in 1985 has been termed the epoch of "stagnation" before a new time of reform and upheaval. In the past decade, however, historians have begun to discover how dynamic this period actually was behind the facade of political stability. One group of citizens whose fate showed a particularly high degree of change was the veterans of the Great Patriotic War. Their feelings of entitlement vis-à-vis the state and society at large had been ignored after demobilization was over. From 1948, only severely disabled former soldiers had a right to some basic help. That help, too, was often not forthcoming. The entire benefits system, such as it was, was geared towards forcing war invalids back to work: the extraction of labor power from their injured bodies was more important than their well-being.

All of this changed in 1978. After a mass letter writing campaign in the context of the discussion of the 1977 constitution, Brezhnev, who fancied himself a war hero, conceded that more privileges were warranted and allowed the legislation of special provisions for "participants in the Patriotic War." This category was subsequently widened to more and more groups until all former servicemen – and women – of World War II were covered.

While the older generation thus received an increasingly elevated status based on their past service to the state, a growing group of young Soviets looked elsewhere for inspiration. Following a Beatles mania (which never really stopped),

Hippies appeared, joined later by Punks and Heavy Metal fans. The more independently minded among Soviet youth thus found other aesthetics than those promoted by bemedaled old timers or the state youth organization. In the end, they, too, had to accommodate themselves to the control of the powers that be, however, because the Komsomol controlled concert and other venues.

However, it was possible now to carve out fairly autonomous spaces for creative activity away from the mainstream. Boiler rooms became centers of thriving intellectual subcultures. They allowed a place of retreat from the gaze of stern communist morality, as a boiler room attendant had a job, even a proletarian one, and was thus not a "parasite," even if he or she wrote philosophical essays on the meaning of drunkenness. While thus shielding the intellectual from the strictures of official norms, the job did not fill the day with more than a modicum of meaningless activity. The rest of the day, or indeed the night, could be devoted to scholarship, music, art, drinking, poetry, friendship, and love. As a result, such jobs were sought after in a certain crowd. To obtain one required good connections and an impressive, if alternative CV, as attendants had fairly far reaching control over who would be hired in "their" boiler room. An entire alternative set of hierarchies and career choices thus emerged in the shadow of the official Soviet world and engaged some of the most creative minds of the Soviet 1970s and early 1980s.

Gerontocracy

Meanwhile, the elite who ran the country aged. The decision makers had, in their majority, made a career in the context of Stalin's revolutions from above. Having survived upheaval, terror, and war, exhausted from the exciting times under Khrushchev, these old men and women became the symbol for the stagnation of the empire. After Brezhnev, increasingly incoherent in his final years, had died in 1982, an unimpressive succession of elders took over the General Secretaryship: Iurii Andropov (1982–1984) and Konstantin Chernenko (1984–1985). It was only a matter of time until this old generation died out and younger hands would take over. This moment came in 1985 with the appointment of Mikhail Gorbachev (born in 1931), the gravedigger of the Soviet Empire.

Notes

1   Mark B. Smith, *Property for Communists. The Urban Housing Program from Stalin to Khrushchev* (DeKalb: Northern Illinois University Press, 2010), 21.
2   Mark B. Smith, "The Withering Away of the Danger Society: The Pensions Reform of 1956 and 1964 in the Soviet Union," *Social Science History* 39, no. 1 (2015): 129–48, here: 136.

3   The Russian terms are *golodalizm* and *dorogovizm*. They were used in an anonymous letter to a member of the Supreme Soviet of the USSR in 1956. Russian State Archive of Newest History (RGANI), fond 5, opis' 30, delo 141, l. 82.

4   *Programme of the Communist Party of the Soviet Union. Adopted by the 22nd Congress of the CPSU, October 31, 1961* (Moscow: Foreign Languages Publishing House, 1961), 61–2.

5   Amir Weiner, "Robust Revolution to Retiring Revolution: The Life Cycle of the Soviet Revolution, 1945–1968," *The Slavonic and East European Review* 86, no. 2 (2008): 208–31.

6   *Toast to the Russian People at a Reception in Honour of Red Army Commanders Given by the Soviet Government in the Kremlin on Thursday, May 24, 1945*, https://www.marxists.org/reference/archive/stalin/works/1945/05/24.htm, accessed January 2, 2018; *Speech at a Reception in the Kremlin*, https://www.marxists.org/reference/archive/stalin/works/1945/06/25.htm, accessed January 2, 2018.

7   Jukka Gronow, *Caviar with Champagne. Common Luxury and the Ideals of the Good Life in Stalin's Russia* (Oxford, New York: Berg, 2003).

8   "Khrushchev on Modern Art. Nikita Khrushchev, Conversation at the Manege Exhibit. December 1, 1962," *Seventeen Moments in Soviet History. An On-line Archive of Primary Sources*, http://soviethistory.msu.edu/1961-2/khrushchev-on-the-arts/khrushchev-on-the-arts-texts/khrushchev-on-modern-art/, accessed January 2, 2018.

9   Edward D. Cohn, "Sex and the Married Communist: Family Troubles, Marital Infidelity, and Party Discipline in the Postwar USSR, 1945–64," *The Russian Review* 68 (2009): 429–30; here: 430.

10   Harrison E. Salisbury, "Russia Re-Visited: Crime Wave Goes Unchecked. Violence, Drunkenness and Graft Plague Communist Ruled Country," *The New York Times*, October 1, 1954, p. 25.

11   Marc Elie, "Khrushchev's Gulag: The Soviet Penitentiary System after Stalin's Death, 1953–1964," in: *The Thaw. Soviet Society and Culture during the 1950s and 1960s*, ed. Denis Kozlov and Eleonory Gilburg (Toronto: University of Toronto Press, 2013), 109–42, here: 133.

12   Vladimir Shlapentokh, *Public and Private Life of the Soviet People. Changing Values in Post-Stalin Russia* (New York and Oxford: Oxford University Press, 1989), 161.

13   Alena Ledeneva, *Russia's Economy of Favours. Blat, Networking and Informal Exchange* (Cambridge, New York, Melbourne: Cambridge University Press, 1998), 71.

14   James R. Millar, "The Little Deal: Brezhnev's Contribution to Acquisitive Socialism," *Slavic Review* 44, no. 4 (1985): 694–706.

15   Mark Edele, "Stalinism as a Totalitarian Society. Geoffrey Hosking's Socio-Cultural History," *Kritika: Explorations in Russian and Eurasian History* 13, no. 2 (2012): 441–52; here: 449.

Bibliography

Adler, Nanci. *Beyond the Soviet System. The Gulag Survivor* (New Brunswick, NJ and London: Transaction Publishers, 2002).

Alexeyeva, Ludmilla, and Paul Goldberg. *The Thaw Generation: Coming of Age in the Post-Stalin Era* (Pittsburgh, PN: University of Pittsburgh Press, 1993).

Bacon, Edwin, and Mark Sandle, eds. *Brezhnev Reconsidered* (Basingstoke: Palgrave Macmillan, 2002).

Barenberg, Alan. *Gulag Town, Company Town. Forced Labor and Its Legacy in Vorkuta* (New Haven, CT and London: Yale University Press, 2014).

Bittner Steven V. *The Many Lives of Khrushchev's Thaw. Experience and Memory in Moscow's Arbat* (Ithaca, NY: Cornell University Press, 2008).

Chumachenko, Tatiana. *Church and State in Soviet Russia. Russian Orthodoxy from World War II to the Khrushchev Years* (Armonk, NY, London: M. E. Sharpe, 2002).

Cohn, Edward. *The High Title of a Communist. Postwar Party Discipline and the Values of the Soviet Regime* (DeKalb: Northern Illinois University Press, 2015).

Dobson, Miriam. *Khrushchev's Cold Summer. Gulag Returnees, Crime, and the Fate of Reform after Stalin* (Ithaca, NY and London: Cornell University Press, 2009).

Edele, Mark. *Soviet Veterans of the Second World War. A Popular Movement in an Authoritarian Society, 1941–1991* (Oxford: Oxford University Press, 2008).

Edele, Mark. "Veterans and the Welfare State: World War II in the Soviet Context," *Comparativ. Zeitschrift für Globalgeschichte und vergleichende Gesellschaftsforschung* 20, no. 5 (2011): 18–33.

Edele, Mark. "The New Soviet Man as a 'Gypsy': Nomadism, War, and Marginality in Stalin's Time," *REGION: Regional Studies of Russia, Eastern Europe, and Central Asia* 3, no. 2 (2014): 285–307.

Edele, Mark. "The Impact of War and the Costs of Superpower Status," *The Oxford Handbook of Modern Russian History* (online), ed. Simon Dixon, November 2015. At: http://www.oxfordhandbooks.com/view/10.1093/oxfordhb/9780199236701.001.0001/oxfordhb-9780199236701-e-028, accessed January 6, 2018.

Evangelista, Matthew. "'Why Keep Such an Army?' Khrushchev's Troop Reductions," *Cold War International History Project Working Papers* 19 (1997).

Evans, Christine E. *Between Truth and Time. A History of Soviet Central Television* (New Haven, CT: Yale University Press, 2016).

Field, Debora A. *Private Life and Communist Morality in Khrushchev's Russia* (New York: Peter Land, 2007).

Filtzer, Donald. *Soviet Workers and De-Stalinization: The Consolidation of the Modern System of Soviet Production Relations, 1953–1964* (Cambridge: Cambridge University Press, 1992).

Fürst, Juliane, and Josie McLellan, eds. *Dropping out of Socialism. The Creation of Alternative Spheres in the Soviet Bloc* (Lanham, MD: Lexington Books, 2016).

Gorsuch, Anne E. *All This is Your World. Soviet Tourism at Home and Abroad after Stalin* (Oxford: Oxford University Press, 2011).

Hardy, Jeffrey S. *The GULAG after Stalin. Redefining Punishment in Khrushchev's Soviet Union, 1953–1964* (Ithaca, NY: Cornell University Press, 2016).

Harris, Steven E. *Communism on Tomorrow Street: Mass Housing and Everyday Life after Stalin* (Baltimore, MD: Johns Hopkins University Press, 2013).

Jones, Polly. *Myth, Memory, Trauma. Rethinking the Stalinist Past in the Soviet Union, 1953–70* (New Haven, CT and London: Yale University Press, 2013).

Kharkhordin, Oleg. *The Collective and the Individual in Russia. A Study of Practices* (Berkeley, Los Angeles, London: University of California Press, 1999).

Koenker, Diane. *Club Red: Vacation Travel and the Soviet Dream* (Ithaca, NY: Cornell University Press, 2013).

Kornai, Janos. *The Economics of Shortage*, 2 vols. (Amsterdam: North-Holland Publishing Co., 1980).

Kozlov, Denis. *The Readers of Novyi Mir: Coming to Terms with the Stalinist Past* (Cambridge, MA: Harvard University Press, 2013).

Kozlov, Denis, and Eleonory Gilburd, eds. *The Thaw. Soviet Society and Culture during the 1950s and 1960s* (Toronto: University of Toronto Press, 2013).

Kozlov, Vladimir A. *Mass Uprisings in the USSR. Protest and Rebellion in the Post-Stalin Years* (Armonk, NY: M. E. Sharpe, 2002).

Khreshchev, Sergei, and William Taubman, *Khrushchev on Khrushchev: An Inside Account of the Man and his Era* (Boston, MA: Little, Brown, 1990).

LaPierre, Brian. *Hooligans in Khrushchev's Russia: Defining, Policing, and Producing Deviance during the Thaw* (Madison: University of Wisconsin Press, 2012).

Lovell, Stephen. *Summerfolk. A History of the Dacha, 1719–2000* (Ithaca, NY and London: Cornell University Press, 2003).

Lovell, Stephen. "Soviet Russia's Older Generations," in: *Generations in Twentieth-Century Europe*, ed. Stephen Lovell (Basingstoke: Palgrave Macmillan, 2007), 205–26.

Lovell, Stephen. *The Shadow of War. Russia and the USSR 1941 to the Present* (Oxford: Wiley-Blackwell, 2010).

Lüthi, Lorenz. *The Sino-Soviet Split. Cold War in the Communist World* (Princeton, NJ: Princeton University Press, 2008).

Madison, Bernice Q. *Social Welfare in the Soviet Union* (Stanford, CA: Stanford University Press, 1968).

Mawdsley, Evan, and Stephen White. *The Soviet Elite from Lenin to Gorbachev. The Central Committee and Its Members, 1917–1991* (Oxford and New York: Oxford University Press, 2000).

Millar, James R., ed. *Politics, Work, and Daily Life in the USSR. A Survey of Former Soviet Citizens* (Cambridge and New York: Cambridge University Press, 1987).

Misiunas, Romuald J., and Rein Taagepera. *The Baltic States. Years of Dependence 1940–1990*, expanded and updated ed. (Berkeley and Los Angeles: University of California Press, 1993).

Nagle, John D. "A New Look at the Soviet Elite: A Generational Model of the Soviet System." *Journal of Political & Military Sociology* 3, no. 1 (1975): 1–13.

Pilkington, Hilary. *Russia's Youth and its Culture. A Nation's Constructors and Constructed* (London and New York: Routledge, 1994).

Raleigh, Donald J. *Soviet Baby Boomers. An Oral History of Russia's Cold War Generation* (Oxford: Oxford University Press, 2012).

Reese, Roger R. *The Soviet Military Experience* (London and New York: Routledge, 2000).

Reese, Roger R. *Red Commanders. A Social History of the Soviet Army Officer Corps, 1918–1991* (Lawrence: University Press of Kansas, 2005)

Reid, Susan E. "Cold War in the Kitchen: Gender and the De-Stalinization of Consumer Taste in the Soviet Union under Khrushchev," *Slavic Review* 61, no. 2 (2002): 211–52.

Reid, Susan E. "In the Name of the People: The Manege Affair Revisited." *Kritika: Explorations in Russian and Eurasian History* 6, no. 4 (2005): 673–716.

Rigby, T. H. "The Soviet Regional Leadership: The Brezhnev Generation," *Slavic Review* 37, no. 1 (1978): 1–24.

Roth-Ey, Kristin. *Moscow Prime Time: How the Soviet Union Built the Media Empire That Lost the Cultural Cold War* (Ithaca, NY: Cornell University Press, 2011).

Shlapentokh, Vladimir. *A Normal Totalitarian Society. How the Soviet Union Functioned and How It Collapsed* (Armonk, NY and London: M. E. Sharpe, 2001).

Shlapentokh, Vladimir. *Public and Private Life of the Soviet People. Changing Values in Post-Stalin Russia* (New York and Oxford: Oxford University Press, 1989).

Siegelbaum, Lewis H., ed. *Borders of Socialism. Private Spheres of Soviet Russia* (New York: Palgrave Macmillan, 2006).

Siegelbaum, Lewis H. *Cars for Comrades: The Life of the Soviet Automobile* (Ithaca, NY: Cornell University Press, 2008).

Slezkine, Yuri. *The Jewish Century* (Princeton, NJ: Princeton University Press, 2004).

Smith, Mark B. *Property of Communists: The Urban Housing Program from Stalin to Khrushchev* (DeKalb: Northern Illinois University Press, 2010).

Taubman, William. *Khrushchev. The Man and His Era* (New York and London: W. W. Norton & Co., 2003).

Taubman, William, and Abbott Gleason, eds. *Nikita Khrushchev* (New Haven, CT: Yale University Press, 2000).

Tsipursky, Gleb. *Socialist Fun. Youth, Consumption, and State-Sponsored Popular Culture in the Soviet Union, 1945–1970* (Pittsburgh, PA: University of Pittsburgh Press, 2016).

Tumarkin, Nina. *The Living & The Dead. The Rise and Fall of the Cult of World War II in Russia* (New York: Basic Books, 1994).

Varga-Harris, Christine. *Stories of House and Home. Soviet Apartment Life during the Khrushchev Years* (Ithaca: Cornell University Press, 2015).

Youngblood, Denise J. *Russian War Films. On the Cinema Front, 1914–2005* (Lawrence: University Press of Kansas, 2007).

Zubok, Vladislav. *Zhivago's Children. The Last Russian Intelligentsia* (Cambridge, MA: Belknap Press, 2009).

Zubok, Vladislav, and Constantine Plashakov. *Inside the Kremlin's Cold War. From Stalin to Khrushchev* (Cambridge, MA: Harvard University Press, 1996).

Part V

Imperial Discontent

9

Reform, Crisis, Breakdown (1985–1991)

The Soviet Union in 1985

In 1985, Mikhail Gorbachev became General Secretary of the Communist Party of the Soviet Union (CPSU), the top position in the Soviet Union. At 54, he was a spring chicken in the context of the regime of septuagenarians who had run the country until that point. Of mixed Russian-Ukrainian heritage, Gorbachev was a survivor of the 1932/1933 famine and World War II, and a typical Soviet social climber. Growing up in a Russian village he learned to drive a combine harvester before graduating with a law degree from the best school in the empire – Moscow State University. Gorbachev became a career apparatchik and honed his political skills in the Communist Youth League. Komsomol officials, as one historian has acidly noted, were good at two types of activities: maintain "tight-knit clan groupings that fought effectively against rivals" and "organize showy events that the leadership liked." They were "poorly suited to solving problems that required competence acquired over years, above all in the production and distribution of industrial goods, science, or serious international affairs." These were left to specialists, while Komsomols made careers in state security, propaganda, or relations with socialist countries. They usually did not make it to the top of the political system until Iurii Andropov, who came via a career in the KGB. His short tenure as General Secretary did not allow him to cause major damage to the complex, if cumbersome political, economic, and social system the Soviet Union had become. His protégé Gorbachev, by contrast, had more time.[1]

The Soviet Union: A Short History, First Edition. Mark Edele.
© 2019 John Wiley & Sons, Inc. Published 2019 by John Wiley & Sons, Inc.

Gorbachev presided over a party and a society that had evolved significantly since the dark years of Stalinism, which continued to hang above them like a shadow. Membership of the CPSU had grown to nearly 19 million full and candidate members, collectively referred to as "communists" to distinguish them from the "non-party" majority of the population. Over the decades, the Party membership had become more educated, as had the population as a whole. The 1937 census recorded half of the empire's residents as unable to read or write, in 1979 only 14% had not completed primary education. The percentage of citizens who had enjoyed higher education had risen from 1% in 1939 to 7% in 1979, and the share of the population with at least some secondary education had exploded from 8% to above 46%. As the vanguard on the march to the communist future, Communists had long been more educated than the rest of the population, and they continued to draw in the best trained sectors of the peoples of the empire. In 1939, 5% of the membership had higher education and 14% completed secondary education; by 1961 these proportions had already reached 13% and 30%, respectively, much higher than in the population at large.

By the time Gorbachev stepped up to take the reins of the CPSU, power within the party was firmly held by leaders of Brezhnev's generation, who had made their career under Stalin and reasserted their leading role after they returned from the war in 1945. They were now all fairly old men, ruling an enormous empire, which had remained constant in size since the war. Its 8.6 million square miles were divided into 15 Union republics: Russia, Ukraine, Belarus, Latvia, Lithuania, Estonia, Moldova, Georgia, Azerbaijan, Armenia, Uzbekistan, Turkmenistan, Tadzhikistan, Kazakhstan, and Kyrgyzstan. The republics were enmeshed in complex ties of mutual economic dependencies, which also encompassed the wider communist bloc in eastern Europe, and indeed the capitalist world economy. The deep integration of the various parts of the Soviet Empire was also expressed by a long and deep history of labor migration between republics, "transnationalism in one country," which would create large ethnic minorities once the union broke apart into nation states.[2]

Within this multinational empire, the relative weight of the two largest Slavic nationalities – Russians and Ukrainians – had continuously decreased as the birth rates of these nations were lower than those of others. Russians had seen their high-point in 1939, after the famine had decimated Ukrainians. In that year, Russians made up over 58% of the Soviet population. From then on, their share had declined. As the westward expansion during World War II added substantial numbers of non-Russians, the largest nationality's percentage dropped to 55% by 1959. From then on the censuses tracked a steady downward trend: 52% in 1979 and just under 51% in 1989. The share of the second largest nationality, Ukrainians, fell from 18% in 1959 to below 16% in 1989. Meanwhile, the rise of Russia and the Russians as the first among unequals had been entrenched by victory in World War II and was never undone thereafter, despite the demographic realities.

The population Gorbachev was in charge of was immense. The number of Soviet citizens had grown from 208.9 million in 1959 to 216 million in 1960 and on to 266.6 million in early 1981. Communist party membership grew even faster, bringing a growing group of the population into the heart of the Soviet political system. The sheer size of the empire and its populations, however, meant that even a massively expanded Party organized only a small, if growing minority. If in 1926, less than 1 in a 100 Soviet citizens had been a party member or candidate member (that is, a "communist"), by 1939, this share had reached 1.4%. Twenty years on, nearly 4 in 100 Soviet citizens were enrolled in the unifying political organization of the Soviet Union, and by 1979 the saturation of the population with communists had reached 5%. The trend continued and in the 1980s between 6% and 7% Soviet citizens were full or candidate members. The vast majority of the population thus remained outside this important pillar of the Soviet order.

Participating in a global trend, the economy, and with it society as a whole, was increasingly urban. The growth of the cities was one of the most far-reaching changes in the empire since the start of the twentieth century when only 13% of the empire's population had lived in the cities. By 1914, this number had risen to 18%, only to decline in the de-urbanization processes of war, revolution, and civil war. By 1926 the share had recovered to the prewar level. Stalin's brutal revolution from above accelerated the process. At the end of the 1930s, city dwellers constituted a third of the Red Empire's inhabitants and by 1959 48% was reached. Urbanization continued, reaching 56% in 1970, 62% in 1979, and 72% in 1989. By the time Gorbachev took control of the Soviet Union, it was a thoroughly urban place.

This place – a Union of 15 republics spanning an unbelievably vast space in both Europe and Asia – was integrated by the sinews of the Communist Party on the one hand, and the empire's economic system, on the other. Different parts of the Soviet Empire produced and consumed different goods and services and exchange between the different parts was essential to the operation of the overall system. Union republics, thus, were interdependent economically. They could not function on their own. Exchange was organized via a complex, centralized economic plan, supplemented by ubiquitous informal mechanisms and small-scale markets, both legal and illegal, which had emerged to circumvent systemic problems built into the system. This interdependence had been one of the reasons for rebuilding the empire after the imperial breakdown of 1917/1918, as discussed in Chapter 3. Once the system began to unravel, this interdependence would exacerbate the economic catastrophe that ensued.

The destruction of the empire under Gorbachev was not a process initially driven "from below." By 1985, there was widespread compliance with a system that had successfully integrated rulers and ruled in an often unhappy and gray but stable existence. Anticolonial armed resistance in Central Asia had been crushed in the 1920s, 1930s, and, this time decisively, during the war. Brutal deportations also ended opposition in the Caucasus. The nationalist insurgencies in Ukraine and the Baltics had been destroyed by the early 1950s through a combination of military action, amnesties, and deportations. Dissent, savagely repressed ever since the civil war, had re-emerged everywhere since Khrushchev's partial liberalization, but was then successfully suppressed again under Brezhnev.

The young were mostly docile. Many youth preferred the Beatles to Soviet pop, while others embraced the bards of the 1960s or the subcultural Victor Tsoi (1962–1990), who sang of love and melancholy, and whose death would trigger a major suicide wave among teenagers. Despite such aesthetic choices, however, most were not oppositional. The Soviet Union they had grown up in seemed like it was there to stay. Only fools would try to fight against such an overwhelming reality, and many were indeed integrated via school and Komsomol into official society.

The Soviet Union thus seemed like it was "forever" – until it suddenly "was no more."[3] Social and ethnic tensions did exist, but at a lower level than under Khrushchev. Hence the widespread consensus among historians, that perestroika and breakdown were yet another "revolution from above." It was not "civil society" that broke the grip of Communism – it was the Communist establishment, "uncivil society," which was primarily responsible for downfall of the Soviet Empire.[4]

The Soviet Economic System

This revolution began with the economy. Poorly described, with terms such as "planned economy" or "state socialism," it was constituted by a complex web of formal and informal structures and practices, which combined to produce shortages in certain fields of the economy while producing surplus in others. The Soviet "economy of shortage" originated in the command system established under Stalin and was merely modified, but never fundamentally reformed, in the subsequent, less violent decades.[5]

The central feature of this economy was that the production and distribution of goods and services was not facilitated by a market (seen as "anarchic" by Marxist-Leninists) but by centralized planning (seen as more "rational"). A market is a fairly decentralized system of information flow between producers and consumers. Producers find out what consumers want through the work done by distributors and sellers who gather data on what goes out the door and what stays on the shelves. Markets are never "perfect," and there are no historical examples of societies where all exchanges are ruled by market forces (although such fantasy worlds continue to serve as dystopias to some and utopias to others). Nevertheless, in more or less functioning market economies, all involved in the economic process have a strong interest in passing on as much information as possible to increase their profits or to obtain what they want. Producers and distributors can try to influence consumer choice by pricing and marketing, and large monopolies can limit the available choices, but consumers' actions and inactions have a strong influence over what is produced, bought, and sold. In such systems, what is in short supply are typically not goods and services, but the money to pay for them. Waste comes from overproduction and under-consumption.

In the Soviet Union, there were small-scale legal markets, especially for food, as we detailed in earlier chapters, and there was a thriving second economy integrated by semi-legal and outright illegal transactions. In addition, there were also quasi-market mechanisms underwriting the official economy. But the overall system of production, distribution, and consumption of goods and services was not coordinated by market relations. The exchange of information between producers and consumers was mediated not via a market system of decentralized information gathering, but through a complex bureaucratic system of target setting, target adjustment, and target fulfillment. This system was meant to be less chaotic than the market, which essentially relies on trial and error, with each error producing waste. Instead, planners would give consumers what they needed on the basis of a rational assessment of what was required, where, and when.

In practice, this attempt created several problems. One was that planners could only know some of the needs of consumers. Take housing as an example. It was obvious that there was a huge housing shortage in the Soviet Union, and the Soviet system was able to deliver an impressive increase in urban housing in a relatively short time under Khrushchev. But because the state became the near-monopoly supplier of housing, consumers had no choice other than to take whatever was offered them, which decreased the incentives to ensure quality construction. "Plan fulfillment" depended on aggregate statistics of square meters built, not on consumer satisfaction. The careers of managers relied on their plan fulfillment and their loyalty to patrons higher up in the food chain. At the top of the system, the careers of the decision makers in the Politburo did not depend on the loyalty or the votes of ordinary citizens who had to live with their decisions, but on the political process they controlled themselves. Nothing forced anybody in the entire chain of command to make sure apartments were built properly. Hence, the impressive housing construction came at the cost of shabbily built apartments.

Information flow between consumers and producers was better in the defense sector, a field of economic activity where state direction and resource allocation by political choice is typical in many twentieth and twenty-first century societies (the Pentagon and NASA are not trading corporations, for example). Here, consumers (that is the military brass) had access to the political decision makers, whose survival depended on their ability to defend the empire both domestically and internationally. They were thus compelled to react to information about the poor quality of tanks, planes, or rifles and put pressure on the producers to rectify the situation. The existence of a feedback loop between producers and consumers in the military sphere, and its absence in the sphere of consumer goods, was one of the reasons why the Soviet Union could win World War II in Europe and later fly the first man into space, while it was never able to produce enough, or decent quality, toilet paper.

The economics of defense point to a second central problem in the Soviet system. Because the empire was a dictatorship, which did not have to react to consumer demand, and because the state effectively owned all assets, politicians were able to decide much more freely than elsewhere how much they committed to warfare or to welfare. Neglect of the latter could lead to riots (as in Novocherkassk in 1962) or even uprisings (as during collectivization), but these could be suppressed with the superior means of violence at the state's command. Thus, the decision makers were free to lower civilian consumption even to starvation levels (as happened under Stalin) or to divert massive amounts to defense even under conditions of severe shortage of items of everyday consumption (as they continued to do under the compulsions of empire until Gorbachev tried to put a stop to this excess spending). In fundamental ways, even with rising consumption and welfare after Stalin, the Soviet Union remained a warfare more than a welfare state. As we have seen in Chapter 8, the Soviets could only afford to continue expanding both sectors in the economy as long as world oil prices floated the Soviet boat. Once commodity prices dropped, the leadership had a serious economic problem, which Gorbachev inherited.

Any attempt to deal with this crisis had to rely on economic leaders whose entire outlook differed fundamentally from capitalist functionaries. In the Soviet system, the task of managers was not to make a profit. Rather than produce something somebody wanted to buy and make sure it would find its way to the consumer while controlling costs in order to create a surplus of capital, the Soviet manager had to first and foremost fulfill a plan. The plan had a deadline, which needed to be reached and a quantitative target to be fulfilled. Quality mattered less to the career of the manager than reaching the target by the deadline. Moreover, because plan targets were subject to political negotiation within the system, they changed over the course of a planning period. Hence, as the deadline approached, a mad rush to get across the line, called "storming," invariably followed, which again did nothing to ensure quality, but also had more wide-ranging implications. Importantly, storming created very strong incentives to hoard both materials and labor. All enterprises stockpiled whatever materials they could, no matter the costs, as one never knew what would come in handy during the "storming periods." All enterprises also kept more workers on the payroll than they needed on average, because they relied on them during the rush to the finish line.

The systemic hoarding was at the center of many of the economic problems of the Soviet system. It was one of the main reasons for the shortage even of goods that were produced in significant quantities: they did not find their way out of the warehouses unless they were exchanged through informal channels with other enterprises that needed them to fulfill their own targets. It also led to a labor shortage, which gave workers significant power vis-à-vis management. Because managers and foremen needed to keep workers in the enterprise but could not provide them with very strong material incentives to stay, they had two choices: they could mobilize the state and its repressive mechanisms to threaten the workers (as happened under Stalin), or they could tolerate absenteeism (time often used to stand in line to purchase ever-scarce consumer goods), slack work discipline, drinking on the job, or the minor pilfering of materials to be used privately, as long as workers would hold up their side of the bargain during storming periods to ensure the enterprise's successful plan fulfillment. Poor productivity, hence, was an integral part of the social contract that emerged at the heart of Soviet socialism, a social contract that had its advantages. Where "we pretend to work, while you pretend to pay us" was the basic maxim, nobody needed to worry about losing a job.

The consumer sector of Soviet society, therefore, presented a paradox where a lot was produced, but in fits and starts and often of poor quality. Because stockpiling was rampant, both producers and consumers needed to find ways to access these stockpiles. They did so by creating systems of exchange outside the official system of distribution. Some of them were outright illegal: there was a black market in goods siphoned off the official economy and distributed against cash payments on the black market. There was also outright corruption of officials with access to scarce goods and services. On the other end of the spectrum, there were legal markets for everyday items (flea-markets or bazaars, which also served as central hubs of the black market) as well as kolkhoz markets where collective farmers were allowed to sell their own surpluses at market prices. But there were other, much more "gray" areas of distribution. All enterprises employed "consultants" who were in reality procurement agents, "pushers" with good connections to other enterprises who could facilitate swapping materials to the benefits to all involved. Thus, subsidiary market mechanisms indeed underwrote the ostensibly "planned" economy.

Private citizens, too, had their networks. Friends and family, the friends of friends of family and friends, and their friends, family, and acquaintances would help each other. One might be in a position to facilitate admission to a prestigious university, another might have rights to buy goods in special stores, and a third might be able to pilfer roofing iron in his enterprise. Each one of them might have a need for one of these goods or services available in the network. Each would provide them on the basis of friendship and trust (which was essential, as at least some of these exchanges were illegal) and on the assumption that should he or she need the help of friends in the future, it would be forthcoming. This practice had a name: "blat" (*connections*), which is what one would call it if one saw others do it. If one was engaged in it oneself, it was called "friendship." Under Stalin, *blat* was said to be "higher than Stalin."[6] Once repression lessened under his successors, it reigned supreme. The Soviet economy of scarcity was also an "economy of favors."[7]

Finally, this was an economy of small-scale land owners who engaged in subsistence agriculture. Collective farmers of course had their private plot, the center of their economic activity. But by the time Gorbachev came to power, the majority of urban residents, too, had access to a small garden where they grew vegetables and raised small animals for consumption by themselves, their families, and their wider network. In some areas, too, there was market gardening for urban consumption.

In its basic outlines, this system of shortages and favors, of lines and job security, of soft budget constraints and hoarding, of subsistence production and small-scale exchange remained the same after the attempt to control it through the threat of prison or worse under Stalin was abandoned. Under Khrushchev, the system was reformed by giving more autonomy to republics and regions, which did help to engender some more responsiveness, but did not fundamentally change the underlying dynamics. Under Brezhnev, this decentralization was undone, and nominal control returned to ministries in Moscow.

The cumulative effects of the economic dysfunctions of the system itself, the long-lasting destructive influence of first revolution and civil war, then Stalin's revolutions from above, and finally World War II, the costs of empire, and the ongoing compulsion to devote significant shares of national wealth to defense in the framework of the Cold War meant that the Soviet population remained poor by international standards. While defense spending ate up, depending on the estimate between 16% and 20% of the budget (or 7% of GDP), male life expectancy had dropped from 66 years in the mid-1960s to only 62 by the late 1970s. By the 1980s, the Soviet Union was 32nd in the world in terms of life expectancy, 75th in terms of share of GDP spent on healthcare, and 77th place with regard to per capita consumption. Despite the massive house-building program started in 1957, housing remained in short supply and of poor quality. Many people continued to live in communal apartments or even barracks and remained on waiting lists to receive their own apartment for years, even decades. Only 30% of housing in the cities and 10% in the villages had telephones. Alcoholism was rampant, and social and ethnic tensions simmered under the surface of "stability" and occasionally broke to the surface.

Economic Reform

Thus, at the time Gorbachev took over as General Secretary, the Soviet Empire was a thoroughly urban, very well-educated place, with an odd, outdated industrial system producing weaponry and shortages. It was politically stagnant, and there was no pressure from below for political change. The dissident movement had been crushed and Soviet society had settled into a social contract, which amounted to a vicious circle of poor productivity and a predictable economy of scarcity and favors. With the end of the oil boom, this social contract had become increasingly hard to pay for, but opportunities existed to further activate a private sector, in particular small-scale gardening, which fed much of the population (and would ensure its survival through the economic breakdown brought about by Gorbachev's reforms).

Instead of tinkering with the system, Gorbachev launched deeply ideological campaigns of "reform" or "re-building" (*perestroika*). They quickly unraveled the complex economic ties that held the empire together (in addition to the tentacles of the Communist Party, an extensive system of myth making, and simple repression, the other three main integrating forces).

The first step was "acceleration" (*uskorenie*), the watchword of the first two years of Gorbachev's tenure as General Secretary. Instead of reform, the argument went, the economic system just needed speeding up – an optimistic assessment if there ever was one. As we have sketched above, "slowness" outside periods of "storming" was an inherent feature of the Soviet social contract, and decrees from above to hurry up and get on with things did little to upset an equilibrium reached over decades between managers and their workforce. Moreover, in practice, acceleration meant massive investment of capital at a time when revenue was rapidly disappearing.

This disappearance of state revenue was caused in part by a fall of the price of the Soviet Union's major export commodity: oil. But the crisis was also self-made. The attempt to speed up production was accompanied by an anti-alcohol campaign, which became one of the least popular aspects of the early Gorbachev years. Beer halls, wine and vodka shops were closed, vineyards destroyed, and the population treated to a sustained education campaign about the evils of drink. The unpopularity of these measures was one thing, their economic impact quite another. Severe alcoholics were not weaned off the bottle, but instead substituted moonshine, industrial alcohol, typewriter cleaning fluid, or eau de cologne for beer, wine, and vodka, as people had done during the world and civil wars earlier in the century. Meanwhile, the destruction of the alcohol industry cancelled one of the state's most potent ways to extract surplus money from the population, and hence control inflation.

While failing to sober up the population (and thus "accelerate" production), the anti-alcohol campaign constricted the state's ability to act in the economic sphere at exactly the time when oil prices were falling. Imported consumer goods disappeared from the shelves because the Soviet Union could no longer afford to buy them abroad. In 1988, the anti-alcohol campaign was thus abandoned, but not before it had led to extraordinary shortages. As goods disappeared from the shelves, the cashed-up population, which could no longer spend its money on vodka or imported goods, began buying whatever was left, just in case. Hoarding, a long established reflex of people with recurrent experiences of war and crises, led to deepening shortages. Rationing had to be introduced.

More popular was the anticorruption campaign, which led to several high-level convictions of apparatchiki. It did not serve any fundamental purpose, because the main problem was not corruption in the sense of giving and receiving bribes, but an economy that fundamentally revolved around the reproduction of scarcity and the provision of favors. Eliminating bribery did nothing to change this system, which benefitted all participants who had learned to live with it even as it punished them with lack of goods, services, and life chances.

Faced with systemic inertia to "acceleration," Gorbachev upped the ante, starting a vicious cycle of call and response between the reformers and the economic and political system they faced. This cycle ultimately led from economic to political reform both contributing to ever deepening crisis. Among the many legal changes of the 1980s the most momentous were the 1987 enterprise law and the 1988 law on cooperatives. Together, they amounted to destruction of central economic control flanked by only partial marketization of the economy. State enterprises continued to fulfil state orders, but saw their subsidies reduced and were forced on a new system of self-financing with potential bankruptcy lurking in the background. Management now was meant to set its own production plans and the enterprise was allowed to market any surplus production after it had fulfilled the state orders. To increase competition, the 1988 law legalized private enterprises, which in theory functioned outside the state sphere, but in practice were also often attached to state enterprises, siphoning off stockpiles and increasing the economic muddle.

To managers who had grown up in the Soviet economy of scarcity and favors, these reforms were disorienting. They had made a career by honing the particular skills of maintaining political connections to influence plan targets and economic connections to other enterprises that could help obtaining scarce goods. They knew how to keep their workers quiet, if not happy, by tending to their needs for housing or other necessities, while allowing them to privatize much of their time and some of the enterprise's assets in exchange for their loyalty during storming periods. Now they were meant to find buyers for their products, make decisions about what to produce and in what quantity, balance the books, and if necessary dismiss workers. Essentially, they were meant to switch to a completely different set of skills and from one established pattern of economic life to another. To make things worse, even if they were able to retool themselves (and motivate their workers to begin producing quality goods day in day out without allowing them to take time off or pilfer from the enterprises, which could no longer be accepted), they could not simply turn to "the market" to make decisions, because there was none. Thus, instead of replacing the economy of scarcity with a thriving surplus economy, the reforms led to a further deepening of the crisis. The economic system, not fully marketized but no longer centrally controlled, collapsed.

Why did marketization not work as expected? Real economic life depends on many and varied concrete actions: information needs to be gathered and passed on in complex networks of actors all over the economic system. Markets often develop spontaneously, as they indeed did within and under the command economy, as we have seen above. But market relations that would spread across the large space of the Soviet Empire and replace the complex imperial division of labor and allocation of resources of the old system with a new one would not be easy or quick to build. A market did not simply emerge from nowhere, while the abolition of the planning system quickly undermined the complex relations of exchange that did exist. The old system thus began to break down and there was nothing there yet to replace it. The response of the population was continuing hoarding of whatever was available, to prepare for the rainy days ahead – completely rational microeconomic behavior with catastrophic macroeconomic results. By the end of the year, the Soviet Union was effectively insolvent.

Faced with increasing pressures on their established way of life and work, larger demands on productivity, job losses, a steadily worsening supply of consumer goods, and massive rises in costs of living, workers began to rebel. With debate more and more open, and with repression scaled back, protest became possible again. In July 1989 a massive strike among coal miners rocked Siberia's Kuzbass, soon spreading to Ukraine's Donbass as well as to Kazakhstan. The movement was renewed with a focus on the Donbass and with increasingly radical demands for an end to communist rule in 1990/1991.

Glasnost

As if economic crisis was not unsettling enough, Gorbachev's reforms also rattled two other pillars of the Soviet system: myth making and dictatorship. Many scholars agree that it was the combination of democratization and somewhat haphazard economic reform that weakened the Soviet system to the extent that it could be exploded by national independence movements led by local elites of the old Soviet system who became increasingly aware of the possibility of increasing their own power. The Chinese example, which avoided, indeed cracked down upon, democratization while moving ahead with economic reform is often cited as a more successful path. Why, then, did Gorbachev push democratization and economic reform at the same time?

The answer is partially ideological and partially tactical. Again, recalling Gorbachev's socialization in the Komsomol is useful in understanding why he behaved the way he did. Ideological sincerity was prized in fields that did not require technical competency, such as the Youth League, and Gorbachev was nothing if not a sincere Communist. He did not set out to destroy the Soviet system but wanted to make it, in reality, live up to its ideal: a society where each would work according to ability and receive according to need. Dictatorship was an essential step in the march towards communism, but not as a goal in itself. It was only necessary, taught Lenin, as long as forces of the old order resisted the takeover of power by the proletariat. Once the suppression of the bourgeois counter-revolution had been accomplished, the state would wither away, because it was no longer necessary. There would be administration of some kind, to be sure, but no repressive apparatus. Free speech would be possible again, once everybody had the same economic interests, and hence no class difference would distort reasonable argument. Such were the convictions of Leninism that Gorbachev had grown up with.

By 1985, it was hard to argue that there was still a bourgeoisie in need of repression in the Soviet Union. The official sociology, developed by Stalin and essentially unchanged thereafter, assumed that there were two "non-antagonistic classes" (workers and collectivized peasants) and a "strata" of white-collar workers of the brain, the "intelligentsia." Gorbachev adjusted this analysis only insofar as he now introduced war veterans and youth as constitutive generational groups in society. Otherwise he accepted Stalin's sketch of the class structure of socialism. If one took this Marxist analysis seriously, as Gorbachev did, then dictatorship was no longer necessary: there was nobody left to repress.

If democratization thus made sense ideologically, it would have done so ever since Stalin developed this view of society in the 1930s. Quite obviously, such ideological compulsion had been without consequence thus far. The liberalization of debate under Khrushchev happened in fits and starts, because the actual results of allowing freer exchange of ideas were so destabilizing that they were quickly limited, Marxism or no Marxism. Ideology, thus, explains everything and nothing. Instead, short-term tactical considerations were what pushed Gorbachev to make good on what ideology should have suggested to Soviet leaders ever since.

The quick and catastrophic economic decline triggered by Gorbachev's reforms led to resistance from within the Party and state apparatus. Thus Gorbachev and his team began to engage in the other major skill of the Komsomol functionary: outsmarting and outmaneuvering the opposition in the apparatus. While working in the Komsomol as lower-level functionaries, Gorbachev's team could mobilize support from superiors. Once at the top of the hierarchy, where could they go for the required aid? Given the magnitude of the problems they had created and the depth of opposition within the apparatus, the logical place was to look outside it. And given the ideological blinkers they wore, they could imagine that the population at large (from whom they just had confiscated the vodka, one of the few consolations in a bleak existence) would support them; thus freeing up discourse and hence democratic reform.

That freedom of information was a tactical measure was shown in 1986, just after the need for "openness" (*glasnost*) had been announced. On April 26, 1986, a nuclear reactor at Chernobyl (Chornobyl) in Ukraine exploded, spreading radiation far and wide. Despite mass evacuations of civilians in the region, Soviet media remained silent about the catastrophe, reverting to the time honored tradition of making bad news disappear by ignoring it. The population was not warned about the danger of radioactive fallout. The festivities of May 1 went ahead in the most heavily affected Ukraine and Belarus as if nothing had happened. Only on May 14 did Gorbachev face the public in a TV address that broke the news blackout. This attempted cover-up enraged not only oppositional figures in the slowly democratizing Soviet Union, it also alienated the political elites in the affected republics, an important moment of national bonding of the elites in opposition to the Soviet center.

Once it went ahead the policy of glasnost was a disaster for a political system dependent on a lacquered reality. Between 1986 and 1989, the acid of free debate and critical inquiry dissolved one foundational myth after another. The victims of dekulakization, famine, and terror became prominent in the public debate about the Soviet past, while those who resisted in whatever capacity were now celebrated as heroes by the new history. The supposed superiority of socialism melted away as economists and sociologists began to compare all kinds of indicators with the West. Food shortages (especially of meat), the ever-crushing housing crisis (despite large steps made since Khrushchev), and the terrible state of medical care all came into focus.

Most damaging of all was probably the assault on the myth of the Great Patriotic War, which had reached bombastic heights under Brezhnev. Even if nobody talked about famine, collectivization, deportations, the Gulag, and the mass shooting operations of the Great Terror, nobody had forgotten them either. But it continued to be possible to make sense of them as maybe terrible, but necessary, sacrifices in preparation for the war against the Nazi invaders, which had touched most families. Commemoration of the war was an official obsession, but it was also integrated into rituals of daily life and the lifecycle. This war cult was deeply embedded in the social structure. The Great Patriotic War, for this and other reasons, became the central foundational myth of Soviet society – the achievement of the Soviet Empire and the pivot around which its entire history revolved. If the Soviet Union had single-handedly rescued Europe, even the world, from fascism, maybe it had all been worth it.

Once intellectuals could openly examine the extent to which the war cult actually reflected historical reality, the positive narrative about this past soon unraveled. Instead of heroic resistance against fascism, the new histories found a morally repugnant pact with Hitler's Germany, mass executions of Polish officers, willful ignorance of the German threat, poor preparation for the Wehrmacht's onslaught, brutality towards the own troops, mass deportations of "enemy nations" and criminal treatment of civilians in "liberated" Eastern Europe. Soon, little was left of this once glorious past – to the shock, horror, and disgust of those who had a personal commitment to it.

Democratization

Freeing discourse, thus, did not create more support for the reformers. Instead, it increased resistance from within the apparatus, as well as from among organized war veterans, who had nothing to gain from a destruction of the war myth. Thus, a more far-reaching opening of the political system was necessary to produce the support Gorbachev and his entourage convinced themselves they would find in the population. What followed was a political liberalization unseen in Soviet life since October 1917. In order to circumvent the entrenched interests in the Communist Party, Gorbachev introduced a new parliament, the Congress of People's Deputies, elected in March 1989. Its composition was still a far cry from adequate representation, but in the Soviet context it was breathtakingly democratic. Only a third of the seats were directly controlled by the CPSU and affiliated organizations, such as (official) trade unions, the Komsomol, or a new veteran organization. The rest could be contested by multiple candidates and many of the seats indeed were. In some cases, runoff elections had to be held.

Suddenly, the Soviet Union had a loyal opposition in parliament. It was nothing less than a cultural revolution: The political monopoly of the Communist Party – a major pillar of the Soviet order ever since the foundation of the Soviet Union – had been abolished. Moreover, the meeting of the Congress was broadcast live on television, and many former Soviets remember how life came to a halt as citizens were glued to the television screens to hear unprecedented truths being told openly in full view of the public.

Rather than creating support for Gorbachev's clique, therefore, democratization began to undermine the very political structure his power was based on: the Union of Soviet Socialist Republics. Elections to republic level parliaments in 1990 led to ever more far-reaching democratization. The opposition won in the Baltic republics, Moldova, Armenia, and Georgia. In Russia, too, the oppositional "Democratic Russia Bloc" gained a majority and elected Boris Yeltsin (1931–2007) Chairman – a major boost for the career of a former apparatchik who had fallen out with Gorbachev and would later win the prize of being the first president of an independent Russia. In Ukraine, meanwhile, the democrats were still in the minority and Communists dominated the Supreme Soviet (*Rada*).

Detente

As the social contract of late socialism thus unraveled in the paradoxes of economic reform, and as the political unity of the empire crumbled under the onslaught of free speech and democratization, in a parallel universe the confrontation with the West, one of the basic structuring principles of all the decisions Soviet leaders had made ever since 1945, also started to melt away. The results were far reaching. Most importantly, detente began the unraveling of the wider perimeter of satellites, with severe repercussions for the empire itself.

As in the field of economics, the destruction of the empire's perimeter was an unintended consequence of a deliberate attempt by Gorbachev and his allies in the leadership to deal with a severe problem holding the Soviet Union back. They rightly perceived that the structure of the economy was only one problem, which depressed the consumption levels of the population. The other was the massive drain on resources by the military-industrial complex, made necessary by the arms race with the United States, which in turn was a necessary outcome of the determination to have a protective ring of satellites to ensure the Soviet Union's safety from Europe. In order to shrink the warfare state and grow the welfare and consumption sectors, therefore, renewed detente with the West was of the essence.

Gorbachev pursued this issue with vigor, making him immensely popular in the West. He stopped the deployment of SS-20 rockets in Europe in 1985, and began a campaign to convince the United States to massively cut nuclear arsenals on both sides. In 1986, the Soviet Union began withdrawing troops from Afghanistan (a move that accelerated in 1988 and was complete in 1989), as well as from the long-term satellite in the south-east: Mongolia. In 1987, the landmarks Intermediate-Range Nuclear Forces Treaty was signed by the United States and the USSR, which eliminated the massive arsenals of missiles with short or intermediate (up to 3400 miles) range. The treaty effectively ended the arms race. The Cold War was over.

1989

Gorbachev's skillful diplomacy managed to end the Cold War and thereby create the conditions under which the warfare state could be demobilized. Resources could then be transferred from guns to butter. However, he was unable to replicate his success at home, where the reforms that were supposed to build this communist welfare state ran deeper and deeper into the mud. With the ideological glue dissolving, the economy in a downward spiral of self-destruction, and democratization demanding a new focus on "the people," local nationalisms, always more accommodated and contained than superseded by a Soviet consciousness, bubbled to the surface. Separatist tendencies were strongest in the latest additions to the Red Empire and its perimeter: first came the satellites in Eastern Europe, added after 1945, then the Baltic states, acquired in 1940. From here, the dissolution spread to other non-Russian republics before hitting Russia itself.

The unraveling began in Eastern Europe. As in the Soviet Union proper, the crisis was at its core an economic one. Rising oil prices, which allowed the

Soviet heartland to expand both welfare and warfare spending throughout the 1970s, paradoxically hit its wider European empire hard. Although the Soviets did not pass on the full amount of the blow to the satellites, the dependence of communist Eastern Europe on Soviet oil severely worsened the terms of trade: they had to export more of their industrial products to the Red Empire to be able to import the same amount of oil, and the discrepancy was rising every day. Hence they began to take up foreign debt to pay for the social contract of low productivity and relatively stable living conditions at the core of mature socialism. The result was a death spiral of breathtaking proportions, which did nothing to change the underlying economic problem that instead it allowed to reproduce.

With the economic situation worsening, it quickly turned out that close to half a century of ideological indoctrination had not anchored the communist system in the minds and souls of Eastern Europeans. Rather, it had been brute force and its threat that kept the perimeter together. True, there was widespread support for the socialist welfare state, such as it was. But then again, free education and healthcare, rental protection, and fairly secure work flanked by unemployment benefits could be found in the supposedly capitalist welfare states of Western Europe as well. Despite all attempts to control information, many in Eastern Europe knew it, too, not least because free-to-air Western television could be watched in many places. In Germany, family connections across the inner-German border continued. People knew that life was better outside of the Soviet bloc.

Again and again, Moscow had to make it clear that it would not allow what it called "counter-revolution" in its backyard. The crackdowns, well remembered by haunting pictures of civilians facing Soviet tanks, had been periodic: Germany in 1953, Hungary in 1956, and Czechoslovakia in 1968. Poland in 1981 had been made to do its own dirty work, but the result was the same: martial law ended a movement for political reform. Faced with regimes of relative scarcity, prohibition of free exchange of ideas, and top-down management, many East Europeans had tried to leave the promised land; the empire reacted by keeping them – by force. The borders to the West were sealed, most symbolic by the erection of the Berlin Wall in 1961.

As long as those in power were willing to employ the means of suppression at their disposal (as the Chinese Communists would do in 1989, the same year communism fell in Eastern Europe), their power was safe enough. Here again, Gorbachev was key, and paradoxically because he, unlike many others, was not a cynic interested in lining his own pockets, but a true believer in the communist creed. And he was not only unwilling to use force, but he also made sure his clients in the satellites would not either. The result was a chain reaction of popular mobilization.

Poland fell first. A country with a well-developed illegal opposition, *Solidarity*, which had been forced underground in 1981 by the imposition of martial law, the country was the most likely of the satellites to leave the Soviet orbit. With reforms underway in the Soviet Union itself, the communist leadership in Poland finally relented and sat down with the opposition. Partially free elections were held as a result, which the opposition won in a stunning success on the very day the democracy movement drowned in blood on Beijing's Tiananmen Square. By the end of August 1989, Poland had a noncommunist prime minister. Hungary would follow a similar path a few months later. Most spectacular was the fall of the Berlin wall on November 9 after massive demonstrations for the right to exit the GDR, which soon transformed into a movement for reunification of the two German states (completed in the following year). The movement for the end of communism now expanded to Czechoslovakia and Bulgaria (where it turned violent), and by the middle of 1990, all satellites had become democratic states. The outer perimeter of the Red Empire, established by Stalin and with the blood of the Red Army in World War II, was no more. And Gorbachev had not only stood by and allowed it to happen, he had actively encouraged it by keeping the communist elites under control, discouraging crackdowns.

Nationalisms

Gorbachev's refusal to use force to keep the satellites under control sent a strong signal to the non-Russian republics. Within the Soviet Union, the Baltic States spearheaded the new drive towards independence. Here, few had ever accepted the annexations of 1940 as legitimate. Once democratization made it possible to voice such feelings, citizens opted to do so in large numbers. On the 48th anniversary of the Hitler-Stalin Pact, on August 23, 1987, large crowds protested against this past in each of the Baltic republics. The pressures from the street were welcomed by many in the corridors of power, who could feel encouraged by the lack of violent response by the Soviet leadership to the European events of 1989. By January 1990, both Lithuania and Latvia had removed article six of the Soviet constitution of 1977 from their own basic laws: The leading role of the Communist Party, the major institutional straightjacket that allowed Moscow to control the empire, had been abolished. About a month later, all three republics had declared their intention to attain independence. On March 11, the Lithuanian Supreme Soviet declared independence; Estonia followed suit on March 30 and Latvia on May 4.

Thanks to the now uncensored media, Baltic independence sent ripples through the democratizing Soviet republics, which all held contested elections in 1990, soon followed by declarations of sovereignty, which limited Soviet laws. Republics now began to pass their own legislation, often contradicting Union rules. These moves further unraveled the economic entanglements within the

Soviet space, deepening the economic crisis, but also clearing the way for negotiations between the Baltic States and not just the Soviet Union (under
Gorbachev) but also Russia (under Yeltsin). In Ukraine, unhappiness with the
Red Empire had become near-universal with the Chernobyl catastrophe and
the callous attempts by Moscow to manage the political fallout to the detriment
of the population of the republic. Now, demands for more autonomy began to
spread over into separatism at a time when Gorbachev was trying to save the day
with a new union treaty promising more autonomy. He was one step behind,
and the negotiations for the new Soviet framework led protesting students to
occupy the central square (later named *Maidan*) in Kyiv in October 1990. This
"first Maidan" (which would be followed by two other "Maidans" in 2004 and
2013/2014) became a mass movement when Kyivans joined the protesters by
the tens of thousands to protect them from government supporters sent to break
up the demonstrations.

When negotiations with the Baltic States dragged on without result, Moscow
finally had enough. In January 1991, Soviet tanks and paratroopers advanced
into Lithuania and Latvia. The civilian casualties this intervention yielded
sparked outrage both in the Baltics and among democrats elsewhere in the
empire and abroad. Moreover, it did not have the desired effect. Instead of
intimidating the elites of the three Baltic States, the force wielded by Moscow
further radicalized them. Referenda for independence were held in February
and March, showing overwhelming support for separation. The Baltics were well
on their way to return to the independence they had won in the wake of World
War I and lost in the opening years of World War II.

Gorbachev now changed tactics. Instead of tanks, he tried the ballot box as a
means to keep the Union together. In March 1991 a referendum was held to ask
the Soviet Union's citizens to approve a new federation of sovereign republics.
Armenia and Georgia, the Baltic States, and Moldova boycotted the elections.
Elsewhere, the overwhelming majority voted in favor. His position thus strengthened, Gorbachev was able to reach agreement with eight of the remaining nine
republics (including Russia) on a new union treaty but the ninth republic, Ukraine,
balked, asking for a much looser confederation of states. Here, skillful maneuvering
of the republic leadership had added a second question on the referendum. If
Soviet citizens elsewhere voted on the question if they wanted "to preserve the
USSR as a renewed federation of equal sovereign republics," residents of Ukraine
were asked also if they preferred this continuation only "on the basis of the
Declaration of State Sovereignty of Ukraine." The result was that nearly 71% voted
in favor of the USSR and over 80% for a sovereign Ukraine, strengthening the
claim to power by the Republic's political elite vis-à-vis Moscow.[8]

Ukraine's resistance led to an unprecedented intervention of the United
States in the internal affairs of the declining empire. This episode would be
quickly forgotten after the breakdown of the Soviet Union, when many in the

West began to think of themselves as the victors in the Cold War. In fact, few in the United States at the time wanted the breakdown of the Soviet Union. Hence, in early August 1991 US President George H. W. Bush visited Kyiv to make the case for Ukraine easing its stance and remaining in the new and reformed Soviet Union. In what would become famous as his "Chicken Kiev speech," he lectured the Ukrainian parliamentarians that "freedom is not the same as independence." The United States, he continued, "will not support those who seek independence in order to replace a far-off tyranny with a local despotism." He would not "aid those who promote a suicidal nationalism based upon ethnic hatred."[9]

Such high-minded rhetoric, as condescending as it was towards his Ukrainian interlocutors, barely concealed not unwarranted panic about the risks of political change within the Soviet space. Like many others, Bush senior preferred the stability the Red Empire offered in international relations to the uncertainty of multiplying nation states in the region. A breakup, he worried, could lead to civil war (as it indeed did in Yugoslavia), a nightmare in a region with massive stockpiles of nuclear weapons. And it was by no means guaranteed that what would follow would be more democratic than what came before. Better to stick with the devil one knew, in particular if Beelzebub came in the guise of Mikhail Gorbachev – 1988 *Time* magazine's man of the year and 1990 Nobel Peace Prize laureate, much more popular abroad than at home.

The Soviet Union, then, broke apart despite, not because of, the actions of the West. The Soviet Union was not "defeated" by the United States. It merely ended. And it ended in farce, which might well have become tragedy, had those initiating the events been more forthright in their actions.

Dual Coup

When US President Bush lectured Ukrainians about "suicidal nationalism" he found a receptive audience not in the democratic Ukrainian opposition, but in communist hardliners in Moscow who had long thought that Gorbachev's reforms had gone too far. As we have seen, the desire to keep the Union together was widespread among the core populations of Russia, Belarus, and Ukraine who had clearly supported the idea of a continued, if democratized Soviet state in the referendum of 1991. Ukrainian resistance was not against a union as such, but centered on the extent to which the constituent parts would have to surrender sovereignty to Moscow. To those who had never accepted that anything major was rotten in Soviet life, however, even such reform-minded Soviet patriotism was anathema. And such reactionaries were prominent in the Soviet power structure, as Gorbachev's reforms had not been a revolution replacing one elite with another but rather a slow transformation of the Soviet ruling stratum.

The hardliners were indeed correct when they denounced democracy as a major danger to the continued existence of the Red Empire. After all, the Soviet Union had been put together not by democratic means but by force of arms in the civil and then the two world wars. Why should it hold together without such violence, or the threat thereof? It had not in Eastern Europe, after all, why should it elsewhere?

We get a glimpse of the ideology animating the conservative insurrectionists in a manifesto of their cause they had published in the arch-conservative newspaper *Soviet Russia* on July 23, 1991. Mobilizing the heroic memory of the Great Patriotic War, an imperial patriotism that equated the Soviet Union with Russia, and resentments against the inequalities in both economics and politics Gorbachev's reforms had fostered, it denounced the results of perestroika in no unclear terms. It was a call to arms:

> Let us unite to stop the chain reaction of the disastrous collapse of the state, the economy, and human personality; to contribute to the strengthening of Soviet power, to the transformation of it into a genuine people's power, and not some manager for the hungry nouveaux riches, who are ready to sell off everything for the sake of their insatiable appetite. ...
>
> The Soviet Union is our home and stronghold, built with enormous efforts of all its peoples and nations. It has saved us from disgrace and slavery at times of horrible invasions! Russia – unique and beloved – is crying for help.[10]

At that point, a conspiracy of eight leading reactionaries had already formed clandestinely. This gang of eight called itself the State Committee on the State of Emergency (GKChP) and united major hardliners from the Soviet State apparatus, the KGB, the Communist Party of the Soviet Union, and the military-industrial complex. Having obtained a copy of the new union treaty on August 17, 1991, they concluded that this document (which was supposed to be signed three days later) would spell the end of the Soviet project. The next day, the conspirators placed the vacationing Gorbachev under house arrest in his holiday home in Crimea, put the KGB on alert, and prepared for mass arrests. In the early morning hours of August 19, the GKChP announced that it had taken control of the government and declared a state of emergency.

While the majority of the USSR ministers supported the coup, few others did. Most importantly, the conspirators failed to arrest Boris Yeltsin, the first President of the Russian Republic (who had been elected in June). Yeltsin emerged as the spokesman of the resistance to the putsch, immediately denouncing it in a press conference. Protesters began to pour into the streets of Moscow, accosting with flowers or tongue-lashings the tanks that had taken position in front of the parliament building. In the middle of the day of August 19, Yeltsin had his maybe most famous moment, when he mounted a tank to deliver a fiery speech against the insurrection – an act of treason against the RSFSR, as he claimed.

That Yeltsin got away with mobilizing Russia against the Soviet Union showed what a pathetic lot of old men he faced in this showdown. The putschists, after all, controlled the mighty KGB, but did not use it to crack down on their opponents. The expected mass arrests did not eventuate. They did not even arrest Yeltsin, an elementary mistake. Later accounts of the conspirators paint a picture of indecision, high blood pressure, and nerves in need of soothing by way of liberal application of alcohol. The army stood aside and the crowds in front in the Moscow streets grew by the hour.

On August 20, the 14th Army went over to Yeltsin's side and soldiers took up position outside the Kremlin. The Russian president now upped the ante by declaring himself in command of all troops on the territory of the RSFSR. This step was, in essence, a counter-putsch, the enlargement of the powers of Russia vis-à-vis the Soviet Union. Covering his international bases, Yeltsin arranged a conversation with the US President, who declared his support for what he perceived to be the side of democracy.

On the night of August 20 minor clashes between GKChP troops and protesters caused several fatalities, but as August 21 dawned, the Emergency Committee was on the verge of breakdown. The conspirators called off their tanks. Yeltsin, meanwhile, decreed himself in control of all enterprises on the territory of the RSFSR, yet another power grab from the quickly disintegrating Soviet Union.

By midday of August 22, several members of the GKChP had been arrested and Gorbachev had returned to Moscow. A victory rally was held outside the Soviet parliament building, the White House. The putsch was over. It had started as a desperate attempt to save the USSR and it ended with a massively strengthened RSFSR and a Soviet Union with only days to live.

The Red Empire Breaks Apart

Like the two revolutions of 1917, the 1991 coup was fought out in the metropole of the empire. If in 1917 the epicenter had been Petrograd, then the capital of the Romanov realm, in 1991 it was the capital of the Red Empire: Moscow. In Ukraine, the government refused to implement the emergency decrees of the putschists, but did nothing to defeat them either. Instead, the government stood aside, counseling its citizen to remain calm, which did not prevent mass demonstrations against the coup. The other republics only reacted once Yeltsin deepened his counter-putsch. He took control of the Union government and forced Gorbachev to resign as General Secretary of the Communist Party, usurping the empire's center for Russia. A democratized Soviet Union was one thing, being part of a new Russian Empire was quite another for elites who had started to get a taste for running their own affairs.

Now the initiative shifted from the center to the periphery, with Ukraine leading the way with an overwhelming parliamentary vote for independence on August 24. The declaration was to be confirmed in a referendum on December 1, which showed how the landscape had shifted. In March 1991 71% of the population of Ukraine had voted to stay in the Union and 80% for a sovereign Ukraine within it, now an even larger majority of 90% voted for independence, including many Russian speakers, ethnic Russians, and Jews in all regions of the country. In the coal mining and steel producing Donetsk area, dominated by Russians ever since industrialization took off in the late years of the Romanovs, 83% voted in favor, and in the heavily Russian Crimea, handed over to Ukraine by Khrushchev in 1954, 54% wanted a break with Moscow. This evidence of a civic patriotism, which identified with the Ukrainian republic rather than the Ukrainian ethnicity silenced, for the time being, Yeltsin's threats to dispute the borders of the republic. Claims that eastern Ukraine and Crimea were "Russian" areas, however, would return two decades later under a different Russian president.

With Ukraine independent, the project of a new Union treaty was dead. Yeltsin opted for independence, as without Ukraine Russia would be at the mercy of the Muslim republics. Once Russia had opted out, there was no more reason to go ahead with a union that excluded the economically strongest and most populous republic. Instead, Belarus, Ukraine, and the Central Asian republics joined Russia in a very weak new Commonwealth of Independent States, formed in December 1991. The Soviet Union, heir of the Romanov Empire, victor in World War II, a major alternative to liberal capitalism, and one of two superpowers jockeying for world supremacy in the Cold War, was history.

Notes

1   Nikolay Mitrokhin, "'Strange People' in the Politburo: Institutional Problems and the Human Factor in the Economic Collapse of the Soviet Empire," *Kritika: Explorations in Russian and Eurasian History* 10, no. 4 (2009): 869–96, here: 892.

2   Lewis H. Siegelbaum and Leslie Page Moch, "Transnationalism in One Country? Seeing and Not Seeing Cross-Border Migration within the Soviet Union," *Slavic Review* 75, No. 4 (2016): 970–86.

3   Alexei Yurchak, *Everything Was Forever, until It Was No More. The Last Soviet Generation* (Princeton, NJ and Oxford: Princeton University Press, 2006).

4   Stephen Kotkin, *Uncivil Society. 1989 and the Implosion of the Communist Establishment* (New York: The Modern Library, 2010).

5   Janos Kornai, *The Economics of Shortage*, 2 vols. (Amsterdam: North-Holland Publishing Co., 1980).

6   Sheila Fitzpatrick, "*Blat* in Stalin's Time," in: *Bribery and Blat in Russia. Negotiating Reciprocity from the Middle Ages to the 1990s*, ed. Stephen Lovell, Alena Ledeneva, and Andrei Rogachevskii (New York: St. Martin's Press, 2000), 166–82.

7   Alena Ledeneva, *Russia's Economy of Favours. Blat, Networking and Informal Exchange* (Cambridge, New York, Melbourne: Cambridge University Press, 1998).

8   Serhy Yekelchyk, *Ukraine: Birth of a Modern Nation* (Oxford and New York: Oxford University Press, 2007), 189.

9   President George H. W. Bush, speech to a session of the Supreme Soviet of Ukraine, 1 August 1991 https://en.wikisource.org/wiki/Chicken_Kiev_speech, accessed January 3, 2018.

10   Slightly corrected translation adapted from https://en.wikipedia.org/wiki/A_ Word_to_the_People, accessed January 3, 2018.

Bibliography

Alexievich, Svetlana, *Secondhand Time* (Melbourne: Text Publishing, 2013).

Aron, Leon, *Roads to the Temple: Truth, Memory, Ideas, and Ideals in the Making of the Russian Revolution, 1987–1991* (New Haven, CT: Yale University Press, 2012).

Bisley, Nick. *The End of the Cold War and the Causes of Soviet Collapse* (New York: Palgrave Macmillan, 2004).

Brown, Archie, *The Gorbachev Factor* (Oxford: Oxford University Press, 1996).

Cohen, Stephen F. "Was the Soviet System Reformable?" *Slavic Review* 63, no. 3 (2004): 459–88.

Colton, Timothy J. *Yeltsin. A Life* (New York: Basic Books, 2008).

Dallin, Alexander, and Gail W. Lapidus, eds. *The Soviet System. From Crisis to Collapse*, 2nd revised edition (Boulder, CO: Westview Press, 1995).

Davies, R. W. *Soviet History in the Gorbachev Revolution* (London: Macmillan, 1989).

de Tinguy, Anne, ed. *The Fall of the Soviet Empire* (Boulder, CO: East European Monographs, 1997).

Edele, Mark. *Soviet Veterans of the Second World War. A Popular Movement in an Authoritarian Society, 1941–1991* (Oxford: Oxford University Press, 2008).

Ellman, Michael, and Vladimir Kontorovich, eds. *The Disintegration of the Soviet Economic System* (London: Routledge, 1992).

Ellman, Michael, and Vladimir Kontorovich, eds. *The Destruction of the Soviet Economic System. An Insiders' History* (Armonk, NY: M.E. Sharpe, 1998).

Filtzer, Donald. *Soviet Workers and the Collapse of Perestorika. The Soviet Labour Process and Gorbachev's reforms, 1985–1991* (Cambridge: Cambridge University Press, 1994).

Filtzer, Donald. "Labor Discipline, the Use of Work Time, and the Decline of the Soviet System, 1928–1991," *International Labor and Working-Class History* 50, no. Fall (1996): 9–28.

Filtzer, Donald. "Atomization, 'Molecularization,' and Attenuated Solidarity: Workers' Responses to State Repression under Stalin," in: *Stalinist Subjects: Individual and System in the Soviet Union and the Comintern, 1929–1953*, ed. Brigitte Studer, 99–116. (Zürich: Chronos, 2006).

Gill, Graeme. *The Collapse of a Single-Party System: The Disintegration of the Communist Party of the Soviet Union* (Cambridge: Cambridge University Press, 1994).

Hanson, Philip. *The Rise and Fall of the Soviet Economy: An Economic History of the USSR from 1945* (London: Routledge, 2003).

Hough, Jerry F. *Democratization and Revolution in the USSR, 1985–1991*, (Washington DC: Brookings Institution Press, 1997).

Kotkin, Stephen. *Uncivil Society. 1989 and the Implosion of the Communist Establishment* (New York: The Modern Library, 2010).

Kotkin, Stephen. *Armageddon Averted. The Soviet Collapse, 1970–2000* (New York and Oxford: Oxford University Press, 2001).

Kramer, Mark, ed. *The Collapse of the Soviet Union,* double special issue of *Journal of Cold War Studies* 5, Nos. 1&4 (2003).

Kramer, Mark, "The Collapse of East European Communism and the Repercussions within the Soviet Union," *Journal of Cold War Studies* pt. 1: 5, no. 4 (2003); 178–256; pt. 2: 6, no. 4 (2004): 3–64; pt. 3: 7, no. 1 (2005): 3–96.

Lane, David. *Soviet Society under Perestroika,* completely revised edition (London: Routledge, 1992).

Ledeneva, Alena. *Russia's Economy of Favours. Blat, Networking and Informal Exchange* (Cambridge: Cambridge University Press, 1998).

Lewin, Moshe. *The Gorbachev Phenomenon. A Historical Interpretation,* expanded edition (Berkeley, Los Angeles: University of California Press, 1991).

Lieven, Anatol. *The Baltic Revolution. Estonia, Latvia, Lithuania and the Path to Independence* (New Haven, CT and London: Yale University Press, 1993).

Lovell, Stephen. *Summerfolk. A History of the Dacha, 1719–2000* (Ithaca, NY and London: Cornell University Press, 2003).

Lovell, Stephen. *The Shadow of War. Russia and the USSR 1941 to the Present* (Oxford: Wiley-Blackwell, 2010).

Marples, David R. *The Collapse of the Soviet Union 1985–1991* (London: Pearson Longman, 2004).

Marples, David R. "Revisiting the Collapse of the USSR," *Canadian Slavonic Papers / Revue Canadienne des Slavistes* 53, no. 2/4 (2011): 461–73.

Mawdsley, Evan, and Stephen White. *The Soviet Elite from Lenin to Gorbachev. The Central Committee and Its Members, 1917–1991* (Oxford and New York: Oxford University Press, 2000).

Misiunas, Romuald J., and Rein Taagepera. *The Baltic States. Years of Dependence 1940–1990,* expanded and updated edition (Berkeley and Los Angeles: University of California Press, 1993).

Mitrokhin, Nikolay. "'Strange People' in the Politburo: Institutional Problems and the Human Factor in the Economic Collapse of the Soviet Empire," *Kritika: Explorations in Russian and Eurasian History* 10, no. 4 (2009): 869–96.

Plokhy, Serhii. *The Last Empire: The Final Days of the Soviet Union* (New York: Basic Books, 2014).

Pons, Silvio, and Federico Romero, eds. *Reinterpreting the End of the Cold War: Issues, Interpretations, Periodization* (New York and London: Frank Cass, 2005).

Shlapentokh, Vladimir. *A Normal Totalitarian Society. How the Soviet Union Functioned and How It Collapsed* (Armonk, NY, London: M. E. Sharpe, 2001).

Slezkine, Yuri. *The Jewish Century* (Princeton, NJ: Princeton University Press, 2004).

Smith, Kathleen E. *Remembering Stalin's Victims: Popular Memory and the End of the USSR* (Ithaca, NY: Cornell University Press, 1996).

Stoff, Laurie, ed., *The Rise and Fall of the Soviet Union* (Farmington Hills, MI: Thomson Gale, 2006).

Suny, Ronald G. *The Revenge of the Past. Nationalism, Revolution, and the Collapse of the Soviet Union* (Stanford, CA: Stanford University Press, 1993).

Taubman, William. *Gorbachev: His Life and Times* (New York: W. W. Norton, 2017).

Verdery, Katherine. "What Was Socialism, and Why Did It Fall?" in: *Beyond Soviet Studies,* ed. Daniel Orlovsky (Washington, DC: Woodrow Wilson Center Press, 1995), 27–46.

Zubok, Vladislav M. *A Failed Empire: The Soviet Union in the Cold War from Stalin to Gorbachev* (Chapel Hill: University of North Carolina Press, 2007).

10

After Empire: Epilogue

The End of (a) History

The Soviet Union is no more. To the relief of some and the chagrin of others, the major alternative to liberal capitalism has abolished itself. For those who lived through this breakdown and its aftermath in the lands of the former Soviet Union, these were hard years economically, and exciting years politically – both in a positive and negative meaning of the word. Many have been disappointed with the results, while a minority amassed wealth and power – only to lose both in sometimes spectacular stories of rise and fall. Today, the legacies of the Soviet order are assessed differently in different successor states, among different groups of society, and in different generations. The multiplication of histories, which the breakdown of the Soviet Union has engendered, has led to disorientation outside the region. Many in the English-speaking world have simply given up trying to understand this new complexity. The hope that history would be over and we would no longer have to deal with what in the olden days one could erroneously call "the Russians" has been disappointed.

Specialists on Soviet history, politics, and culture are rarer today than they were 25 years ago, as universities and think tanks deploy their resources elsewhere. Among the remainder, the overwhelming majority are "Russianists" – scholars like myself who entered the field with training in Russian language and culture often have at best a limited understanding of life outside Russia. Specialists in Ukrainian, Belarusian, Baltic, Transcaucasian, or Central Asian history are few and far between. As history turned out to not be over in the lands of the former Soviet Union, we will need more of them.

The Soviet Union: A Short History, First Edition. Mark Edele.
© 2019 John Wiley & Sons, Inc. Published 2019 by John Wiley & Sons, Inc.

This book has tried to give a nonspecialist audience a general framework for understanding the complex imperial history the 15 successor states shared for most of the twentieth century. This book attempted to resist the imposition of one national narrative on the Soviet past. It has tried to avoid telling the story of the Soviet Union as the history of one of its successor states, be that Russia, Ukraine, or any of the smaller nations. Instead, what interested me was the historical unity of this particular formation: the Soviet Union, the successor state to the Romanov Empire, a state that is no more, despite the ghosts that haunt the lands it once controlled.

In this respect, 1991 was a more decisive break than 1917. In 1917, the ruling elite and the ideology of the empire changed, but much of its territory and population were regathered. Thus, the widespread convention in the West to speak of "Russia" when one meant the Soviet Union made some sense in the seven decades between 1921 and 1991: Russia was the largest republic, Russians were the largest group in the communist party, the lingua franca of the empire was Russian, and its borders were, with a few exceptions, similar to the ones of the old Russian Empire. Today, this matter of speaking is no longer adequate.

In 1991, while initially the ruling elite in most successor states remained in place, the economic and ideological transformation also included the shattering of the political landscape. Unless we see a neo-imperial takeover of its neighbors by a resurgent Russia, the territorial discontinuity between the Soviet and post-Soviet Eurasia is so strong, that we must accept that this history has come to an end. The last empire in Europe has finally been decolonized. With the breakdown of the Soviet Union in 1991 the unified history of the 15 successor states ended. New histories began, histories of nation states with a common past, but not necessarily a common future.

Paths

Different countries took different paths after 1991. At the most extreme, the three Baltic States joined the European Union and NATO, exiting the Russian dominated space completely. They did remain of course economically entangled with their neighbors, as they found out painfully once sanctions cut them off after Russia's invasion of Ukraine in 2014. Others, such as Kazakhstan or Belarus forged careful relationships of interdependence with Russia while guarding their sovereignty, while Georgia and Ukraine stood between these two groups, not managing to be admitted to the Western club of privileged nations while refusing to see themselves as parts of the "Russian World."

All successor states struggled with the economic fallout, which came with the unscrambling of the empire's economic system and the transition from state socialism to some type of capitalism. After major crashes wiped out much national wealth everywhere, GDP per head increased overall in the region from 1995 onwards. Recovery was slower in some places, most notably Russia and Ukraine, but here, too, an economic boom began in 1999 and 2000, interrupted only by the global financial crisis of 2007/2008, which led to a major reversal everywhere. Soon, however, GDP per head recovered and continued to grow. Only with the hybrid war fought by Russia in eastern Ukraine, the annexation of Crimea, and the following economic sanctions and counter-sanctions did this trend come to an end. At the time of writing, GDP per head has dramatically declined everywhere with the exception of the economic backwater of Uzbekistan.

Politically, the countries of the former Soviet Union include several dictatorships (most famously Belarus), authoritarian "managed democracies," most notably in Russia, but also vibrant democracies, such as in the Baltic states or Ukraine. Often one type of system transforms into the other, sometimes quite quickly as in the so-called "colored revolutions," sometimes more slowly, such as in the many cases of authoritarian creep. A quarter of a century after the breakdown of the Soviet Union, history is clearly not over. Things still evolve, sometimes for the better, often for the worse.

Legacies

The 15 post-Soviet republics might have emerged from the Soviet Union with a consciousness of their own national identity, but none of them is ethnically homogenous. The 70 years of economic and political entanglement in the Red Empire have left deep marks everywhere. All of the successor states have significant minority populations, and in some of them – Kazakhstan, Kyrgyzstan, and Latvia – the titular nationality is in the minority. Everywhere, then, civic nationalism and a tolerant attitude to neighboring nations would appear necessary to ensure domestic and international peace. Tragically, however, in many places instead ethnic fundamentalism, and a hostile attitude to the outside world became increasingly entrenched once the region emerged from the period of post-breakup upheaval. If commentators in the early 1990s spoke of the breakup of the Soviet Union as a surprisingly peaceful process and the beginning of a new wave of democratization; if some particularly triumphalist liberals in the west declared this to be not only a US victory in the Cold War but even the "end of history," a quarter century later it appears that the major alternatives for the region are authoritarian democracy, dictatorship, or kleptocracy. Ukraine and the Baltics remain the last bastions of some hope, but here, too, the open society has not remained unchallenged by its enemies.

National histories in all states have taken a jingoistic turn, which makes communication across borders difficult, if not impossible. War has become not only a threat, but a reality in several regions, and respect for civil liberties and established border lines between sovereign states cannot be taken for granted. Where this situation will lead is anyone's guess, but it is clear that the legacies of the past heavily determine both the present and the future. We can only hope that the elites in the countries concerned will orient themselves more on the positive aspects of this past. This was a past, after all, which, while embroiled in war making and the preparation for it for much of the time, also included serious attempts to provide for the welfare of the population, however flawed the results of these efforts might have been. It was welfare rather than warfare that was genuinely popular among all the peoples of the Soviet Union; it was the Soviet welfare state, not its warfare sibling, which formed the core of the fascination of many outside of the Soviet Union with the Red Empire.

Time will tell. In late 2017, when this book was finished, there seemed little reason for optimism. However, the future is always open. Few predicted in 1917 that the Bolsheviks would be able to hold on to power and reassemble the crumbled empire; fewer still expected in 1941 that the Soviet Union would survive the Nazi onslaught and go on to save Europe from fascism; and nobody predicted in 1985 that the Soviet functionary Mikhail Gorbachev would turn out to be the gravedigger of the Red Empire. We can expect this region and its peoples to have surprises in store in the future as well.

Index

The Soviet Union: A Short History, First Edition. Mark Edele.
© 2019 John Wiley & Sons, Inc. Published 2019 by John Wiley & Sons, Inc.